1968 + 50

Looking back at the historic, tumultuous year of 1968

Tony Edwin

Contact: 1968plus50@gmail.com

About This Book

George Santayana summed it up: "History is nothing but assisted memory." As we go through life, our memories continue to play an important role. A distinguishing trait of mankind is that we do indeed have a recorded, assisted memory—our common history—from which we can choose to better ourselves and our world.

That's where this book comes in. It's a reflection of a short piece of history: the year 1968. One lap of our planet around the sun. But it was a particular year so full of historic events that I think we would do well to remember what happened during those 366 days. And of course, it was George Santayana who also wrote: "Those who cannot remember the past are condemned to repeat it."

This book was created to commemorate events that took place in 1968, a year like no other. The year 2018 marks the 50th anniversary of each of these events.

Before you read any further, I want you to know what this book is, and what it isn't. It is a presentation of the major events of the year, as well as interesting facts (sometimes not-so-major) about entertainment, sports, politics, science, technology, pop culture, and other areas. There's at least one entry for every day. It is *not* an expert analysis about what each of those events means, and how it impacts our world today. With the chronological, "compartmentalized listing" manner in which events from 1968 are presented this book, you may wish to read it just a day or a month at a time, to provide a more real-time picture of how the events of 1968 transpired. Whether you read it a day at a time, or read the entire book in a day, I'm confident that you'll find 1968 to have been a historic, fascinating, tumultuous, and interesting 366 days.

This small book is intended to be a brief, high-level listing of the events of 1968. For a much deeper look at that historic year, the impact of the events, and reasons why they were important, I strongly recommend the book *1968: The Year That Rocked the World* by Mark Kurlansky (New York, Ballantine Books, 2003). And although much of the information in this book is publicly available, if you're doing professional work, I recommend consulting multiple sources, as I did for this book. Some online encyclopedias and other sources are maintained by people who used the best information available, but it's not uncommon to find incorrect dates or other details. So it's useful to check information if it's critical, usually as close to the original source as possible (for example, for information about the American space program, the NASA website is a good one to check).

Having lived through 1968 as a teenager, the information in this book comes from two general places: my own knowledge, and a number of sources for public information. To be sure, I consulted with various sources to confirm my own experiences. Although it's somewhat unusual to include a significant amount of public information in a book such as this, I was unable to find any book that does what this book does, namely, describing events that happened on a day-to-day basis, in addition to providing details about the more important or interesting ones. Although I utilized public information on these pages, I expanded on entries with other sources and added substantial information. In the Acknowledgements section at the end of this book, I've listed the major sources used to verify information.

With credit to Charles Dickens, it was the best of times, and the worst, but also a time of war, revolution, and changes in society.

More significant events seemed to be packed into a single year than we might otherwise expect in decades.

This book is written for those of you who are old enough to have lived through them, and to those of you who want to learn more about them. It's for my fellow history and trivia buffs, and if you like sports, or art, or aviation, or music (and who doesn't like some kind of music?) 2018 marks exactly 50 years since something unique in your area of interest took place. I trust that whatever your background, there will be something in this book that you'll find interesting, and especially worth knowing about that historic, tumultuous year.

I enjoyed researching, compiling, and writing this book, and I hope you enjoy reading it. Although I remember first-hand many of the events listed here, my research reminded me of many others, and I learned tons more that was brand new to me. Age, and I hope wisdom, have suggested that it was as important for me to relive, just a little bit, those tragic events as much as it was the good ones.

Please feel free to review the book online, or e-mail me at 1968plus50@gmail.com if you'd like to share additional information, or let me know your thoughts or experiences.

1968 + 50

Looking back at the historic, tumultuous year of 1968

To those who strive to make our world a better place.

1968 + 50

Looking back at the historic, tumultuous year of 1968

We human beings track time, and have a need to organize events and activities according to time. We celebrate birthdays and anniversaries of events, including events that have impacted us personally, as well as events that have impacted thousands or even millions of people.

The year 2018 marks the 50th anniversary—half a century—since the tumultuous, sometimes unprecedented, frequently important events of the year 1968.

For those of us who are old enough to remember the year 1968, the year stands alone. The United States and the world experienced civil wars, declared and undeclared. At times, it seemed as if the glue that held society together was dissolving. Hot wars, cold wars, riots, assassinations, and cultural upheaval previously unimagined was becoming real. In some ways—such as the first journey of human beings outside of Earth's gravity, and seeing the far side of the moon for the first time—it truly was a unique year. Tragic events would make 1968 memorable, including the assassinations of Rev. Martin Luther King, Jr., Sen. Robert F. Kennedy, and the loss of 16,592 American troops in Vietnam.

Norms and standards were changing globally. Rebellions took place. In addition to many that took place in the United States, protests or riots would also take place in many other countries, including Czechoslovakia, Poland, Germany, France, Italy, Belgium, Brazil, Japan, and the United Kingdom. Seeds planted decades earlier were sprouting: In Africa and Central America, revolutions and the beginnings of new nations took place with regularity. Many new nations had, until their independence, been colonies of other nations. Authoritarian leaders such as Generalissimo Francisco Franco in Spain and Josip Broz Tito in Yugoslavia, who were key players in World War II, remained firmly in power, and new leaders such as Nicolai Ceaușescu in Romania came onto the world scene. The leader of North Vietnam, Ho Chi Minh, largely held his communist philosophy because the great world powers would not support his country against France colonialism at the end of World War I. (President Woodrow Wilson refused to meet with Ho Chi Minh at Versailles in 1919 to address his concerns, almost 100 years ago now.) Unrest originated from many different causes; in the United States, the Vietnam War and civil rights were prominent drivers. However, despite many movements having defined leadership, many others were decentralized. Even within the U.S. civil rights movement, there was a spectrum of movements ranging from peaceful civil disobedience espoused by Dr. Martin Luther King, Jr., to the desire to change things much more rapidly, as was an objective of leaders such as Stokely Carmichael and H. Rap Brown.

In the United States, the news event of the decade was the war in Vietnam. Our military involvement in that Southeast Asian country began in 1964, when President Johnson and the Department of Defense began operations to keep communism from spreading from North Vietnam into South Vietnam. By 1968, the war half a world away was part of everyday life in America. Young men were enlisting and being drafted, and by the beginning of 1968, nearly 500,000 Americans were there. The evening news reported casualties on a weekly basis. The United States' involvement in the war in Vietnam was costing the United States $2-3 billion per month.

When 1968 began, the world was fresh from upheavals the previous year (including continued escalation in Vietnam, and cultural phenomena such as organized rebellion by youth), but there was hope for peace in 1968. Culture was changing in obvious but seemingly less important ways: The length of men's hair, which was perceived as long when the Beatles came to America four years earlier, now went down to the shoulders and beyond. Women's skirts varied from very long to very short. In this year of change, United Artists would remove, from television distribution, eleven Looney Tunes and Merrie Melodies cartoons made from 1931 to 1944 due to the stereotypical depiction of African-Americans. These cartoons are informally called the Censored Eleven.

In politics, Democratic incumbent President Lyndon Johnson, who had been elected in a landslide in 1964—a year after taking office upon John F. Kennedy's assassination—was still heavily favored to win the '68 nomination, in August in Chicago. That was despite Eugene McCarthy, an anti-war senator from Minnesota, having announced in 1967 his intention to run. Among the Republicans, the Michigan Republican governor, George Romney, was no longer the front-runner in the polls, having told Detroit talk show moderator Lou Gordon in 1967 that "When I came back from Vietnam, I just had the greatest brainwashing that anybody could get, not only by the generals, but also by the diplomatic corps over there." (Romney, of course, was the father of future governor and presidential candidate Mitt Romney. That was a time when a candidate could be knocked out of a political campaign because of a single mistake.) Republican New York governor Nelson Rockefeller, who represented the moderate wing of his party, was supported by many, but thought to be too liberal by others. Richard Nixon conveyed a more conservative message that many Republicans welcomed, but he had lost to John Kennedy for president in 1960 and to Democrat Edmund "Pat" Brown for governor of California in 1962, and he was deemed by many to be a guy who couldn't win.

Tensions existed in the Middle East, as they had for centuries. Relations between Israel and its neighbors were never completely normalized after the Arab-Israeli war of 1948, and conflicting territorial claims led to a high state of tension by 1967. In late May of that year, Egyptian president Gamal Abdel Nasser ordered the Straits of Tiran closed to Israeli ships, and also mobilized Egyptian troops along their border with Israel. As a result, on June 5, Israel staged what it called a pre-emptive attack, and soon destroyed virtually the entire Egyptian Air Force. Nasser convinced Syria and Jordan to join in battle against Israel, but the Israeli Defense Forces were overwhelming. As a result, Israel won the war in six days, and as a result it held the Golan Heights (a strip between Israel and Syria), the West Bank (a tract between Israel and Jordan), and the entire Sinai Peninsula with its 23,000 square miles (60,000 square kilometers) as well as more than one million Sinai residents.

In theaters and on television, films and shows spanned from westerns, which were still very common, to science fiction that described more and more realistic exploration of the moon and beyond. In the real world, the Soviets and the United States remained in a heated space race to see who would first land on the moon. Both countries frequently conducted tests of fission (atomic bomb) and fusion (hydrogen bomb) weapons underground, and under the sea, although most atmospheric testing had stopped five years earlier.

Aircraft safety was a very different thing in 1968 than today. Crashes of commercial aircraft and military aircraft (that weren't involved in combat) were virtually weekly events, with hundreds of lives lost. As just one example of the losses that occurred, five U.S. Air Force KC-135 Stratotanker refueling aircraft crashed in separate events throughout1968, taking the lives of 43 people. (According to listings available as of December 2017, a total of 46 KC-135 Stratotankers crashed between 1958 and 2013.) The year was also a tragic one for submarine crews and their families, as four submarines were lost with all on board: The Israeli submarine *Dakar* with 69 on board, the French sub *Minerve* with 52 on board, the Soviet sub *K-129* with its crew of 98, and the American sub *USS Scorpion* with its crew of 99. In addition, travel by bus or train was a higher risk than today; a number of them were involved in accidents with great loss of life.

It was a year of shocking news, shocking events, and surprises. Like most people, I heard about many of them on the television or radio, and remember where I was when I heard the news. We were surprised by the Tet Offensive. We were shocked and angered when North Korea captured our patrol boat, the USS *Pueblo*. We were shocked and saddened when Dr. Martin Luther King, Jr. was killed, and we followed the news as America and the world kept a lookout for his killer or killers. Just two months later, Sen. Robert F. Kennedy was shot immediately after declaring victory in the California primary; he died the following day. One of the saddest scenes that some of us remember was watching the funeral train carrying Sen. Kennedy from New York City to Washington, DC, from where the casket would be carried to Arlington National Cemetery. Whether you supported Bobby or not, we all knew that killing our leaders was not the way to create change. We were shocked at seeing angry people screaming at the Democratic National Convention in Chicago, not just inside the International Amphitheatre, but also out in the streets and parks of the Windy City. Like a prize fighter who had endured punch after punch until a numbness starts to set in, the events at campuses in the United States and across the world in 1968 might have simply led to disbelief by the time we saw reporters and students teargassed and struck with clubs in Chicago, and even saw armored vehicles rolling down the street.

To be sure, most of the surprises of 1968 weren't good ones. But baseball fans saw one of the greatest seasons ever, as players— primarily pitchers—achieved marks seldom seen before and never since (notably, the St. Louis Cardinals' Bob Gibson's 1.12 earned run average [ERA] and Detroit Tigers' Denny McLain's 31 wins). In the American League, Luis Tiant of the Cleveland Indians had an ERA of 1.60, and allowed opposition hitters a batting average of just .168, still a record. The "Year of the Pitcher" also saw the Los Angeles Dodgers' Don Drysdale set the modern baseball record for consecutive scoreless innings pitched (which held until the Dodgers' Orel Hershiser broke it in 1988). October brought a World Series victory of the Detroit Tigers over the St. Louis Cardinals, as well as some shocking performances, on the track and off, at the Games of the XIX in Mexico City. Professional football and basketball also saw changes and great performances. A final pleasant surprise during the year for many was watching Apollo 8 orbiting the moon on Christmas Eve, an event that many of us who were around won't forget.

As mentioned, I hope that this book will be useful to students and younger people as well as by people who lived through 1968. Perhaps the next generations will learn from the mistakes made by previous ones.

January 1968

January 1 (Monday)

The New Year began on a Monday, with the traditional college football bowl games taking place in the U.S. The Division 1 college football playoff tournament would not take place for another 46 years, but all four teams ranked #1 through #4 in the polls were playing in the Rose and Orange bowls. Each of those teams went into their bowl game with identical 9-1-0 records. The Rose Bowl had invited the champions of the Pacific Eight and Big Ten conferences, #1 University of Southern California (USC) and #4 Indiana, respectively. Later that evening, the Orange Bowl matched the #2 ranked Tennessee Volunteers of the Southeastern Conference against the #3 Oklahoma Sooners of the Big Eight Conference. In the Rose Bowl, USC defeated Indiana, 14-3, to retain its #1 ranking for the season. Both USC touchdowns were scored by O.J. Simpson, who would win the 1968 Heisman trophy, and would later go on to professional football and acting careers. Years later, Simpson would stand trial for the 1994 murder of his ex-wife, Nicole Brown, and her friend Ron Goldman. In the Orange Bowl, Oklahoma lost its 19-0 halftime lead over Tennessee, but held on to win the game, 26-24. USC and Oklahoma would eventually be ranked first and second, respectively, in the final coaches' and sportswriters' polls.

The United Nations announced that 1968 would be the International Year for Human Rights. This announcement, which ordinarily might not receive a great deal of attention, would play into events later in the year…including the Olympic Games.

In the Soviet Union, a new military service law went into effect that would require all able-bodied men to report for service on their 18th birthday.

Cecil Day-Lewis was named Poet Laureate of the United Kingdom, replacing the John Masefield, who had died the previous 12 May.

According to vietnamwarcasualties.org, 10 American service personnel were declared killed on the first day of 1968. They represented 10 different states; five were in the Army, three in the Navy, and two in the Marine Corps.

January 2 (Tuesday)

In Cape Town, South Africa, Dr. Christiaan Barnard performed the first heart transplant that was successful enough that the recipient could go home from the hospital. It was history's third heart transplant overall. (Barnard had performed the very first heart transplant about a month before, on December 3, 1967.) The recipient, 58-year-old Philip Blaiberg of Cape Town, would leave the hospital after 73 days and would survive for another 17 months until his death in August 1969. By the end of 1968, more than 100 heart transplants would take place across the globe.

In Jackson, Mississippi, Robert G. Clark was sworn in as the first black representative in the Mississippi state legislature since 1894. Clark, now age 89 (as of late 2017) served in office until 2004.

U.S. President Lyndon Johnson signed into law the Bilingual Education Act (BEA). At the signing, Johnson said, "Thousands of children of Latin descent, young Indians, and others will get a better start, a better chance in school... We are now giving every child in America a better chance to touch his outermost limits. We have begun a campaign to unlock the full potential of every boy and girl, regardless of his race, or his religion, or his father's income." The bill had been introduced the previous year by Ralph Yarborough, the liberal senator from Texas who, five years earlier, had ridden in the car with President Johnson during President Kennedy's tragic motorcade through Dallas.

In Vietnam, the 36-hour New Year's ceasefire expired. During the New Year's Day truce, there had been 64 major violations by the Viet Cong and North Vietnamese Army (NVA).

The American Independent Party (AIP) qualified for inclusion on the California election ballot. Former Alabama Governor George C. Wallace would run for president on that ticket, leading up to the November 5th general election.

Born: Cuba Gooding, Jr., American film actor who won the Academy Award for Best Supporting Actor in *Jerry Maguire*, was born in New York City.

January 3 (Wednesday)

In Cuba, the government of Fidel Castro started to ration gasoline for the first time since Castro took power in 1959. The night before on the revolution's anniversary, Castro announced in a speech that drivers would be allowed to purchase between eight and 25 gallons per month, depending on the horsepower of their vehicle.

U.S. Senator Eugene J. McCarthy of Minnesota officially announced that he would run for the Democratic Party's nomination for president, and that he would directly challenge President Johnson for the party's nomination. McCarthy took steps to place his name on the New Hampshire primary ballot.

Furniture manufacturer Herman Miller, Inc. of Zeeland, Michigan, introduced the Panton chair to the market. The highly stylized and frequently very colorful chair was designed by Danish furniture and interior designer Verner Panton.

January 4 (Thursday)

The U.S. 4th Infantry Division, conducting an operation in the Dak To area of South Vietnam, captured a classified five-page North Vietnamese document titled "Urgent Combat Order No. 1," which described the strategy for conducting a series of attacks in Pleiku during the upcoming Tet holiday.

During a cabinet meeting, British Prime Minister Harold Wilson presented a proposal for the United Kingdom to withdraw from defending Singapore and Malaysia by the end of March 1971, and to withdraw British troops stationed east of the Suez Canal by mid-1972.

In Gothenburg, Sweden, American rock guitarist and singer Jimi Hendrix was arrested for vandalism after performing at the Lorensberg Cirkus arena. Police said that Hendrix vandalized his room at the Opelan Hotel. Hendrix was kept in jail overnight, then released to continue his tour of Sweden.

Died: Joseph Pholien, who had been the prime minister of Belgium from 1950 to 1952, died at age 83.

January 5 (Friday)

Alexander Dubček, age 46, became the First Secretary of the Communist Party of Czechoslovakia, after the party's Central Committee voted to remove Antonín Novotný from the position because of his perceived ineffective leadership of the country. The previous day, a 21-person "Consultative Group" had been divided between preferring Dubček, Prime Minister Jozef Lenárt, Deputy Premier Oldřich Černík and National Assembly Chairman Bohuslav Lastovička. The choice was narrowed down on Friday morning to

Dubček or Lenárt, and the Consultative Group selected Dubček by "a decisive majority" of the 21 members.

American pediatrician Benjamin Spock, Yale University chaplain William Sloane Coffin Jr., and three others were indicted for giving advice to young men about avoiding the draft.

Weekly Vietnam War casualties continued to be announced on the evening news, and the casualties announced on the first Friday of 1968 listed 185 Americans killed along with 227 South Vietnamese and 37 from other countries. The number of enemy soldiers killed was given as 1,438.

Born: Carrie Ann Inaba, dancer and television host, was born in Honolulu, Hawaii.

January 6 (Saturday)

The Agartala Conspiracy Case arose in East Pakistan with the indictment and arrest of 35 people charged with plotting the secession of the eastern part of Pakistan from the rest of the nation. Sheikh Mujibur Rahman, identified as the leader of the plot, was charged with traveling to Agartala in India to meet with P. N. Ojha, India's representative to the East, in hopes of obtaining military support. East Pakistan, whose residents primarily spoke Bengali, comprised more than half of Pakistan's population, but only 10 percent of its government officials. West Pakistan residents primarily spoke Urdu. Sheikh Mujib and the other defendants would be put on trial on June 19, leading to mass demonstrations, a civil war, and the eventual separation of East Pakistan as the nation of Bangladesh, with Sheikh Mujib as its first President.

Dr. Norman Shumway performed the first successful heart transplant in the United States, operating at the Stanford University Hospital in California. The donor was 43-year-old Virginia May White, who had suffered a cerebral hemorrhage while celebrating her 22nd wedding anniversary; the recipient was Mike Casparak, a 54-year-old steelworker with terminal viral myocarditis. Casparak survived for 15 days, dying on January 21 from liver failure. Shumway, who was born in Kalamazoo, Michigan, would later become the president of the American Association for Thoracic Surgery (1986-87) and along with Bruce Reitz, would perform the world's first heart-lung transplant (1981, at Stanford Hospital).

An Aeroflot An-24B airliner exploded in midair, killing all 45 people on board, while flying from Olyokminsk to Lensk in eastern Russia.

The first successful separation of conjoined twins who were joined at the head took place at Transvaal Memorial Hospital for Children in Johannesburg, South Africa, as a team of 27 surgeons separated Catherine and Shirley O'Hare. Two previous attempts to separate twins conjoined at the head had ended with only one of the twins surviving.

In Hixon, Staffordshire in the UK, an express train collided with a truck that was stalled on the tracks, killing 13 people, all of them passengers on the train. The truck driver and his-coworker were uninjured. The truck was slowly hauling a 125-ton electrical transformer over the crossing when the Manchester-to-London southbound express train arrived with 500 people on board. The crossing gates lowered automatically, preventing the truck from completing its move off of the crossing, and the locomotive and eight cars derailed.

In South Korea, President Park Chung-hee agreed to honor the petition submitted by the nation's Hangul Society, requesting the phasing out the use of Chinese language that had been taught in schools and published in conjunction with the Korean alphabet (hangul), and replacing Chinese symbols with Korean symbols. Chinese words would be phased out, and eliminated altogether by the end of 1972.

The Beatles song "Hello, Goodbye" became #1 on the U.S. charts, and would remain there for a second week.

Born: John Singleton, African-American director (Boyz N the Hood), was born in Los Angeles.

Died: Karl Kobelt, President of Switzerland in 1946 and again in 1952, died in Bern, Switzerland at age 76. Kobelt was a member of the Swiss Federal Council from 1940 to 1954.

January 7 (Sunday)

The cost of a First-Class stamp in the United States increased from five cents to six cents. The increase went into effect exactly five years after the 1963 increase from four cents to five.

Forty-three passengers on a bus in South Korea were killed near Jinju when their bus lost one of its front wheels and fell over a 33-foot high cliff and sank in the Nam River.

Surveyor 7, the seventh and last of NASA's Surveyor lunar probes, was launched from Cape Kennedy at 1:30 am Eastern U.S. time. (See entry for Surveyor landing on the moon on January 10.)

A group of 500 California Institute of Technology ("Caltech") students demonstrated in front of NBC's studios in Burbank, California, in an effort to convince NBC to renew the original Star Trek television series for a third season. The protest was intended to be perceived as a grassroots campaign, but was actually orchestrated by series creator Gene Roddenberry. The efforts of the students and letter writers were successful as the series would be picked up for a third and final season.

Born: James Brokenshire, British Member of Parliament and Secretary of State for Northern Ireland, was born in Southend-on-Sea, Essex.

Died: Gholamreza Takhti, a popular Iranian wrestler who won a gold medal for his country in the 1956 Summer Olympics, was found dead at the age of 37. Officially, the death was ruled a suicide by an overdose of sleeping pills in his hotel room. However, after the 1979 Iranian revolution, it was revealed in court testimony that Takhti had been arrested for belonging to a moderate anti-government group, and that he was tortured to death. He is considered by many to be the most popular Iranian athlete of the 20th Century.

Died: Hugo Butler, the screenwriter of approximately 15 films, died of a heart attack at age 53 after suffering from arteriosclerotic brain disease for several years. Butler, whose father had acted and written scripts for silent films, had been born in Calgary, Alberta, but blacklisted during the McCarthy era of the early 1950s while working in Hollywood.

Died: Ephraim Longworth, English soccer football star who played for Liverpool Football Club from 1910 to 1928, died at age 80.

Died: Gen. Mario Roatta, former Italian Army Chief of Staff during World War II, died at age 80, two years after his return from a post-war exile in Spain.

January 8 (Monday)

Pierre Guillard, a mentally ill French man, used a knife to gouge several holes in Peter Paul Rubens' *The Virgin and Child Surrounded by the Holy Innocents* at The Louvre in Paris.

Italy and Yugoslavia signed a treaty to set their nations' respective boundaries in the Adriatic Sea.

A collision between two Boston subway trains injured 61 people. There were no fatalities.

Otis Redding's single "(Sittin' On) The Dock of the Bay" was released posthumously. Redding recorded the song, which he had written with Steve Cropper, less than a month before its release; he and six others were then killed when their charter airplane crashed into Lake Monona outside Madison, Wisconsin on December 10, 1967. The song would become #1 on the U.S. charts, becoming the first posthumously released song ever to do so.

The Undersea World of Jacques Cousteau, a televised documentary series that focused on marine biodiversity, made its debut on the ABC television network in the United States.

January 9 (Tuesday)

In Australia, an election of Liberal Party leadership was held to elect a successor to the late Prime Minister Harold Holt, who disappeared while swimming in rough conditions on December 17, 1967. Initially, four candidates vied for the leadership of the party, which was also essentially the prime ministership: Les Bury, John Gorton, Paul Hasluck, and Billy Snedden. No candidate received a majority, and Bury and Snedden were eliminated from further consideration after receiving the fewest votes. On the second ballot, Gorton won an absolute majority over Hasluck. Gorton was sworn in as prime minister the following day.

The Israeli submarine INS *Dakar* departed Portsmouth Harbor, England, on its first voyage for the Israeli Navy after having been purchased from Great Britain, renovated and refit. All contact with the submarine would be lost near Crete 15 days later with 69 hands on board. More than a year later, items from the submarine would wash ashore, but the main wreckage on the bottom of the Mediterranean Sea would not be found until May 1999.

For the first time since 1955, the clocks in the tower housing Big Ben in London were stopped by the weather. Snow drifts and intense cold caused the clocks' hands to stop at 6:28 a.m. Maintenance crews restarted the clock four hours later.

The Organization of Arab Petroleum Exporting Countries (OAPEC) was formed by Saudi Arabia, Kuwait and Libya, which were members of both the Organization of Petroleum Exporting Countries (OPEC) and the Arab League.

The National Football League Players Association (NFLPA) formally established itself as an independent labor union. The players would strike just six months later, leading to the league's first collective bargaining agreement.

The Secret Service confiscated $4.1 million in counterfeit money at John F. Kennedy Airport in New York City. At the time, it was the largest such seizure in history.

Born: Joey Lauren Adams, American actress and director who has appeared in at least 40 films including *Dazed and Confused* and *Chasing Amy,* and television series such as *The United States of Tara*, was born in North Little Rock, Arkansas.

January 10 (Wednesday)

With tensions between India and Pakistan rising, India rescinded its approval of the Tashkent Declaration, which it had signed with Pakistan exactly two years earlier (January 10, 1966) to resolve the Indo-Pakistani war of 1965.

In South Vietnam, 15 U.S. battalions were relocated from the border with North Vietnam and moved to new positions around Saigon (now called Ho Chi Minh City) and other major cities by order of Gen. William Westmoreland, the head of U.S. forces in Vietnam. Although the U.S. would benefit from the decision later in the month during the surprise Tet Offensive, American military leaders "failed to anticipate the timing and, more particularly, scale and character" of the Tet full-scale attack.

At 7:05 p.m. in Houston, Texas NASA Mission Control successfully soft-landed Surveyor 7 on the moon. It landed on the rim of the crater Tycho, and would remain operational until February 21. During its time on the moon, Surveyor 7 sent 21,091 photographs back to Earth, and successfully detected two laser beams aimed at it from the night side of the crescent Earth, from Tucson, Arizona and Wrightwood, California.

In the Bay of Biscay off the west coast of France, the British submarine HMS *Grampus* was ensnared in the nets of the fishing trawler *Formalhaut*, immobilizing both vessels. The *Formalhaut* was dragging its nets deep in the bay when it unexpectedly hit the *Grampus*, bringing it to a halt. Ninety feet below the surface, the *Grampus* could not maneuver. Complicating matters, nobody on the *Formalhaut* spoke English and nobody on the *Grampus* spoke French. After a few hours, the trawling cable was cut and the *Grampus* sailed onward, "with her conning tower still draped with nets, "to continue in a scheduled naval exercise."

Born: Zoe Tay, Singaporean actress, was born as Tay Hui Gek in Singapore.

Born: Lyle Menendez, who along with his brother Erik would be convicted in 1994 of the 1989 murder of their parents, Jose and Kitty Menendez, was born in Woodbury, New Jersey.

Died: Eben Dönges, South African President-elect and former Prime Minister; died on June 1, at the age of 69. Dönges had been elected to the honorary post of State President, but had suffered a stroke before he could take office and fell into a coma from which he never awoke.

January 11 (Thursday)

The Israeli government expropriated 838 acres (3.39 sq. km) of former Jordanian land in East Jerusalem in order to restore the city's Jewish Quarter.

In Geneva, the International Red Cross announced that Israel and Egypt had agreed to conditions for releasing prisoners of war who had been captured during the Six Day War in June 1967. At the time, there were 4,000 Egyptian prisoners of war (POWs) and only 20 Israeli POWs to be exchanged, because agreements had already been worked out with Jordan, Syria, Lebanon and Iraq. The transfers took place between Ismailia on the west side of the Suez Canal, and El Qantara on the east side, with the exchange controlled by Israel's occupation forces.

Salomon Tandeng Muna was appointed new Prime Minister of West Cameroon, while Simon Pierre Tchoungui continued as the Prime Minister of a reorganized East Cameroon. Both positions were under the direction of Ahmadou Ahidjo, the President of the Federal

Republic of Cameroon. In 1972, the offices of Muna and Tchoungui would be eliminated.

British Foreign Secretary George Brown met with his American counterpart, U.S. Secretary of State Dean Rusk, to tell him that Britain's economic problems had led it to decide that it could no longer police the Middle East or Southeast Asia. In a meeting that Brown would refer to as "bloody unpleasant," Rusk reportedly said, "Be British, George, be British. How can you betray us?"

The U.S. Navy electronic surveillance ship USS *Pueblo*, under the command of Commander Lloyd M. Bucher, was dispatched from the port of Sasebo, Nagasaki, Japan toward North Korea for a 17-day mission to collect intelligence. (Later in the month, on January 23, the *Pueblo* and its crew would be captured by North Korea. See the subsequent entry below for that date.)

Died: Rezső Seress, a Hungarian composer whose 1933 song "Gloomy Sunday" was blamed for multiple suicides, took his own life in Budapest. He was 78.

Died: Marcello Pirani, German-born physicist who invented the Pirani vacuum gauge, based on the principle of heat loss measurement, died at age 87.

Died: Moshe Zvi Segal, eminent Israeli rabbi and Talmudic scholar, died at age 88.

January 12 (Friday)

The American Telephone and Telegraph Company (AT&T), which controlled nearly all of the telephones in the United States, announced plans to provide a universal emergency telephone number that could be dialed quickly from any telephone in the country, and said that it would allocate $50,000,000 to install the routing equipment in American cities over a period of several years, starting with the exchanges in New York City and Washington, D.C. According to AT&T, a computer search found that the number most likely to have no conflict with an existing area code or exchange, and to also meet the requirement of not being misdialed from a rotary phone, was 9-1-1.

Norman M. Yoder, a Pennsylvania Department of Human Services commissioner from the office that provided services to the blind and visually impaired, told the Associated Press that six college students "at a western Pennsylvania college" which he declined to identify, had permanently lost their eyesight after taking the hallucinogen LSD and staring at the sun, not realizing what they were doing. Skeptical reporters began investigating, and Pennsylvania Governor Raymond P. Shafer ordered an inquiry, which determined that Yoder had made the story up.

The trial of four Soviet writers ended with the defendants being found guilty of subversion, with sentences ranging from one to seven years. Poet Yuri Galanskov received the longest term after being convicted of sedition for working with the anti-Communist organization Narodno-Trudovoy Soyuz (NTS, the "People's Labor Union"), with author Alexander Ginzburg sentenced to five years. Vera Lashkova was sentenced to one year incarceration, but was given credit for nearly a year of detention. Alexei Dobrovolsky received a reduced two-year sentence in exchange for testifying against Galanskov and Ginzburg.

Zambia released five South African police who had been held in the jail in Livingstone since December 27, 1967. The five men had driven across the Victoria Falls Bridge from Rhodesia into Zambia, then ignored an order by border police to stop. The release followed an apology by South Africa's foreign minister, Hilgard Muller, to Zambia's President Kenneth Kaunda.

The Kampuchean Revolutionary Army, which would carry out a genocide program in Cambodia between 1975 and 1979, was established by the orders of Pol Pot, the leader of the southeast Asian nation's Communist party, the CPK.

Born: Keith Anderson, American country music singer, was born in Miami, Oklahoma.

Born: Rachael Harris, American actress who portrayed the mother in the *Diary of a Wimpy Kid* film series, was born in Worthington, Ohio.

January 13 (Saturday)

Johnny Cash performed his historic concert at Folsom State Prison in California. The location was selected by his manager because of Cash's 1955 hit song "Folsom Prison Blues." The concert wasn't the first that Cash had performed at a penal institution, nor was Cash the only artist to appear that day (the Statler Brothers, Carl Perkins, The Carter Family, and The Tennessee Three were also present), but it was the first time that Cash had recorded a live album inside a prison. *Johnny Cash at Folsom Prison* would become the number one country music album in the United States after going on sale in May.

Bill Masterton, a center for the Minnesota North Stars of the National Hockey League, was fatally injured during a game against the Oakland Seals after a body check by two defenders. After Masterton was taken from the rink and blood cleaned from the ice, play continued in a game that would end in a 2-2 tie. Masterton (who was known for scoring the North Stars' very first goal when the team began play on October 11, 1967) would die 30 hours later from brain hemorrhaging caused by severe head trauma.

Standing Naval Force Atlantic (STANAVFORLANT), a multinational naval force with ships from the Netherlands, Norway, the United Kingdom, and the United States, was activated for the first time, with a base at England's Portland Harbor. Within six months, Canada, West Germany and Portugal would also contribute ships and crews.

At Minot Air Force Base in North Dakota, a U.S. Air Force KC-135 Stratotanker crashed. The subsequent investigation determined that during a snowstorm, the pilot over-rotated the aircraft during takeoff. All 13 crew members were killed. It was the first of five U.S. Air Force KC-135 Stratotankers that would crash in 1968.

Born: Patrick Stewart "Pat" Onstad, Canadian soccer goalkeeper and national team member, was born in Vancouver, British Columbia.

January 14 (Sunday)

In Super Bowl II, the Green Bay Packers defeated the Oakland Raiders, 33-14, before 75,546 fans at the Orange Bowl in Miami. Packers quarterback Bart Starr was selected as Most Valuable Player in the game, as he was for the first Super Bowl. Packers head coach Vince Lombardi retired after the game, which was still officially called the AFL-NFL World Championship Game until the following year.

The Battle of Nam Bac, which had been waged since August 1966, ended in Vietnam. The battle was fought between the Royal Armed

Forces of Laos and attackers from the North Vietnamese Army and the Communist Pathet Lao group. The battle ended with the 3,000 remaining Nam Bac defenders being killed or captured.

Born: LL Cool J, the American rapper and actor, was born as James Todd Smith in Bay Shore, New York.

January 15 (Monday)

An earthquake in Sicily killed 380 people and injured 1,000 more. Occurring in the valley along the Belice River, the 6.4 magnitude quake struck at 2:01 in the morning and destroyed the villages of Gibellina, Montevago and Salaparuta, and caused heavy damage to Santa Margherita di Belice, Poggioreale, Santa Ninfa and Salemi. The quake came to be known in Italy as *Il Terremoto del Belice.*

On this, the first day that the U.S. Congress would meet in 1968, former Congresswoman Jeanette Rankin from Montana led a group of 5,000 women from Washington D.C.'s Union Station to the steps of the U.S. Capitol Building in an anti-war protest. Previously, in 1917, Rankin would be one of only 50 members of Congress who would vote against U.S. involvement in World War I, and on December 8, 1941, she would be the only member of Congress to vote in opposition to declaring war against Japan. When asked to reconsider her vote that day to make the declaration of war against Japan unanimous, pacifist and women's rights advocate Rankin replied "As a woman, I can't go to war, and I refuse to send anyone else."

In Belgium, the campus of the Catholic University of Leuven erupted in violence that spilled into the city, after the clergy administering the 440-year-old institution announced that they would continue to hold classes in French (spoken by the Walloon minority in the school) in addition to Flemish Dutch language. Hundreds of students were arrested, and the revolt would spread to other universities and towns in the northern part of the kingdom, leading to the resignation of the Belgian government on February 7. At the end of the spring semester, the university would split into two institutions, with the Flemish-speaking students and professors continuing at the Katholieke Universiteit Leuven, and the opening of a new campus 30 kilometers (19 mi) away at Louvain-la-Neuve for the French-speaking *Université Catholique de Louvain*.

The NBC spy adventure *The Man from U.N.C.L.E.* aired its final episode. The series had premiered in September 1964, and led to spy-crazed television schedule that eventually included 12 different series, including *Mission: Impossible*, *I Spy*, *The Avengers*, and even the Mel Brooks spy spoof *Get Smart*. The series was so popular that several double episodes were released in theaters; in addition, the spinoff *The Girl from U.N.C.L.E.* aired from September 1966 to April 1967, and a series of U.N.C.L.E. toys and novels were very popular. The international spy agency U.N.C.L.E. (an abbreviation for the United Network Command for Law and Enforcement), as well as some of the character names and many gadgets, were the brainchild of James Bond creator Ian Fleming, as well as series creator Sam Rolfe. The two main characters were American agent Napoleon Solo (played by Robert Vaughn) and Soviet agent Illya Kuryakin (played by David McCallum). The series would be replaced the following week by the innovative NBC sketch comedy series *Rowan & Martin's Laugh-In*.

Born: Chad Lowe, American actor known for playing roles in television series including *Life Goes On*, *Melrose Place*, *24*, and *Pretty Little Liars*, was born in Dayton, Ohio.

Died: Bill Masterton, 29-year-old Canadian hockey player, became the first and only NHL player to die of injuries received in a game.

The league now awards the Masterton Trophy annually to the player "who best exemplifies the qualities of perseverance, sportsmanship, and dedication to ice hockey."

January 16 (Tuesday)

A team of 31 North Korean infiltrators undertook a mission in South Korea to attack the Blue House (the residence of the president of South Korea) and kill President Park Chung-hee. (See entry below for January 21.)

South Vietnam's President Nguyen Van Thieu and U.S. Army commander William C. Westmoreland decided to end the scheduled Tet holiday truce with North Vietnam, four days ahead of schedule, though the announcement of the decision would not be made until January 30. According to the written logs of a North Vietnamese spy who had infiltrated Thieu's offices, North Vietnam's military leaders had moved the date of a major offensive from February 5 to January 31.

British Prime Minister Harold Wilson announced to the House of Commons the British government decision to remove its military presence from the Persian Gulf and all of Asia (with the exception of Hong Kong) by January 31, 1971.

Urho Kekkonen was re-elected to a third term as President of Finland. Kekkonen received votes from his own Centre Party as well as those of the Social Democratic Party and the Finnish People's Democratic League. Kekkonen received 56% of the popular vote.

The Prime of Miss Jean Brodie, starring Zoe Caldwell, premiered on Broadway. The play was based on the novel by Muriel Spark. Caldwell would win a Tony playing the title role.

Born: Stephan Pastis, an American cartoonist known for the comic strip "Pearls Before Swine" was born in San Marino, California.

Born: Atticus Ross, an Oscar-winning English film composer whose work was featured in films *The Social Network* and *The Girl with the Dragon Tattoo*, was born in London. (In 2016, Ross would join the band Nine Inch Nails).

Died: Bob Jones Sr., American evangelist and religious broadcaster who founded Bob Jones University, died in Greenville, South Carolina at the age of 84.

January 17 (Wednesday)

President Lyndon Johnson gave his constitutionally mandated State of the Union address to the 90th United States Congress at the U.S. Capitol Building. Johnson reported that "I believe, with abiding conviction, that this people—nurtured by their deep faith, tutored by their hard lessons, moved by their high aspirations—have the will to meet the trials that these times impose."

British auto manufacturers British Motor Holdings and Leyland Motor Corporation announced a merger to become British Leyland. The new corporation became the largest car company in the United Kingdom and the sixth largest in the world (after General Motors, Ford Motors, Chrysler, Fiat, and Volkswagen). British Leyland vehicles included Jaguar, MG, Triumph, and Land Rover.

The Kampuchean Revolutionary Army launched its first attack, with three guerrillas storming a police post at Bay Damram in Cambodia to steal weapons. The following day, weapons were seized in other villages and three policemen were killed in ambushes. An attack at Thvak took place the following week. The Kampuchean revolutionaries would take control of Cambodia seven years later and begin a reign of terror that took the lives of an estimated 2-3 million Cambodian people.

Born: Women's middle-distance runner Svetlana Masterkova was born in Achinsk, Russia. In August 1996, Masterkova would set the women's world record for one mile (4 minutes, 12.56 seconds) and one kilometer (2:28.98); both records still stand as of December 2017. Masterkova also won the 800m and 1500m races in the 1996 Olympics and the 1999 world championships.

January 18 (Thursday)

Singer and actress Eartha Kitt was a guest at a White House luncheon hosted by Lady Bird Johnson to honor a group of "Women Doers," influential women who were invited by the First Lady to talk about specific issues. When President Johnson entered the room, Kitt asked him a question to which she evidently didn't like the president's answer. Although Kitt did not respond to the President himself, she confronted the First Lady about the Vietnam War in what became one of the first public in-person disagreements with the president's war policy.

Born: David Ayer, American film director (*Fury, Suicide Squad*) and writer (*Training Day*) was born in Champaign, Illinois.

Died: Bert Wheeler, an American comedian who was part of the vaudeville act of Wheeler & Woolsey until Robert Woolsey's death in 1938, died in New York City at age 72.

January 19 (Friday)

An experiment called "Project Faultless" was conducted; it was designed to determine whether an earthquake could be triggered by detonating an underground nuclear weapon along a fault line. After the residents of the Central Nevada Test Site towns of Tonopah and Eureka, Nevada were briefed about what to expect, an atomic bomb was detonated in Nye County at a depth of 3,200 feet (980 m). The blast, which the Atomic Energy Commission said had a one megaton yield, was believed to be the most powerful nuclear weapon ever exploded in the United States. The explosion caused upheavals of the ground in a wide area, breaking windows 87 miles (140 km) away at a high school in Ely. Because of the surface damage, the test site would eventually be declared unsuitable. Reports the following day would say that buildings in Salt Lake City and San Francisco swayed from the explosion. University of California at Berkeley scientists estimated the blast to be 6.0 on the Richter scale.

U.S. President Lyndon Johnson completed the installation of a tape recording system in the Cabinet Room of the White House to preserve his discussions with staff and government leaders. Roughly 200 hours of recordings would be delivered to the Johnson presidential library after Johnson's death in 1973. Despite Johnson's own wish that the recordings be sealed for 50 years after his passing (i.e., until 2023), most were released beginning in 1992.

In Japan, thousands of people protested as the American aircraft carrier USS *Enterprise* made the first visit to that nation by a nuclear-powered ship. The *Enterprise* docked at the U.S. Navy base at Sasebo, about 50 miles (80 km) from Nagasaki, which had been devastated by the second U.S. atomic bomb on August 9, 1945. Permission to dock had been granted by Prime Minister Eisaku Sato, who had made the decision without consultation with his Foreign Minister or other cabinet members.

Born: Matt Hill, Canadian voice actor known for portraying the character Ed on *Ed, Edd, 'n' Eddy* was born in North Vancouver, British Columbia.

Died: Ray Harroun, the American race car driver who won the first Indianapolis 500 in 1911, died in Anderson, Indiana at age 89. In that first Indy 500, Harroun drove a bright yellow Marmon Wasp to victory at an average speed of 74.602 miles per hour (120.060 km/h). The winning vehicle remains on display at the Indianapolis Motor Speedway Museum, located on the infield of the race track.

January 20 (Saturday)

In South Vietnam, a defector from the North Vietnamese Army surrendered to U.S. Marines at the Khe Sanh Combat Base and warned them that the NVA was preparing to launch a large attack there the next day, starting with an assault after midnight against Hill 861 overlooking the area.

Singer/guitarist/songwriter Bob Dylan performed at the Woody Guthrie Memorial Concert at Carnegie Hall in New York City. Guthrie had died three months earlier from complications from Huntington's Disease. Other performers at the concert included Robbie Robertson, Levon Helm, Rick Danko, Richard Manuel, and Garth Hudson. Dylan was performing in public for the first time since being badly injured 18 months earlier in an accident while riding his Triumph motorcycle near his home in Woodstock, New York. Mystery continues to surround the accident, as friends reported that Dylan provided them with different causes of the crash, including Dylan having sun in his eyes or hitting an oil spot on the road. Dylan's account of his injuries also reportedly varied.

In the first regular-season college basketball game to be shown live on national television, the second-ranked University of Houston Cougars defeated the top-ranked University of California at Los Angeles (UCLA) Bruins, 71-69. Played inside the Houston Astrodome baseball stadium, the game set a college basketball attendance record of 52,693, and was billed as "The Game of the Century." Both teams came in undefeated, with UCLA having a 13-0 record and a 47-game winning streak, and Houston having a 16-0 record. Both teams had a well-known player, with Houston being led by Elvin Hayes and UCLA being led by Lew Alcindor (who would later change his name to Kareem Abdul-Jabbar).

Married: Actress Sharon Tate married film director Roman Polanski at a ceremony in London, a little more than a year before they moved to their home in Los Angeles. At that home, Tate, age 26 and two weeks from giving birth to a son, would be murdered by members of the Manson group in August 1969.

January 21 (Sunday)

The Battle of Khe Sanh began under cover of fog at 5:30 a.m. as the North Vietnamese Army started shelling a U.S. Marine base from positions in South Vietnam and across the border in Laos. On the first day, shells destroyed the American base's main ammunition dump, along with 98% of its ammunition. The battle would last for 77 days, with the compound finally being freed in April. However, 274 U.S. troops were killed, and American forces were diverted prior to the Tet Offensive.

North Vietnamese Army (NVA) General Vo Nguyen Giap gave the go-ahead to NVA and Viet Cong commanders in South Vietnam to begin the Tet Offensive on the eve of the Vietnamese New Year celebration. The attacks would begin five days earlier than originally planned, after the Tet holiday ceasefire was shortened.

A U.S. B-52 jet bomber crashed in Greenland, losing its four Mark 28 nuclear bombs. The crash occurred while the Stratofortress was monitoring the U.S. Air Force's Thule Air Base, flying back and forth at an altitude of 35,000 feet (11,000 m) over the base's early warning system. Four cushions had been placed beneath an uncomfortable seat and were blocking a vent; when the co-pilot switched on a backup heating system that relied on warm air that had been pulled in through the plane's intake manifold, the cushions caught fire. The seven-man crew ejected, but the airplane crashed into the ice-covered Bylot Sound near the base. The conventional explosives inside the four thermonuclear weapons exploded on impact, contaminating three square miles of ice with radioactive plutonium. However, because of the "one-point safe" design that had been developed in the mid-1950s to avoid a crash such as this, a larger catastrophe was averted. A historian would later note: "If the Mark 28 hadn't been made inherently one-point safe, the bombs that hit the ice could have produced a nuclear yield. And the partial detonation of a nuclear weapon, or two, or three— without any warning, at the air base considered essential for the defense of the United States— could have been misinterpreted" at the headquarters of the Strategic Air Command, starting a nuclear conflict.

The group of 31 North Korean guerillas who began their mission on January 16 to attack President Park Chung-Hee's presidential home, Blue House in South Korea, carried out their mission of attempting to assassinate the president. Although the guerillas were unsuccessful in completing their mission, they came within 800 meters of the Blue House before a firefight began, initially with South Korean police. Twenty-Eight North Koreans, 26 South Koreans, and four Americans were killed in the operation.

The Israeli Labor Party was created by the merger of three existing parties, Prime Minister Levi Eshkol's Mapai; Yitzhak-Meir Levin's Ahdut HaAvoda; and David Ben-Gurion's Rafi.

Born: Charlotte Ross, American TV actress best known for her roles in the daytime soap opera *Days of our Lives* and the police drama *NYPD Blue*, was born in Winnetka, Illinois.

Died: Will Lang Jr., American journalist, war correspondent, and bureau head for *Life* magazine, died in St. Anton, Austria, at age 53.

January 22 (Monday)

Rowan & Martin's Laugh-In, which would become the number-one rated television show in the U.S. by its second season, began as a weekly program on NBC. *Laugh-In*, hosted by comedians Dan Rowan and Dick Martin, was a fast-paced variety show that featured a regular cast of comedians including Goldie Hawn, Arte Johnson, Ruth Buzzi, Judy Carne, Henry Gibson, and Jo Anne Worley. The title was a play on words of the cultural phenomenon of "sit-ins," "be-ins," "love-ins" and similar terms used for forms of civil protest. The show introduced a number of guest celebrities including Tiny Tim, and well-known celebrities made cameo appearances. The show also featured catch phrases that would become popular, including "Sock it to me!" "Ver-r-ry interesting!" and "Here come da' judge!"

The unmanned Apollo 5 was launched to test the Lunar Module (LM) that would take two astronauts from lunar orbit to the lunar surface, and then back again for a return to Earth. The LM, less its spindly landing gear, was loaded into the nose of a Saturn 1B rocket, and was launched from Cape Kennedy at 5:48 p.m. After it reached an orbit of 138 miles (222 km), the LM separated from the rocket and testing was performed on its descent engine (which would eventually lower astronauts to a soft landing on the moon). The LM would return to Earth the following day, damaged during its fiery reentry into the atmosphere.

Nigerian one-pound banknotes that had been circulated since 1958 became worthless as the deadline expired for exchanging them for newly printed currency. The decision to replace the notes had been made in August 1967 after the secession of Biafra, in order to prevent Biafra from trading its holdings of Nigerian pounds on foreign exchanges. Biafra would introduce its own coins and currency, the Biafran pound, one week later.

Born: Guy Fieri (born Guy Ramsay Ferry), American chef and TV personality, was born in Columbus, Ohio.

Died: Duke Kahanamoku, the Hawaiian athlete who popularized surfing, died at the age of 77 in Honolulu. Kahanamoku had won gold medals in swimming in the 1912 and 1920 Summer Olympic games. Kahanamoku was also credited with saving the lives of eight men in 1925, after a fishing vessel overturned trying to enter the harbor in Newport Beach, California. Kahanamoku was able to use his surfboard to make repeated trips out and back into shore to rescue sailors. A total of 29 sailors went into the water and 17 died. As a result of the rescues, lifeguards in the U.S. began using surfboards for rescues.

Died: U.S. Air Force Captain Lance Sijan died in North Vietnam's Hoa Lo prison camp from pneumonia, malnutrition and multiple injuries. Sijan, age 25, had spent 40 days eluding his captors after his F-4C Phantom II fighter was shot down over Laos on November 9, 1967. He had been captured, escaped, and then recaptured. Captain Sijan would be posthumously awarded the Medal of Honor.

January 23 (Tuesday)

North Korea seized the U.S. Navy vessel *USS Pueblo*, claiming the ship violated its territorial waters while spying. The *Pueblo* was a *Banner*-class environmental research ship being used by the U.S. Navy for surveillance. At 12:27 p.m. local time, a North Korean SO-1 patrol boat approached the *Pueblo* and gave the sign for "Heave to or I will open fire." *Pueblo* commander Lloyd M. Bucher ordered his crew to signal back that it was in international waters and that it intended to remain at its location until the next day. Three North Korean P-4 torpedo boats then arrived from Wonsan Harbor, with the first patrol boat signaling for the *Pueblo* to follow. At 1:27, the North Korean vessels fired their guns as the crew of the slower *Pueblo* attempted to escape. At 1:45, Bucher surrendered the ship. (Later in the year, on December 23, after an apology from the U.S., the North Koreans would release the 82 members of the *Pueblo* crew but would keep the American ship, which is now on display in Pyongyang.)

Elections took place for Denmark's parliament, the *Folketing*, ending the government of Prime Minister Jens Otto Krag of the Social Democratic Party.

The government of state of Madras in southern India became the first to eliminate a requirement that students learn Hindi, the most commonly spoken language in the country. Students had the option to learn Hindi, but required instruction was in the Tamil language spoken by most of people in Madras (now called the Tamil Nadu state). The only remaining required language for students in Madras was English.

The student strike at Belgium's Catholic University of Leuven that had begun a week earlier was joined by other Flemish speakers, and high school students in Flanders walked out of their classrooms.

Born: Eric Metcalf, American professional football running back and collegiate long jumper, was born in Seattle, Washington.

January 24 (Wednesday)

France conducted its first test of the experimental *Ludion* jet pack, which was propelled by isopropyl nitrate and designed to lift a soldier for a short distance. The *Ludion* project was abandoned after 64 flights.

Charlie Wilson, a participant in of the Great Train Robbery in England in August 1963, was recaptured more than three years after he had escaped from prison. Police found him near Montreal in the Canadian town of Rigaud, Quebec. Wilson had been living in Rigaud for two years under an assumed name. Wilson would be released in 1978 after spending 10 more years imprisoned in England, would retire to Spain, and would be murdered on April 23, 1990, at his home in Marbella in a contract killing.

The western film *Firecreek*, starring James Stewart and Henry Fonda, was released in theaters.

Born: Mary Lou Retton, American gymnast who would win five medals at the 1984 Olympics in Los Angeles, including a gold medal in the individual all-around competition, was born in Fairmont, West Virginia.

Died: Yvor Winters, American poet and literary critic from Chicago, died at age 67.

January 25 (Thursday)

The Israeli submarine INS *Dakar* sank in the Mediterranean Sea on its first voyage since being purchased from the United Kingdom, killing the 69 crew members on board. The wreckage would be located more than 30 years later, in 1999. The probable fault was determined to be structural failure in one of the torpedo tubes.

I Never Sang for My Father, starring Hal Holbrook and Lillian Gish, premiered on Broadway. It ran for 124 performances at the Shubert Theatre, and the story would be made into a film in 1970.

January 26 (Friday)

Rioting began in Caen, France after police broke up a protest march by roughly 10,000 protesters and striking workers from the Saviem truck factory. Police used large amounts of tear gas in what was described as an unprovoked attack. The marchers, angered by the use of tear gas, began to throw rocks and Molotov cocktails; the riot would go through the night until 5:00 the following morning. One hundred people were hurt, 36 of them badly enough to require hospitalization, and another 85 were arrested.

Flying a Lockheed A-12 Blackbird reconnaissance jet at 80,000 feet (24,000 m) above North Korea, CIA pilot Jack Weeks located the missing USS *Pueblo*, anchored at Wonson. The A-12, predecessor of the SR-71 Blackbird, was flying as part of the Asian reconnaissance program called Operation Black Shield. In the same mission, Weeks also took photos that showed that North Korea was not massing troops near the demilitarized zone, easing fears of a new Korean War.

Born: Ravi Teja, Indian actor in Telugu cinema, was born as Ravi Shankar Raju Bhupatiraju in Jaggampeta, Andhra Pradesh.

Born: Eric Davis, American football cornerback, was born in Anniston, Alabama.

Born: Novala Takemoto, Japanese fashion designer, was born in Uji, Kyoto Prefecture, Japan.

Died: Merrill C. Meigs, American journalist and publisher of the *Chicago Herald and Examiner*, died at age 84. Meigs was also an aviator who strongly supported Chicago as a center of aviation. Advocating for a third airport in Chicago in addition to O'Hare and Midway, Meigs fought for the airport in Chicago's loop that was named after him in 1949. Meigs Field was removed in 2003.

January 27 (Saturday)

Two days after the loss of the Israeli submarine *Dakar* with all 69 on board, the French submarine *Minerve* sank in the Mediterranean Sea, killing all 52 aboard. The last contact from *Minerve* was while it was in the Mediterranean approaching its home port at Toulon, just 25 miles (40 km) away. At the time, the submarine was 40 feet (12 m) below the surface, shallow enough that it was using its snorkel to take air into its diesel engine. To date, the cause of the sinking is not known, and the wreckage has never been found.

The official Tet holiday ceasefire began in South Vietnam and North Vietnam, in the days leading up to the New Year's Eve celebrations to welcome the start of Mau Than, the Year of the Monkey.

In the Indian state of Bihar, the government of Chief Minister Mahamaya Prasad Sinha was removed from power by a censure motion that passed 163-150.

Born: Mike Patton, American rock music singer known for his work with the group *Faith No More*, was born in Eureka, California.

Born: Tricky, British hip hop musician, was born as Adrian Nicholas Matthews Thaws in Bristol, England.

Born: Tracy Lawrence, American country music singer and songwriter, was born in Atlanta, Texas.

Born: Matt Stover, American football placekicker who became one of most accurate kickers in National Football League history, was born in Dallas, Texas.

January 28 (Sunday)

Political organizer Anibal Escalante and 36 other members of Cuba's Communist Party were arrested and charged with being a "microfaction" which was working outside of governmental channels with eastern European governments, particularly the Soviet Union via the Soviet Embassy. In reaction, the Soviets, who provided the support to the Cuban government's programs, began to establish relations with governments that Cuba regarded as unfriendly.

Born: Sarah McLachlan, Canadian singer, instrumentalist, and songwriter, was born in Halifax, Nova Scotia.

Born: Rakim, American hip hop musician, was born as William Griffin, Jr. in Wyandanch, Long Island, New York.

January 29 (Monday)

Eight days after four hydrogen bombs were lost in the B-52 Stratofortress crash in Greenland, the U.S. Strategic Air Command ordered all nuclear weapons removed from its patrol bombers in order to prevent further accidents.

Born: Edward Burns, American actor, film producer, writer, and director, was born in Woodside, Queens, New York City.

Born: Aeneas Williams, American professional football cornerback, was born in New Orleans, Louisiana.

Died: L. P. Jai, Indian cricket player who was a major star between the First and Second World Wars, died at age 65.

January 30 (Tuesday)

The Tet Offensive, one of the most significant events and a major turning point in the Vietnam War, began when Viet Cong forces launched a series of surprise attacks across South Vietnam. The attacks began with an assault shortly after midnight on the Nha Trang Air Base and the headquarters of the U.S. Army's I Field Force. Attacks followed next at the American I Corps and II Corps bases at Ban Me Thuot, Kontum, Hoi An, Tuy Hoa, Da Nang, Qui Nhon, and Pleiku. The North Vietnamese Army had planned for the offensive to begin on January 31, but Viet Cong forces in the South started a day in advance.

Ford's Theatre in Washington, D.C., held its first entertainment program since April 14, 1865, the night that President Abraham Lincoln was assassinated there during the comedy *Our American Cousin*. For the reopening, Henry Fonda, Harry Belafonte, Helen Hayes, and Andy Williams were among the performers on hand for the celebration. Television viewers at home could watch a videotaped performance that night.

Assistant Postmaster General Richard Murphy ruled that hippies could work for the United States Postal Service "but they must have neat haircuts and get rid of their beards and sandals" and wear proper attire. According to Murphy, the largest number of hippies worked at post offices in San Francisco and some had been "walking their routes barefooted with shaggy beards, hair down to their shoulders, and wearing everything from bearskin coats to dungarees."

Born: King Felipe VI of Spain, who would become head of state in Spain in 2014, was born in Madrid.

Died: Robert Wood Johnson II, 74, American businessman who built the Johnson & Johnson Company into one of the world's largest health care suppliers. He left most of his $400 million estate to the Robert Wood Johnson Foundation.

Died: Pete Calac, Native Indian former National Football League player from the Mission Indians tribe of California, who played for five NFL teams during the 1920s, died in Canton, Ohio at age 75.

January 31 (Wednesday)

Following sporadic attacks on American bases the day before, the Tet Offensive expanded to nearly all of South Vietnam's military bases and major cities simultaneously, with the Viet Cong and North Vietnamese Army coordinating an extensive assault that was much larger than U.S. intelligence had expected. An estimated 84,000 troops had invaded provincial and district capitals during the Tet holiday ceasefire to strike in what would become the most significant turning point of the Vietnam War. More American soldiers were killed in action on this day than on any other day of the Vietnam War, with 245 deaths. Viet Cong commandos attacked the U.S. Embassy in Saigon. At 2:45 a.m., a truck and a taxi cab pulled out of a repair shop in Saigon and drove to the U.S. Embassy compound. At 3:00, fifteen commandos set explosives and blew a large hole in the compound's wall, then scrambled through and killed the two U.S. military police guarding the six-story embassy building. Antitank guns and rockets were fired at the doors. U.S. Ambassador Ellsworth Bunker was awakened and taken to a secret hiding place. U.S. soldiers counterattacked and retook the compound by 9:15 a.m. Fortunately for the Americans, the embassy had been fortified less than a year earlier with shatterproof windows and a thick, 8-foot wall. The 1,000 guerrillas who had infiltrated Saigon seized the government radio station and surrounded the presidential palace, where fierce fighting would take place in an attempt by the guerillas to capture the palace. Simultaneously, the old imperial capital at Hué was taken over by 3:40 that morning, and more than 2,000 residents would be executed over the next three weeks. Another 6,000 residents would be killed in the bombing and shelling of the city in the American counterattack, which would destroy 90 percent of Hue's 20,000 houses. Overall, 36 of the 44 provincial capitals and 64 of the 245 district government seats were attacked on the first full day of the Tet Offensive. One of the capitals, Ben Tre, was virtually destroyed while being captured and recaptured.

The small island nation of Nauru, having a population of 5,560 (including 2,734 natives) was granted independence from Australia, with Hammer DeRoburt serving as the country's first president.

The first television broadcasting took place in Turkey, with test transmissions for the national network Türkiye Radyo Televizyon Kurumu (TRT, the Turkish Radio and Television Corporation).

February 1968

February 1 (Thursday)

The Royal Canadian Air Force, Royal Canadian Navy, and Canadian Army merged to form the unified Canadian Armed Forces. All combined 105,000 members would begin wearing the same uniform, replacing their traditional uniforms for sailors, soldiers, and airmen.

The Pennsylvania Railroad and New York Central Railroad merged to form "Penn Central." The merger became effective at 12:10 a.m. Eastern time, and, at $4.29 billion, was the biggest corporate merger in history by that time. The United States Supreme Court had concluded on January 15 that the merger would not violate antitrust laws.

Former U.S. Vice President Richard M. Nixon announced his candidacy for the Republican Party nomination for president. Nixon had previously been the Republican candidate for president in 1960, losing to Democrat John F. Kennedy, and had lost the California governor's race to Edmund "Pat" Brown in 1962, telling the press after the '62 loss that "you don't have Nixon to kick around anymore."

One day after widespread attacks on South Vietnam's capital to start the Tet Offensive, Saigon's police chief, General Nguyen Ngoc Loan, publicly displayed a captured Viet Cong officer, Nguyen Van Lem, to a group of reporters. As the journalists watched, the chief pulled out a .38 caliber revolver and executed the Viet Cong prisoner with a single shot to the head at point-blank range. Photographer Eddie Adams captured the moment in a photo that was viewed throughout the U.S. and around the world. In addition, a film crew for the NBC television network filmed the event and the footage was included on the network's *Huntley-Brinkley Report* the following evening.

In Memphis, Tennessee, two Memphis sanitation workers, Echol Cole and Robert Walker, were crushed to death by a malfunctioning garbage truck. Twelve days later, frustrated by the city's inaction and long-standing pattern of mistreating its black employees, workers from the Memphis Department of Public Works would go on strike. (See entry for February 12.) The strike would loom large nationally in 1968, as Rev. Martin Luther King Jr. would come to the city later to support strikers.

The federal minimum wage in the United States was raised from $1.40 per hour to $1.60 per hour.

The USS *Rowan* collided with the Soviet merchant ship *Kapitan Vislobokov* in the Sea of Japan, about 95 miles east of the South Korea port of Pohang. The collision left a six-foot wide hole in the Russian vessel's stern. No injuries were reported.

Two weeks after his Green Bay Packers won Super Bowl II, Vince Lombardi resigned as head coach of the team. Lombardi retained his job as the Packers' general manager.

Born: Mark Recchi, Canadian hockey player and Hockey Hall of Fame member who would play 22 seasons in the National Hockey League, was born in Kamloops, British Columbia.

Born: Lisa Marie Presley, American singer and songwriter who is the only heir of her father, Elvis Presley, was born in Memphis, Tennessee.

Born: Pauly Shore, American comedian, actor, director, and writer whose films include *Encino Man*, was born in Hollywood, California.

Died: Lawson Little, American golfer who won the U.S. Open in 1940, died in Monterey, California at age 57.

February 2 (Friday)

Hilmar Baunsgaard became the Prime Minister of Denmark after King Frederik IX approved of forming a coalition government. The coalition consisted of Baunsgaard's leftist Social Liberal Party, the Conservative People's Party, and the center-right Venstre Party. The new party comprised a majority in Denmark's parliament (99 of 179 seats), the *Folketing*.

The U.S. 1st Cavalry Division took back the Vietnamese city of Quang Tri from the Viet Cong two days after the provincial capital was captured during the Tet Offensive.

In the Central African Republic (CAR) capital of Bangui, President Jean-Bedel Bokassa, President Joseph Mobutu of the Congo, and President Francois Tombalbaye of Chad agreed to form the Union of Central African States (UEAC, the *Union des etats de l'Afrique centrale*). Ten months after setting up the alliance, CAR would withdraw.

British group Jethro Tull performed together for the first time. The group consisted of British musicians Ian Anderson, Jeffrey Hammond and John Evan, who had played previously under various billings such as "Navy Blue," "Ian Anderson's Bag o'Nails," and "Bag o'Blues." The group used the name of an 18th Century agriculturalist and inventor, the Viscount Jethro Tull (1674-1741), who had invented the innovative horse-drawn seed drill.

Deputy U.S. Secretary of Defense Paul H. Nitze initiated a program to halt the growing use of marijuana among U.S. troops in the Vietnam War.

Born: Kenny Albert, American sportscaster and son of sportscaster Marv Albert, was born in New York City.

February 3 (Saturday)

One of Europe's most prominent music competitions, the Sanremo Music Festival, was won by songwriter Sergio Endrigo for "Canzone per te" ("Song for You"), and the song's performer, Roberto Carlos. The festival took place at the Sanremo Casino in Sanremo, Imperia, Italy.

Married: In Copenhagen, Denmark, Princess Benedikte, second in line to the throne as the daughter of King Frederik IX and the younger sister of Crown Princess Margrethe, married Richard zu Sayn-Wittgenstein-Berleburg. Two hundred guests were in attendance.

Born: Vlade Divac, Serbian basketball player and executive who played in Yugoslavia for six seasons, followed by 17 seasons in the National Basketball Association (NBA), was born in Prijepolje, SR Serbian, Yugoslavia. Divac would become the first player born and trained outside the United States to play in more than 1,000 games in the NBA.

February 4 (Sunday)

Eleven students at the Jesuit University of Guadalajara in Mexico died when an unexpected snowstorm overwhelmed their group of 29 hikers who were attempting to climb the 17,343-foot (5,286 m) Iztaccihuatl volcano in southern Mexico. The group had gone as far as the 14,100-foot (4,300 m) level when the storm hit.

Nine residents of the Hotel Roosevelt on Boston's skid row died in a fire, and another 15 were injured. All deceased residents were transients.

The Saunders-Roe Nautical 4 (SR.N4), the world's largest hovercraft, was launched. The craft was built by British Hovercraft Corporation, and had a capacity of 254 passengers. The SR.N4 would enter service carrying passengers across the English Channel on August 1, and would run for 22 years, with service ending on October 1, 2000.

After traveling to a number of cities as part of his work with the civil rights movement, Rev. Martin Luther King, Jr. returned to the Ebenezer Baptist Church where he had been pastor, and delivered what would be his final sermon there. Given to his congregation just two months before his assassination on April 4, his sermon "The Drum Major Instinct" was about the human desire for recognition of one's good works. King spoke of his own desire for recognition for doing what was right. King would say that a person's ambition should be a life of service, adding, "I just want to leave a committed life behind." The recording would be played at King's funeral.

Porsche racecars finished first, second and third places at the 24 Hours of Daytona race. The winning car, a new Porsche 907, was far enough ahead of all other teams that a number of driver changes were made late in the race just so all members of the team could participate directly in the victory. At the end of the event, all three Porsches raced across the finish line together.

Died: Neal Cassady, 43, a major figure in America's Beat Generation, was found in a coma beside a railroad track outside of

San Miguel de Allende in Mexico after attending a wedding party. Found on a cold, rainy evening, Cassady was carried by future El Paso Community College professor Anton Black to the local post office. Cassady died in a hospital a few hours later without regaining consciousness.

February 5 (Monday)

A tragedy involving fishing trawlers from the British fishing port of Kingston upon Hull worsened when the *Ross Cleveland*, the third of three trawlers in less than a month, capsized in a storm and sank off the coast of Isafjordur at Iceland. The only survivor among a crew of 19 was the ship's first mate, who escaped on a life raft before the ship sunk. Two other fishing trawlers from Kingston upon Hull had sunk near Iceland in January; the *St Romanus* had disappeared on January 11 and the *Kingston Peridot* was lost approximately January 26. The latter two trawlers each had a crew of 20.

The Greek legislature passed a law to end the practice of "baby marketing," in which parents in Greece could legally sell their infants to third parties who would then resell them to buyers in the U.S. and the Netherlands. It was believed that the number of babies exported from Greece prior to the law was approximately 1,000 per year.

Born: Roberto Alomar, Major League Baseball player, was born in Ponce, Puerto Rico. Alomar would be regarded as one of the top second basemen in the game from 1988 to 2004. He was inducted into the Baseball Hall of Fame in 2011.

Born: Han Ong, Philippine-born American playwright and MacArthur Genius Grant recipient, whose novels include Fixer Chao and The Disinherited, was born in Manila, The Philippines.

Born: Marcus Grönholm, Finnish rally and rallycross driver and 2000 and 2002 world champion, was born in Kauniainen, Finland.

Died: Luckey Roberts (who had been born Charles Luckyth Roberts), African-American stride pianist and composer known for his work in jazz, ragtime, and blues, died in New York City at age 80.

February 6 (Tuesday)

The 1968 Winter Olympics opened in the French Alps, with 1,350 athletes from 37 nations. The Olympic torch was lit by French skier Alain Calmat, who had won the 1965 World Skiing Championship.

Lebanon Prime Minister Rashid Karami and his cabinet resigned as the country prepared for elections. Karami would be replaced on February 8 by Abdallah El-Yafi, whose staff would form a caretaker government to supervise the voting process.

The Beatles began their trip to India to visit Maharishi Mahesh Yogi. The trip led to an increase in the practice of Transcendental Meditation and acceptance of Indian spirituality and culture in the West. Others on the trip included actress Mia Farrow, musician Donovan, Beach Boys singer Mike Love, the Beatles' wives, girlfriends, and family friends (Maureen Starkey, Jane Asher, Cynthia Lennon, and Pattie and Jenny Boyd) and a number of others from Europe and the U.S.

February 7 (Wednesday)

An Indian Air Force Antonov An-12 disappeared in the Himalayan mountains while flying from Chandigarh to Leh. All 102 people aboard were lost, including members of the Garhwal Rifles. There would be no trace of the wreckage for 33 years until members of a mountaineering expedition discovered several Garhwal Rifle badges in 2001.

In the Vietnam War, the North Vietnamese Army used tanks and other armored vehicles for the first time. The NVA troops and vehicles attacked a U.S. Army Special Forces camp at Lang Vei with Soviet-built tanks. At the camp, 316 American, South Vietnamese, and Laotian troops were killed.

Allied commanders unleashed a severe bombing and shelling operation in Ben Tre, a southern city about 53 miles southeast of Saigon. The operation was intended to destroy the 2,500 Viet Cong who had overrun and taken control of the city. Bombing was performed by American aircraft as well as by U.S. Navy ships off the coast, and according to military officials, it was done knowing that it would cause deaths and injury to civilians and their town. Arising from the operation was a quote that would seem to reflect the confusion of the American presence in Vietnam, as military leaders told Associated Press correspondent Peter Arnett, at Arnett's prompting: "It became necessary to destroy the town to save it."

Born: Peter Bondra, Slovak hockey player who would play 17 seasons in the National Hockey League (1990-2007), was born in Lutsk, Ukrainian SSR, Soviet Union. Bondra later became the general manager of the Slovakia national team (2007-11).

Died: Nick Adams, American television and film actor, died in Hollywood, California at age 36 of a drug overdose. Adams, born Nicholas Aloysius Adamshock, was best known for starring in the TV series *The Rebel*. In addition to acting in more than 30 television shows, Adams also acted in more than 30 films, including two of the three films that starred his friend James Dean (*Rebel Without a Cause* and *Giant*). After Dean died during filming of *Giant*, Adams was brought in to overdub some of Dean's lines that were incomplete. The inquest into Adams' death could not determine whether his overdose death was by accident or suicide.

February 8 (Thursday)

The "Orangeburg Massacre" took place in Orangeburg, South Carolina, when South Carolina Highway Patrol officers fired into a crowd of African American students on the South Carolina State College campus. Three students were killed, and another 27 were wounded. One of the three who was killed, high school student Delano Middleton, had been visiting friends on the campus, and was shot four times. Earlier in the week, the college's NAACP chapter had organized a move to desegregate the All-Star Bowling Lanes near campus, and a fight ensued the following day when more African-American students arrived at the bowling alley. Just prior to the fatal shooting on campus, a group of students had built a bonfire on the edge of the campus, when an object was thrown at an officer, and officers who witnessed the object being thrown opened fire.

In a speech in Chicago, New York senator Robert F. Kennedy said that the war in Vietnam was "unwinnable." Kennedy was considered by many to be a potential presidential candidate.

Born: Gary Coleman, American child actor and star of the situation comedy *Diff'rent Strokes*, was born in Zion, Illinois. (Coleman, who would suffer from health issues throughout his life, would die in 2010.)

Born: April Stewart, American voice actress, was born in Truckee, California. Stewart is best known for voicing a number of female characters on the animated comedy series *South Park*, including Liane Cartman, Mayor McDaniels, Principal Victoria, Carol

McCormick, and Sharon Marsh. April Stewart's father, Freddie Stewart, was a singer in the Tommy Dorsey Orchestra.

Died: Three students died in the fatal shooting by South Carolina Highway Patrol officers, in an encounter that would be called the "Orangeville Massacre." The students were Samuel Hammond Jr., 18, Delano Middleton, 17, and Henry Smith, 19.

February 9 (Friday)

The first subway system in the Netherlands, the Rotterdam Metro, opened. It was one of the world's shortest subway systems, at 3.7 miles (5.9 km) in length. The metro was opened by Crown Princess Beatrix. For some local residents, the subway significantly reduced driving times at rush hour.

The Soviet state-controlled newspaper *Komsomolskaya Pravda*, which was aimed at young Communist Party members, published a candid story expressing that the Soviet Union was lagging behind the Western nations in most economic areas. (In 1961, former party leader Nikita Khrushchev—who would be replaced by party leaders in October 1964—had predicted that the Soviet Union would economically surpass the U.S by 1970, but it had become evident that the prediction would greatly miss its mark.) In 1968, Soviet citizens owned less than 10 percent of the number of automobiles owned by the U.S., and significantly fewer goods such as electronics, clothing, and food products.

Born: Alejandra Guzmán, Mexican singer-songwriter and actress who would sell 60 million albums, was born in Mexico City. She is the daughter of actress Silvia Pinal and singer Enrique Guzmán.

February 10 (Saturday)

The Boeing 737—which would become the best-selling commercial jet aircraft in history—was used for flying commercial passengers for the first time. The first flight of the short-to-medium range, narrow-body twin-engine 737 was by West German carrier Lufthansa, flying out of Hamburg, as it initiated its CityJet service. Many 737s remain in service, and as of the end of October 2017, more than 14,000 of the aircraft had been ordered throughout its history, with 4,430 still to be delivered (per the official Boeing website).

American women's figure skater Peggy Fleming won the Women's Singles figure skating competition at the Winter Olympic Games in Grenoble, France. With her victory, the 20-year-old Fleming, from San Jose, California, became the only U.S. athlete to win a gold medal at the games. Historians viewed the win by Fleming as "particularly meaningful" because the sport in the U.S. was being rebuilt after a 1961 plane crash (Sabena 548) killed the entire U.S. figure skating team of 18, as well as 16 coaching staff members and family, while the team was on its way to the World Figure Skating Championships in Prague. Following her Olympic championship, Fleming would perform in television specials and the Ice Capades, and would give performances in the Soviet Union and China during the Cold War years. Fleming would later become an ice skating commentator.

The instrumental "Love is Blue" by French orchestra leader Paul Mauriat became number one on U.S. charts, and would remain there for five weeks.

Born: Garrett Reisman, U.S. astronaut who would spend more than 107 days in space aboard the space shuttles *Discovery* and *Atlantis* and the International Space Station on several missions, was born in Morristown, New Jersey. Reisman would spend more than 21 hours outside the spacecraft while in orbit, during Extra Vehicular Activity (EVA). Later, he would also spend fourteen days underwater as an aquanaut in the Aquarius underwater laboratory.

Born: Atika Suri, Indonesian television newscaster, was born as Indragiri Hulu Regency in the province of Riau, Indonesia.

Died: Retired Lieutenant General Harry Schmidt, who commanded the U.S. Marines Fifth Amphibious Corps in the successful campaigns in the capture of Tinian Island, the Marshall Islands, and the Battle of Iwo Jima, died at the age of 81. He had previously served in China in 1911, in the Philippines in 1912-13, in an intervention in Guantanamo, Cuba in 1917, and in World War I.

February 11 (Sunday)

The new Madison Square Garden in New York City opened to the public. "The Garden," or "MSG" would become the oldest major sports facility in the greater New York area. Four previous venues on the site or nearby were called by the same name. The new arena was opened with a "Salute to the U.S.O." show by Bob Hope and Bing Crosby.

CBS News anchor and correspondent Walter Cronkite landed in Saigon on a fact-finding mission to report on the status of the war in Vietnam. The results of his mission would be reported later in the month, on February 27th (see entry for February 27 for details).

Born: Mo Willems, award-winning American writer, animator, and creator of books for children, was born in Des Plaines, Illinois. Willems is known for several series of children's books, including the *Pigeon*, the *Knuffle Bunny,* and the *Elephant and Piggie* series.

Willems would also win six Emmy Awards as a writer and animator on Sesame Street from 1993 to 2002.

Born: Lavinia Agache, who would win 10 major gymnastics medals competing for Romania, including gold and silver medals in the Olympic Games and World Championships, was born in Căiuți, Romania.

Died: Howard Lindsay, American theatrical producer, director, playwright, and actor, died in New York City at the age of 78. Lindsay was particularly known for the productions *Life with Father*, *State of the Union*, and *The Sound of Music*.

Died: Muriel Lester, the British social reformer and peace activist, died at age 84. Lester had toured earthquake-damaged areas in Bihar, India in 1934 with Mahatma Gandhi, during his "anti-untouchability" work, and actively worked for peace during the Spanish Civil War later in the decade.

February 12 (Monday)

In South Vietnam, the 2nd Division of the South Korean Marines shot and killed 80 unarmed civilians in the village of Phong Nhi. The incident took place after the South Koreans had come under sniper fire during their patrol of the Quang Nam Province.

Two weeks after the Tet Offensive began, U.S. Army General William C. Westmoreland asked President Johnson to send an additional 10,500 troops to South Vietnam.

In Memphis, Tennessee, a sanitation strike would begin, as the city's 1,300 sanitation workers walked off the job due to low pay, unsanitary conditions, and to express anger about the two workers who had been killed by defective equipment on February 1. Civil rights leader Rev. Martin Luther King, Jr. would come to Memphis in support of the strikers. He would be assassinated in the city on April 4.

The 25th Golden Globe Awards were held. In the film category, *In the Heat of the Night* starring Best Actor - Drama winner Rod Steiger won the award for Best Picture - Drama, while *The Graduate* won for Best Picture - Comedy. Anne Bancroft won the award for Best Actress - Musical or Comedy for her role in *The Graduate*. Both best pictures won multiple awards, as did *Camelot* with its Best Actor - Musical or Comedy, Richard Harris. *Mission: Impossible* won as Best TV Show, with the show's Martin Landau being selected as Best Actor, and Carol Burnett winning as Best Actress for her comedy and variety series *The Carol Burnett Show*. Awards for New Stars of the Year went to Katherine Ross and Dustin Hoffman, both of whom starred in *The Graduate*.

Born: Josh Brolin, American film actor who would go on to make at least 45 films, was born in Santa Monica, California. Brolin is the son of actor James Brolin.

Born: Christopher McCandless, subject of the 2007 Bruce Lamothe film documentary *Call of the Wild* about an American adventurer who adopted a minimalist lifestyle and went by the name "Alexander Supertramp," was born in El Segundo, California.

Born: Chynna Phillips, American singer, actress, and member of the vocal group Wilson Phillips, was born in Los Angeles. She is the daughter of musician/songwriters John and Michelle Phillips of The Mamas & the Papas.

February 13 (Tuesday)

The Westminster Kennel Club Dog Show was the last event to be held at the old Madison Square Garden prior to its closing and replacement by the new Garden. The older structure was demolished later in the year.

Born: Kelly Hu, who would become Miss Teen USA 1985 and Miss Hawaii USA 1993 before becoming an actress in films including *The Scorpion King*, *Nash Bridges,* and *Cradle 2 the Grave,* was born in Honolulu, Hawaii.

Died: Mae Marsh, American film actress who starred in nearly 100 films beginning in 1910 with silent movies, died in Hermosa Beach, California at age 83. Her career had spanned five decades. Marsh worked with famed silent film director D.W. Griffith and appeared in *The Birth of a Nation* in 1915, *Intolerance* in 1916, *The Grapes of Wrath* in 1940, and decades later in *Donovan's Reef* in 1963 and *Cheyenne Autumn* in 1964. Marsh had been born in Madrid, New Mexico Territory in 1894.

Died: Ildebrando Pizzetti, Italian classical music composer, music critic, and musicologist, died in Rome, Italy at age 87.

February 14 (Wednesday)

The KXJB (now KRDK) Television transmitting tower near Galesburg, North Dakota, was accidentally knocked over by the rotor of a U.S. Marine helicopter that struck and cut the guy wires holding the tower in place. The tower was the second tallest man-made structure in the world at the time. All four men on the helicopter were killed, and the television station that used the tower went off the air. The 2,068-foot (630 m) tower was rebuilt, and remains the fifth tallest structure in the world as of 2017. (The tower was knocked over again in April 1997 after an ice storm deposited four inches of ice on its surface and combined with 70 mile-per-hour winds to cause its structural failure.)

The Chairman of the U.S. Joint Chiefs of Staff, Army Gen. Earle G. Wheeler, held a press conference following rumors that he had told members of Congress that he would not rule out the use of nuclear weapons in Vietnam. At the press conference, Gen. Wheeler did not completely reject using atomic bombs, saying, "I do not think they will be required to defend Khe Sanh, but I refuse to speculate any further."

Born: Scott McClellan, who would become White House Press Secretary for U.S. President George W. Bush (2003-05), was born in Austin, Texas. McClellan replaced Ari Fleischer as press secretary, and would be the longest-serving press secretary under the 43rd president.

Died: Pierre Veuillot, Roman Catholic Archbishop of Paris and cardinal, from France, died of leukemia at age 55 after having served as cardinal for only six months.

February 15 (Thursday)

The United Kingdom tested its first submarine-launched ballistic missile when HMS *Resolution* test-fired an unarmed Polaris missile off the U.S. coast near Cape Kennedy, Florida (now Cape Canaveral).

Born: Gloria Trevi, Mexican pop singer, was born as Gloria de los Ángeles Treviño Ruiz, in Monterrey, Nuevo León, Mexico.

Died: Little Walter (Marion Walter Jacobs), American blues musician, singer, songwriter, and harmonica player, died at age 38 in Chicago. Jacobs died of coronary thrombosis believed to have been caused by injuries suffered in a fight the night before. Jacobs' innovative style in playing the harmonica led to his being the only artist inducted into the Rock & Roll Hall of Fame specifically as a harmonica player.

February 16 (Friday)

Following the establishment of the nation's first 9-1-1 emergency telephone system, the world's first 9-1-1 call was placed in Haleyville, Alabama. The call was placed from City Hall by Alabama Speaker of the House Rankin Fite. (Great Britain had introduced its 9-9-9 emergency call system in 1937 after five people were killed in a fire.)

The U.S. Selective Service System changed its rules for the military draft. Under the new rules most graduate students (i.e., those who had already obtained their bachelor's degrees) could now be inducted. Students in the medical, dental, and other health fields generally remained exempt. Many theology students also remained exempt.

Twenty-one of 63 passengers on a Taiwanese Civil Air Transport (CAT) Boeing 727 were killed after the crew attempted an emergency landing on a flight from Hong Kong to Taipei. CAT was a Nationalist Chinese airline that often participated in covert activities on behalf of the U.S. Central Intelligence Agency, and the CIA would later purchase the airline. CAT had begun operations in 1946; it was created by U.S. diplomat and attorney Whiting Willauer in partnership with Lt. Gen. Claire Chennault. (Chennault had previously recruited and commanded the First American Volunteer

Group, the "Flying Tigers," as part of the Chinese Air Force at the beginning of World War II.)

In Moberly, Missouri, William Edward Coleman intentionally started a fire that killed 12 people at a bar in the Randolph Hotel. During Coleman's trial, it was revealed that he had walked a short distance from the hotel to a filling station, borrowed a 5-gallon bucket and filled it with gasoline, then want back to the bar where he threw the gasoline around the bar and then lit it.

Born: Warren Ellis, British comic book writer, novelist, and screenwriter, whose work has included *Transmetropolitan*, *Global Frequency,* and the feature films *Red* and *Red 2*, was born in Essex, England.

February 17 (Saturday)

The Naismith Memorial Basketball Hall of Fame opened in Springfield, Massachusetts. The Basketball Hall of Fame is named after Dr. James Naismith, the Canadian-American physician, chaplain, physical educator, and coach, who invented the game of basketball in 1891, when he was 30 years old.

At the Winter Olympics in Grenoble, France, skier Jean-Claude Killy won the men's slalom event, his third gold medal of the Games. Killy was only the second (and most recent) skier to win the triple crown of alpine skiing; Toni Sailer of Austria had won all three events at the 1956 Winter Olympics at Cortina d'Ampezzo, Italy.

The English progressive rock band Pink Floyd launched its World Tour with a concert in Patronaatsgebouw, The Netherlands. The tour would include two legs in Europe and one in the United States, and would finish on December 28.

The 1968 legislative elections began in Papua New Guinea.

Died: Kailash Nath Katju, Indian politician and minister who served in the administration of Prime Minister Jawaharlal Nehru, died at age 80. He also served as Governor of Odisha (1947-48) and West Bengal (1948-51), and Chief Minister for Madhya Pradesh (1957-62).

Died: Donald Wolfit, British stage, film and television actor, died at age 65 in Hammersmith, London. Wolfit was particularly known for portraying King Lear.

February 18 (Sunday)

The first actions were taken to create the United Arab Emirates as the emirs of Abu Dhabi and Dubai met at the village of as-Sameeh and announced the consolidation of their two emirates.

The first snowboarding contest was held, at Muskegon State Park near Muskegon, Michigan. The new sport of snowboarding involved skiers going downhill on snow, on a curved plank similar to a small surfboard. The sport that would become snowboarding had been created by Muskegon engineer Sherman Poppin who, in 1965, had fastened two skis together and attached a rope that could be handheld for control. (Snowboarding would become a Winter Olympic sport at the Nagano games in 1998.)

Born: Molly Ringwald, American actress, singer, dancer, and author, who starred in a number of films including *Sixteen Candles* (1984), *The Breakfast Club* (1985), and *Pretty in Pink* (1986) was born in Roseville, California.

Born: Dennis Satin, German film and television director and screenwriter known for *Dangerous Dowry*, *Heroes and Other Cowards* and others, was born in Sofia, Bulgaria.

February 19 (Monday)

The World Court ruled to divide land during a border dispute between India and Pakistan regarding the 10,000-square-mile Rann of Kutch salt marshes shared between the two nations.

The Florida Education Association, the primary schoolteachers' labor union in Florida, staged the first statewide teachers' strike in U.S. history. The walkout forced the schools in 51 of Florida's 67 counties to be closed. The walkout of 25,712 teachers would last for a month, though small groups of them would only strike for a few days, with some striking past the call for return that was observed by the majority of striking teachers.

The Panamanian cargo ship *Capitaine Frangos* collided with an unidentified ship at the entrance to the Dardanelles in Turkey, killing 15 members of the crew of 20.

In Canada's House of Commons, a measure to raise income taxes by five percent failed by a vote of 82 to 84.

National Educational Television (NET, later to become Public Broadcasting Service) aired the first episode of *Mr. Rogers' Neighborhood*. The show would run until 2001.

February 20 (Tuesday)

The first telecommunication devices for the deaf (TDDs) units, which included teletypewriters (TTYs) and were designed to allow deaf persons to communicate text over telephone lines, were provided by American Telephone and Telegraph (AT&T). Concurrent with their release in 1968, Paul Taylor, a deaf engineer and associate professor at the National Technical Institute for the Deaf, formed the first advocacy group in St Louis, Missouri to distribute and maintain teleprinters for deaf persons.

West Bengal in India was declared to be under President's rule as called out in India's constitution, following the collapse of its coalition government. West Bengal would remain under national control for over a year, until February 1969, when a new government would be formed.

Canadian Prime Minister Lester Pearson gave the first televised address to the nation by a Canadian leader, announcing that he would postpone a confidence motion scheduled for the following day to demonstrate that his Liberal Party could continue to maintain the government. After filibustering by the opposition leader John Diefenbaker's Progressive Conservative Party of Canada for a week, the confidence motion was passed.

The China Academy of Space Technology (CAST), the primary facility for developing and producing spacecraft in China, was founded in Beijing. (In April 1970, China would launch its first satellite, Dong Fang, and it would launch numerous satellites and astronauts ["taikonauts"] as the program developed. China has also landed a lunar robotic lander and rover, and may be planning to land taikonauts on the moon.) Note that in 1968, many Western media and people called China's capital "Peking." The more correct name of "Beijing" began to be phased in as early as 1958, and was planned for official phase-in beginning in 1979.

Died: Judge Arthur G. Klein, American politician, U.S. Representative from New York (1946-56) and state Supreme Court justice beginning in 1957, died in New York City at age 63.

February 21 (Wednesday)

University students in Egypt's two largest cities of Cairo and Alexandria started an outbreak to support an ongoing workers strike. It was the first arrest of a large number of students in Egypt in 15 years. Over the following week, 635 people would be arrested in Cairo, two workers would be killed, and 223 civilians and policemen would be injured.

In Belgium, King Baudouin dissolved the Belgian parliament and called for ad hoc "snap" elections following his acceptance of the resignation of Prime Minister Paul Vanden Boeynants and his government ministers. The elections would take place on March 31.

A British expedition team led by English explorer Wally Herbert, with a team of three others (Roy Koerner, Allan Gill, and Kenneth Hedges) and 34 huskies, departed from Point Barrow, Alaska as part of their "Trans Arctic Expedition" to cross the "top of the world." The team was delayed at times due to storms and needed supply replenishment by air drop, but they finally reached the Norwegian island of Vesle Tavleøya on May 29, 1969 after travelling 3,620 miles (5,830 km).

NASA's lunar probe Surveyor 7 was deactivated, six weeks after landing softly on the moon. Surveyor 7's batteries were damaged during the first lunar night, and did not reactivate successfully. It would turn out to be the last transmission of signals from the moon before Apollo 11 landed there on July 20, 1969.

The American jazz-rock band Blood, Sweat & Tears released its first album, *Child Is Father to the Man*. The band played a fusion of jazz, blues, and rock, and recorded music from songwriters including Laura Nyro, James Taylor, the Rolling Stones, and Billie Holiday. Like the group Chicago which also performed a fusion of different genres, BST used a horn section in their songs.

American publishing and learning science company McGraw-Hill, Inc. obtained the U.S. rights to Hunter Davies' authorized biography of the Beatles.

Died: Howard Florey, the Australian pathologist and pharmacologist who shared the 1945 Nobel Prize in Physiology or Medicine with Alexander Fleming and Ernst Boris Chain for their role in developing penicillin, died in Oxford, England, at age 69.

February 22 (Thursday)

With Soviet Communist Party leader Leonid Brezhnev visiting, Czechoslovakian Communist Party First Secretary Alexander Dubček announced that his government would engage in creating "the widest possible democratization of the entire socio-political system." Dubček's announcement would be an early indicator of the short-lived liberalization of Czechoslovakian policies to come later in the year, a phenomenon that would be called "Prague Spring."

The United Kingdom announced the intent to implement laws limiting the influx of people from British Commonwealth countries entering the United Kingdom. The measure came in response to 7,000 Asian refugees who had been expelled from Kenya but who, as citizens of a British Commonwealth nation, possessed British passports. The law would pass both Houses of Parliament on February 27.

Born: Jeri Ryan, American television and film actress who would play the character "Seven of Nine" on *Star Trek: Voyager*, was born as Jeri Lynn Zimmermann in Munich, West Germany. Ryan also had regular or recurring roles in television's *Boston Public*, *Dark Skies*, and *Leverage*.

Born: Bradley Nowell, American musician and founder, lead singer, and guitarist of the band Sublime, was born in Long Beach, California. (Nowell would die in 1996 of a drug overdose, at age 26.)

Died: Peter Arno, American cartoonist for The New Yorker magazine, died at age 64 in Port Chester, New York. Arno created 99 covers for the magazine between 1925 and 1968.

Died: Dudley Murphy, American film director, died in Mexico City at age 70.

February 23 (Friday)

Chung Ju-yung, president of the Hyundai Motor Company who had founded the company the year before, signed into agreement with Ford Motor Company whereby Ford would provide Hyundai with technology at its Ulsan, South Korea plant, and Ford would take a portion of the profits. Hyundai would build the Hyundai Cortina and Hyundai Ford 20M automobiles, and the Hyundai Ford D-Series trucks.

Died: Fannie Hurst, American novelist and short story writer who was one of the highest paid American authors, died in New York City at age 82.

February 24 (Saturday)

A Royal Air Lao DC-3 airplane crashed into the Mekong River while on a routine domestic passenger flight from Vientiane to Sainyabuli. All 37 passengers on board were killed. Royal Air Lao was the national carrier of the Kingdom of Laos from 1962 until it ceased operations in 1976.

The British-American rock band Fleetwood Mac released its first album, titled simply *Fleetwood Mac*. Two of the band's co-founders, Peter Green and Jeremy Spencer, performed lead vocals on most of the album's songs.

Born: Mitch Hedberg, American stand-up comedian, was born in Saint Paul, Minnesota. (Hedberg would die in 2005 of a drug overdose at the age of 37.)

February 25 (Sunday)

The Archbishop Makarios III (Michael Mouskos) was re-elected as President of Cyprus by a large majority of voters. Makarios won 220,911 of the 231,438 valid ballots cast.

The first president of Senegal (beginning in 1960), Léopold Sédar Senghor, was re-elected without opposition. Senghor was a poet, cultural theorist, and politician. A member of the Académie française (French Academy), Senghor is regarded by many as one of the most significant intellectuals in Africa in the 20th Century.

Czechoslovakian Major General Jan Šejna of the Czechoslovak Army fled Czechoslovakia for Italy upon hearing that he would be arrested on corruption charges, and falling out of favor with President Antonin Novotny. Šejna would eventually defect to the

U.S., becoming the second-highest officer to defect from the Eastern bloc to the West.

Cambodia's Communist guerilla group, the Khmer Rouge, began its first widespread campaign, with simultaneous attacks on military installations in six Cambodian cities, where the group seized weapons and ammunition.

The historic Imperial Palace in Hue, which had been captured by Viet Cong forces during the Tet Offensive less than a month earlier, was recaptured by South Vietnamese troops in conjunction with the U.S. Marines and Army.

The first issue of *Zap Comix*, the first of the *underground comix* genre, was published. *Zap Comix* was an alternative to traditional comic books, and was directed at the youth counterculture movement. The book was created by San Francisco cartoonist Robert Crumb, working with his wife Dana as staff, and the title would spread throughout the Bay Area and the country.

Born: Thomas G:son, Swedish song composer, was born as Thomas Gustafsson in Skövde, Sweden. In addition to being a multiple-genre performer, G:son has written at least 69 songs for 12 different countries for the Eurovision Song Contest, which had previously been won by world-known performers such as Lulu and ABBA.

Born: Sandrine Kiberlain, French film actress and singer, was born in Boulogne-Billancourt, France.

Died: Camille Huysmans, who had served as Prime Minister of Belgium (1946-47), died in Brussels at age 96.

February 26 (Monday)

In South Vietnam, the city of Hue was declared as secured and recaptured from the Vietcong, who had captured the city less than a month earlier during the Tet Offensive.

A fire swept through the women's ward at Shelton Hospital near the English city of Shrewsbury, killing 21 patients. Investigators determined that doors for the ward, which housed severely disabled patients, were locked from the outside and could not be opened from the inside.

The Communist Party of Czechoslovakia adopted its first draft of an "Action Program" to allow greater freedom of the press.

The best-seller *The Double Helix: A Personal Account of the Discovery of the Structure of DNA* by U.S. Professor James D. Watson was published for the first time, by Atheneum Publishers. Watson's own school, Harvard University, had previously declined on the opportunity to publish the book. The book was an autobiographical account of the discovery of DNA by Watson and Francis Crick.

February 27 (Tuesday)

The historic one-hour CBS News special "Report from Vietnam" with Walter Cronkite aired. The purpose of the program was to communicate Cronkite's findings and opinions about the war in Vietnam (with his editorializing being a deviation from his normal role), based on his trip there earlier in the month. At the close of the program, the host of the *CBS Evening News* told the nine million viewers, "It seems now more certain than ever that the bloody experience of Vietnam is to end in a stalemate...it is increasingly clear to this reporter that the only rational way out then will be to negotiate, not as victors but as an honorable people who lived up to their pledge to defend democracy, and did the best they could. This is Walter Cronkite. Good night." U.S. President Lyndon Johnson is said to have told staff the following day "If I've lost Cronkite, I've lost the war" (or by some reports, "…I've lost the American people."). However, some political experts and historians feel that the conclusion is somewhat of a myth, saying that opposition to the Vietnam War was already rapidly increasing.

U.S. President Lyndon Johnson visited Dallas, Texas for the first time since November 22, 1963, when he was sworn in as president upon the death of President John F. Kennedy. Johnson spoke to delegates at the National Rural Electric Cooperative convention.

Born: Matt Stairs, former Major League Baseball player from Canada, was born in Saint John, New Brunswick. Stairs would play for more teams (13) than any other position player (i.e., non-pitcher) in MLB history. Stairs' career would span from 1992 to 2011.

Died: American rock and roll/rhythm and blues singer Frankie Lymon died in New York City at age 25 from a heroin overdose. Lymon had sung as part of the group Frankie Lymon and the Teenagers, and recorded his biggest hit, "Why Do Fools Fall in Love" at the age of 13.

February 28 (Wednesday)

Gov. George Romney of Michigan became the first major candidate to formally withdraw from the 1968 presidential race. Romney had previously announced that he planned to seek the nomination of the Republican Party, and was even considered the front-runner by some. However, after several statements that were perceived as gaffes negatively impacted his public approval, Romney determined that he was far behind Richard Nixon in fund-raising for the upcoming New Hampshire primary.

Twenty-two of the 23 servicemen on board a U.S. Marine CH-46 Sea Knight helicopter were killed when it was hit by enemy ground fire and crashed near the Marine base at Khe Sanh.

Canadian Prime Minister Lester Pearson won a vote of confidence in Canada's House of Commons by a vote 138 to 119. The successful vote brought an end to the crisis that had begun nine days earlier, after his tax proposal failed.

The four-day annual Rio Carnival in Rio de Janeiro ended with 83 deaths, 14 of which were murders, and at least 5,000 injuries. The carnival is perennially the largest in the world, drawing more than 2 million celebrants per day.

African-American political activist Eldridge Cleaver's memoir, *Soul on Ice*, was published by McGraw-Hill Publishing Company.

Died: Nikolay Voronov, Soviet field marshal and World War II hero, died in Moscow at age 68. Voronov had been commander of Red Army artillery forces from 1941 to 1950. He commanded Soviet artillery during the Battle of Stalingrad and oversaw fronts during the Battle of Leningrad and the Battle of Kursk.

Died: Laurence Stallings, a multi-faceted American playwright, screenwriter, novelist, lyricist, literary critic, and photographer, died in Pacific Palisades, California at age 73. Stallings wrote the 1924 play *What Price Glory* with Maxwell Anderson, wrote the autobiographical novel *Plumes* about his service in World War I, and also published a book of World War I photographs, *The First World War: A Photographic History*.

February 29 (Thursday)

The 1968 Brussels Convention treaty was signed in the Belgian capital by representatives of France, Italy, West Germany, Belgium, the Netherlands, and Luxembourg. The treaty was an agreement to recognize and enforce judgements in civil and commercial disagreements.

The 1968 Polish Political Crisis began when the Union of Polish Writers voted to condemn restrictions on the freedom of speech. As was happening in other parts of Europe, students and intellectuals would escalate protest in order to gain further rights.

As the reforms called the Prague Spring continued to expand in Czechoslovakia, the Writers' Union published the first copy of the magazine *Literární listy,* which was significant in that censors did not review its content in advance.

The Kerner Commission (named after its chair, Gov. Otto Kerner of Illinois, and officially named The National Advisory Commission on Civil Disorders) released its report on the U.S. riots of the previous summer. The report cited racial discrimination as a major cause. The largest 1967 riots had taken place in Detroit, Michigan, where 43 people were killed, and in Newark, New Jersey, where 26 were killed. The 426-page Kerner Commission report became a national bestseller, with two million copies sold. The commission concluded: "Our nation is moving toward two societies, one black, one white— separate and unequal."

A farewell party took place at the Pentagon for Robert S. McNamara, the U.S. secretary of defense who had announced his retirement in late November of 1967 after President Johnson had rejected McNamara's strong recommendations to stop the bombing and U.S. troop involvement in Vietnam. McNamara had worked in the U.S. Army Air Force Office of Statistical Control during World

War II, and began working at Ford Motor Company soon after that war's conclusion. He became president of Ford in November 1960, but was then quickly called on by the newly elected President Kennedy to become his secretary of defense. McNamara initially was a strong supporter of the war, but he resigned late in 1967 when he had believed increasingly that the U.S. should no longer be in Vietnam. President Johnson made a surprise visit to the Pentagon for McNamara's farewell ceremony. After his departure, McNamara became president of the World Bank.

The Grammy Awards were held in Chicago, Los Angeles, Nashville, and New York City, to recognize musicians for 1967. The Beatles and producer George Martin won the Grammy for Album of the Year (*Sgt. Pepper's Lonely Hearts Club Band*). The single "Up, Up and Away" was a big winner, leading to awards for The Fifth Dimension (performers), Johnny Rivers & Marc Gordon (producers), and Jimmy Webb (songwriter). Bobbie Gentry was chosen as Best New Artist, and acting veteran Boris Karloff won for best recording for Children, *Dr. Seuss: How the Grinch Stole Christmas.*

Died: Norwegian poet Tore Ørjasæter, whose poetry was greatly influenced by his country's folk traditions, died in Skjåk, Norway at age 81.

March

March 1 (Friday)

In Rome, violent protests between students and police began outside the Faculty of Agriculture building at La Sapienza University. The violence was believed to have begun when students threw Molotov cocktails and projectiles at police, who were equipped with hoses and nightsticks. Hundreds were injured in the protesting.

In Vietnam, U.S. and South Vietnamese forces continued to engage in Operation Market Time, an initiative started in 1965 to stop supplies from reaching Viet Cong troops in South Vietnam. U.S. Navy and South Vietnamese forces destroyed three North Vietnamese fishing trawlers and turned back a fourth. Once the fourth vessel traveled further than 12 miles (19 km) from the coast and reached international waters, the U.S. Navy was could no longer fire upon the vessel under the existing rules of engagement.

The United States and South Vietnam weren't alone during the Vietnam War. Operation Coburg, a military action led by Australia and New Zealand in Bien Hoa province, ended on this day after six weeks. Seventeen Australian troops, two from New Zealand and one from the U.S. were killed in action during the operation.

Joseph and the Amazing Technicolor Dreamcoat was performed by pupils of Colet Court preparatory school in Hammersmith, London, UK. The event would mark the first performance anywhere of an Andrew Lloyd-Webber-Tim Rice musical.

Married: Musicians Johnny Cash and June Carter were married in Franklin, Kentucky. The best man was Merle Kilgore, who had co-written Cash's hit "Ring of Fire" with June Carter.

Born: Kunjarani Devi, Indian weightlifter, was born in Imphal, Manipur. She is the most decorated woman in Indian weightlifting history, having won more than 50 international medals, in addition to numerous medals for domestic competition.

March 2 (Saturday)

Zond 4, a Soviet Union space mission developed to test the USSR's new Soyuz 7K-L1 space capsule for a lunar fly-by mission, was launched. The capsule would travel the same distance from Earth as the distance to the moon, but in the opposite direction, likely to avoid the effect of lunar gravity.

The United States conducted its first test of the LIM-49 Spartan anti-ballistic missile. The Spartan was designed to carry a five-megaton nuclear warhead to intercept and destroy incoming missiles while they were still outside Earth's atmosphere. The use of the Spartan missile was part of the U.S. Army's Safeguard anti-ballistic missile (ABM) program that began in the 1950s with the use of the Nike Zeus missile.

At Wembley Stadium in London, Leeds United Football Club defeated Arsenal F.C. to win the 1968 Football League Cup Final, 1-0, in front of 97,887 fans.

A state election took place in South Australia. After a close election that resulted in 19 seats each for Steele Hall's Liberal and Country League party and Don Dunstan's Australian Labor Party, independent candidate Tom Stott joined with Hall's party to form a coalition government, thereby giving the prime minister seat to Hall.

Born: Daniel Craig, English film and television actor who would play Agent 007 in the James Bond spy series beginning in 2006, in addition to other major films, was born in Chester, Cheshire, England.

Died: Frank Erickson, American gambling bookmaker who would become wealthy by conducting nation-wide gambling operations throughout the US, died during bleeding ulcer surgery at age 72. Many of the operations of Erickson, who grew up in an orphanage, were legal when he first began them, but became illegal during his career.

March 3 (Sunday)

The newly formed Oriental Actors of America began speaking out against the casting of white (Caucasian) actors in Japanese or Chinese roles. A press conference by a group of Asian American actors took place that day to publicize their concerns, and that evening, protesters picketed the Broadway opening of the musical *Here's Where I Belong*. The producers of the musical had selected white actors in makeup over Chinese-American actors.

Television Wales and the West (TWW), a commercial British TV network that had been in service since 1958, broadcast its last original programming. The network had served south Wales and southwestern England.

In Iraq, Prime Minister Tahir Yahya imposed a new regulation that prohibited Jews from selling their property without government permission. The regulation was part of a continuing campaign by Yahya against Iraqi Jews. Following the Six Day War some nine months before, Jews in Iraq had lost jobs and had their bank accounts frozen.

The tanker *Ocean Eagle*, manned by a Greek crew and registered in Liberia, ran aground and split in two at San Juan, Puerto Rico, then spilled oil on the beaches in San Juan Harbor. The Ocean Eagle blocked the channel leading out from harbor, which trapped 15 ships, including three U.S. submarines.

Born: Brian Leetch, American professional hockey defenseman who would play 18 seasons with the New York Rangers, Toronto Maple Leafs and Boston Bruins, was born in Corpus Christi, Texas. Leetch would be inducted into the U.S. Hockey Hall of Fame in 2008, and in early 2017 would be named one of the "100 Greatest NHL Players" in history.

March 4 (Monday)

The Communist Party leadership in Czechoslovakia voted to discontinue censorship of the press, which had not been done in a Communist nation before. Later that week, newspapers in the country would already begin demanding that President and former party leader Antonin Novotny resign.

Rev. Martin Luther King Jr., who led the 1963 March on Washington, said that a "Nonviolent Poor People's March on Washington" would take place on April 22, and was intended to display the problems of poor people of all races. King prepared for the Poor People's March through most of the month of March.

The film version of William Shakespeare's *Romeo and Juliet* by Franco Zeffirelli (Italian director, producer, and legislator) was shown for the first time. The film starred Leonard Whiting as Romeo and Olivia Hussey as Juliet. The showing took place in London's Leicester Square, with Queen Elizabeth II, her husband Prince Philip, Duke of Edinburgh, and Prince Charles in attendance.

At the new Madison Square Garden, American Joe Frazier knocked out fellow American Buster Mathis in the 11th round to win a share of the world heavyweight boxing title. The heavyweight championship title had previously been vacant, as boxing associations had stripped champion Muhammad Ali of the title a year earlier when he refused to be inducted into the U.S. military.

Died: Einar Sissener, Norwegian actor, producer, and director, died at age 70. His acting career had spanned from 1919 to 1967, during which time he played at least 125 different roles in the Norwegian National Theater.

March 5 (Tuesday)

Air France Flight 212 crashed into La Grande Soufrière mountain on the island of Guadeloupe, killing all 63 on board. The Boeing 707 was flying at nighttime from Caracas, Venezuela. (The following year, another Air France Flight 212, also a Boeing 707 on the same route, would crash into the sea shortly taking off from Caracas to Pointe-à-Pitre, killing all 62 people on board. Six years earlier, Air France Flight 117, another Boeing 707, had crashed into a mountain further north on Guadeloupe, claiming all 113 passengers and crew.)

Thousands of Hispanic students walked out of two high schools in East Los Angeles, California, beginning what would come to be known as the "East L.A. Walkouts." Students at Garfield High School left school when classes were dismissed for lunch, and did not return until the end of the day. Students also walked out of Jefferson High School, where a majority of students were African American.

Born: Gordon Bajnai, who would serve as prime minister of Hungary from 2009 to 2010, was born in Szeged, Hungary. Four years after serving as prime minister, Bajnai founded the Together party (officially called Together – Party for a New Era) as he returned to politics during an anti-government One Million for Press Freedom Rally.

March 6 (Wednesday)

U.S. President Lyndon Johnson extended the War on Poverty program that he started in January 1964 by signing Executive Order 11399, which created the National Council on Indian Opportunity. The council was developed to help 800,000 Native Americans in the United States. In announcing the executive order, Johnson said "The American Indian, once proud and free, is torn between white and tribal values; between the politics and language of the white man and his own historic culture. His problems, sharpened by years of defeat and exploitation, neglect and inadequate effort, will take years to overcome."

In North Sumatra, Indonesia, the brakes of a bus failed and it continued into the path of an approaching train. Twenty-six people on the bus were killed and 25 more were injured.

Born: Moira Kelly, American actress, was born in Queens, New York. Kelly would portray characters in *The Cutting Edge*, *One Tree Hill*, and *Twin Peaks: Fire Walk with Me*.

Died: Léon Mathot, French film actor and director whose career would span from 1916 as an actor to 1953 as a director, died in Paris at age 82. Among his other roles, Mathot played the role of Edmond Dantès in the 1918 silent film serial *The Count of Monte Cristo*.

March 7 (Thursday)

In Geneva, Switzerland, delegates from the United States, the Soviet Union, and the United Kingdom announced that they had agreed to a "superpower umbrella," which was described as "a plan to protect nations without nuclear weapons against atomic attack." The three nuclear powers offered to provide protection to any nation that would ratify the Treaty on the Non-Proliferation of Nuclear Weapons.

Chemical agents were used for the first time in cleaning up an oil spill in the Caribbean Sea after the tanker ship *General Colocotronis* struck a reef in the Bahamas and spilled 37,500 barrels (6,000 cubic meters) of oil. Although some oil reached the nearby beaches, most was successfully diluted by the agents. A subsequent study by British marine biologists concluded that following the use of the agents, there was "no damage to the intertidal marine life."

The drunk driver of a car killed himself and 19 passengers on a bus liner near Baker, California when he drove the wrong way on Interstate 15 eastbound lanes and struck the bus, causing the bus to overturn, and causing his car and the bus to burst into flames. The incident was the first wrong-way collision to be studied by the U.S. National Traffic Safety Board (NTSB), which in 2012 would issue and publish a consolidated report of similar accidents that have taken place across the U.S.

The newly re-elected president of Cyprus, Makarios III, removed restrictions on Cyprus's Turkish Cypriot community, in addition to ordering the removal of roadblocks and barricades that had limited the Turkish-speaking minority from leaving their neighborhoods.

Born: Jeff Kent, who would become an American major league baseball player and second baseman, was born in Bellflower,

California. Kent played in the major leagues from 1992 to 2008 and was voted the Most Valuable Player in the National League in 2000.

March 8 (Friday)

The Soviet ballistic missile submarine *K-129* sank in the North Pacific Ocean, about 90 nautical miles (104 miles or 167 km) southwest of Hawaii. Although several theories for the sinking were developed, the actual cause remains unknown. Beginning in 1974, the U.S. Central Intelligence Agency would begin attempting to salvage the sunken submarine, and was able to salvage part of it.

In Poland, the same type of political dissension that had started in Czechoslovakia began. The political crisis, now known in Poland as "March 1968" or "The March Events," became the first such protest in Poland since the country's Communist takeover. The expulsion of dissidents Adam Michnik and Henryk Szlajfer four days earlier from the University of Warsaw triggered a protest rally involving more than 5,000 students. The protest, which was large but peaceful, was broken up by the government. Once the word of the crackdown spread, protests continued in Warsaw and spread to the universities in Krakow, Lublin, Poznan, Wroclaw, and other cities. (Years later, Michnik would become a renowned essayist, historian, and editor-in-chief of the Polish newspaper Gazeta Wyborcza. Szlajfer would work for the Ministry of Foreign Affairs.)

The term *green revolution* was used for the first time in a speech by William S. Gaud, Administrator of the United States Agency for International Development (USAID). Gaud used the term to describe the use of new technologies to increase agricultural production throughout the world, in order to address starvation.

Fillmore East in New York City, the East Coast equivalent of The Fillmore theater in San Francisco, was opened by rock music promoter Bill Graham. Many of the period's biggest artists performed at the Fillmore East, including Jimi Hendrix, Cream, The Kinks, John Lennon and Yoko Ono, Frank Zappa, The Allman Brothers Band, The Grateful Dead, Jefferson Airplane, Led Zeppelin, Iron Butterfly, The Byrds, Albert King, Taj Mahal, Ten Years After, Derek and the Dominoes, and Crosby, Stills, Nash, and Young. The acoustics of the theater were such that a number of performers recorded live albums at the theater.

In Afyonkarahisar, Turkey, 22 people, mostly students, were killed when the bus in which they were riding skidded on a slippery highway and fell 600 feet (180 m) into a ravine.

March 9 (Saturday)

The unmanned Zond 4 spacecraft that had been launched by the Soviet Union on March 2 re-entered Earth's atmosphere after data was gathered for a possible Soviet manned mission to the moon. Although the flight path was successful, the capsule was automatically detonated on re-entry after the guidance system failed and it became evident that the spacecraft would not land in Soviet territory.

England defeated the Netherlands 1-0 in women's field hockey at Wembley Stadium in London.

March 10 (Sunday)

In North Vietnam, a decree signed by President Ho Chi Minh took effect that would outlaw a number of actions that were "counterculture" to the Communist government. Once such action now banned would be local opposition to the nation's conduct of the war against South Vietnam.

Jacek Kuroń, a former Communist party member and University of Warsaw professor, was among a large group arrested for organizing and participating in student demonstrations. He was sentenced to three and a half years in prison. He would be arrested again over the years, but his diligence over the years would help lead to the collapse of communism. In 1989-90 and again in 1992-93, Kuroń would serve as Poland's Minister of Labor and Social Policy.

On CBS television, the weekly comedy and variety series *The Smothers Brothers Comedy Hour* had as a guest Glen Campbell, with cameo appearances by Woody Allen, Andy Williams, Sen. Robert Kennedy, Robert Morse, former press secretary Pierre Sallinger, and Sen. George Murphy. The following year, Campbell would host his own show, *The Glen Campbell Goodtime Hour*.

In Wyoming, the town of Acme was sold to a group of Chicago investors. Acme, located in Sheridan County and having a population of about 100, had been founded in 1910 as a company town by the Acme Coal Company. The selling price was $100,000.

Died: In Ireland, the country's minister of education, Donogh O'Malley, collapsed and died while speaking in Limerick, where he had been campaigning for re-election to the Irish Parliament. He was 47. O'Malley was in the process of making a number of education reforms. He had previously served as Ireland's minister of education as well as minister of state at the department of finance.

Died: Helen Walker, American film actress of the 1940s and '50s, died of cancer in North Hollywood, California, at the age of 47. She made more than 15 films including *Call Northside 777* and the 1945 version of *Brewster's Millions*, and had starred in an early (1956) episode of the Los Angeles police drama *Dragnet* with Jack Webb.

March 11 (Monday)

In Laos, North Vietnamese and Pathet Lao (Laotian communist army troops) captured an American radar and navigation beacon site atop a 5,500-foot-high (1676 meters) mountain, Pho Pha Thi, which overlooked the North Vietnamese frontier. The fight would be called the Battle of Lima Site 85. At this point, American involvement in the Laotian Civil War was secret. Most of the sensitive electronic equipment located at the American-run Lima Site 85 complex is thought to have been confiscated by the Soviet Union. Eleven U.S. Air Force technicians disappeared in the battle, representing the single largest loss of life of U.S. Air Force troops in ground combat during the Vietnam War.

In an attempt to codify standardization of computer systems, U.S. President Lyndon B. Johnson signed a memorandum requiring that all computers purchased by the U.S. federal government would need to support American Standard Code for Information Interchange (ASCII) character encoding. The measure would formalize existing practice, as ASCII had been the de facto standard for encoding data since 1963.

In the Democratic Republic of the Congo, a landslide buried 260 people in the village of Kazipa.

In Italy, President Giuseppe Saragat ordered that parliament and the government of Prime Minister Aldo Moro be dissolved, and ordered that new elections take place on May 19. (Ten years later, in March 1978, as Moro was on his way to a meeting, he would be kidnapped by the Red Brigades and held captive for 55 days before being killed.)

After one year as acting president of Indonesia, Gen. Muhammad Suharto was elected to a full five-year term as president. He was the second president of Indonesia, replacing President Sukarno. Suharto would hold the office of president for 31 more years before being forced to resign in 1998 during an uprising.

Born: Lisa Loeb, American singer, songwriter, actress, author, and philanthropist, was born in Bethesda, Maryland. Loeb would have a successful recording career, and would act in a number of films including *Helicopter Mom*, *Hot Tub Time Machine 2*, and *Fright Night*.

March 12 (Tuesday)

Mauritius became independent from British rule. Sir Seewoosagur Ramgoolam, who had served as chief minister when Mauritius was a colony, became the first prime minister of the small island nation in the Indian Ocean. Twenty-four years later, Mauritius would become a republic.

In the first U.S. presidential primary of the 1968 election season, President Lyndon B. Johnson narrowly defeated antiwar candidate Eugene McCarthy in the New Hampshire Democratic primary (by a mere 230 votes). Although Johnson won, the closeness of the vote demonstrated that winning re-election would be increasingly difficult for him. The vote highlighted deep divisions in the country, and the party, over the Vietnam War, and would reflect President Johnson's increasing unpopularity. McCarthy's strong performance came despite being relatively unknown outside of his home state of Wisconsin. Importantly, the result would prompt others candidates to challenge the President. On the Republican ballot, New York Governor Nelson Rockefeller had a disappointing finish, after which the Republican Party was faced with the real possibility of another nomination for Richard Nixon.

Born: Aaron Eckhart, American actor, was born in Cupertino, California. Eckhart portrayed District Attorney Harvey Dent in *Batman: The Dark Knight*, the U.S. President in *Olympus Has Fallen* and its sequels, as well as roles in *Sully*, *Nurse Betty*, and other films.

Born: Jason Lively, American actor known for playing Rusty Griswold in *National Lampoon's European Vacation*, was born in Carrollton, Georgia.

March 13 (Wednesday)

In Utah, six thousand sheep were killed on a farm located 27 miles from the U.S. Army's Dugway Proving Ground. The deaths were caused by the release of VX nerve gas by an A-4 Skyhawk jet aircraft that was testing the gas. The aircraft had sprayed about 320 gallons of the nerve gas deep within the restricted proving ground, then released the emptied tanks. Nearby ranchers then began reporting that their sheep had become ill. The Army initially denied that it had conducted the outdoor nerve gas tests. Over time, it would be learned that the Army had also conducted open-air tests of biological weapons and more than 74 dirty bomb tests. Although no humans were known to be affected by the VX contamination, the U.S. Army paid the farmers more than $500,000 (equivalent to $3.4 million in late 2017) in compensation for their sheep and damage to their grazing areas.

The world's first Rotaract club was chartered in Charlotte, North Carolina. The club was formed as a youth auxiliary (for ages 18-30) to the Rotary Club service group. Its name was formed by the combination of the terms "Rotary" and "Interact." By its 50th anniversary of 2017, there would be 9,522 Rotaract clubs across 177 nations, with 291,006 members called "Rotaractors."

After learning the results of the New Hampshire presidential primary the day before, U.S. President Johnson, who had previously decided to deploy 30,000 additional troops in South Vietnam, would rescind the deployment order. By the end of March, he would revise the new deployment to 13,500 troops.

The first of three Record Plant recording studios, founded by recording engineer Gary Kellgren and music businessman Chris Stone, opened in New York City with innovative recording and mixing techniques. The first album cut by the new studio would be *Electric Ladyland* by the Jimi Hendrix Experience.

Born: Akira Nogami, Japanese professional wrestler known as "Akira," was born in Narashino, Chiba, Japan.

Born: Masami Okui, Japanese pop music singer and songwriter, was born in Itami, Hyogo, Japan. She has sung themes for many anime movies and television shows.

March 14 (Thursday)

Child-proof caps for medicines were publicly introduced at a press conference in Chicago, days before National Poison Prevention Week. Such child-resistant mechanisms for opening bottles are now required for prescription and over-the-counter medications, and certain other chemicals. The development of child-resistant lids was led by Dr. Henri J. Breault in Canada. Since the introduction of the caps, a reduction of up to 91 percent in the number of accidental poisonings by children has been observed.

The Southern Christian Leadership Conference (SCLC), which had worked to advance African-American rights under the leadership of Dr. Martin Luther King, began fighting for the rights of all impoverished Americans. Dr. King convened a meeting in Atlanta with people of many minority groups to develop a strategy for fighting poverty.

As the U.S. planned to sell gold reserves to the United Kingdom to maintain the price of $35.20 per ounce of gold, record purchases were being made on the international gold markets. In one day, $400,000,000 of gold was sold on the London Gold Exchange. The U.S. requested that trading be suspended on the London Gold Market, and the market was closed the next day.

The last episode of ABC TV's camp superhero show *Batman*, starring Adam West as Batman and Burt Ward as Robin, aired its final episode.

Born: Megan Follows, Canadian-American film, television, and theater actress, was born in Toronto. Follows starred in the Canadian film series *Anne of Green Gables,* and in the American TV series *Reign.*

Born: James Frain, English television, film, and stage actor, was born in Leeds, West Riding of Yorkshire. Frain is known for portraying Franklin Mott in the television series *True Blood*, as the character Theo Galavan (who is secretly Azrael) in the Batman universe-themed *Gotham*, and as Ferdinand in the science fiction series *Orphan Black.*

Died: Ada Gobetti, Italian journalist, women's rights activist and anti-Fascist, died in Turin, Italy at age 65.

Died: Josef Harpe, German general of the *Wehrmacht* (German army) who commanded panzer (armored) divisions on Germany's Eastern Front during World War II, died at age 80.

Died: Erwin Panofsky, German Jewish art historian, died in Princeton, New Jersey at age 75. Panofsky was particularly an expert in iconography, the branch of art history and study that deals with the interpretation and description of image elements. (Fictional iconography dealing with Leonardo da Vinci and other artists would later be a main premise of the Dan Brown thrillers.) Panofsky and his friend Albert Einstein had some similarities in that they were both German Jews who visited Princeton in the early 1930s but did not return to Germany after the Nazi party came to power there.

March 15 (Friday)

Roy Jenkins, Britain's Chancellor of the Exchequer, announced that the London Gold Market would be closed at the request of the U.S. Government. Queen Elizabeth II approved a proclamation that would make the day a Bank Holiday throughout the country in order to help stabilize gold. Officials also requested that stock exchanges also be closed.

Prime Minister Indira Gandhi of India announced that India would not sign the Nuclear Non-Proliferation Treaty. (India would continue with its atomic weapons program, and would successfully detonate the country's first atomic bomb, named "Smiling Buddha," on May 18, 1974.)

Britain's Foreign Secretary George Brown of the Labour Party resigned. Brown was replaced by Michael Stewart, also of the Labour Party.

Philip Blaiberg of South Africa returned home after his heart transplant on January 2, becoming the first person to leave a hospital after a heart transplant.

Near Madrid, Spain, 26 people were killed and 30 injured in a train collision.

Born: Mark McGrath, American rock singer the rock band Sugar Ray and co-host of the entertainment news program *Extra*, was born in Hartford, Connecticut.

Died: Khuang Aphaiwong, who had served as prime minister of Thailand on three separate occasions between 1944 and 1948, died in Bangkok.

March 16 (Saturday)

In Vietnam, the My Lai Massacre took place as a group of the U.S. Army's 23rd Infantry (Americal) Division killed as many as 504 unarmed civilians—men, women, and children—in the village of My Lai. The Army would cover up the incident for more than a year, until helicopter pilot Ron Ridenour learned of and reported the incident. The U.S. Army officer who gave the order to fire, 2nd Lieutenant William Calley, would be charged with multiple counts of premeditated murder in September 1969, and found guilty by a six-officer jury. Calley was sentenced to life in prison, of which he served three and a half years under house arrest. Of the 26 officers and soldiers who were first charged with either the My Lai event or a subsequent cover-up, Calley was the only one convicted. Public reaction to the My Lai Massacre had a negative impact on public support of U.S involvement in Vietnam.

U.S. Senator Robert F. Kennedy of New York, former U.S. Attorney General and younger brother of the late President John F. Kennedy, entered the Democratic Party race for the presidential nomination, announcing that he would challenge U.S. President Johnson at the August 26-29 national party convention in Chicago. Kennedy's announcement came in the same U.S. Senate caucus room where his brother had entered the race eight years before. Sen. Kennedy said that he was running "not to oppose any man, but to propose new ideas."

The U.S. freighter *African Star* collided with the oil barge *Intercity No. 11* on the Mississippi River in Louisiana, igniting a fire that killed 17 people.

The University of Denver won the 1967-68 NCAA Division I Men's Ice Hockey championship by defeating the University of North Dakota, 4-0, in the final game of the championship tournament. The finals were held at the Duluth Arena Auditorium in Minnesota.

"(Sittin' On) The Dock of the Bay" by Otis Redding, who had died in a plane crash three month before, became number one on the U.S. Billboard charts, and remained there for four weeks. It became the first song to posthumously top the U.S. charts.

Died: Mario Castelnuovo-Tedesco, Italian guitarist, pianist, and composer, died at age 72. He was regarded as one of the most prolific guitar music composers of his day, having written 100 guitar compositions. After moving from Florence to the U.S. in 1939, he composed music for roughly 200 films while working for Metro-Goldwyn-Mayer Studios.

Died: June Collyer, American film actress, died in Los Angeles at age 61. After starring in 11 silent films starting in 1927, she successfully transitioned to sound movies. She was the sister of Bud Collyer, prominent radio announcer who would become one of the first major game show hosts on television.

March 17 (Sunday)

In London, a demonstration against the U.S. involvement in Vietnam became violent. Ninety-one people were injured and 200 arrested.

The London Gold Pool was dissolved following the instability of gold reserves in recent weeks.

Compared to today, there was a greater risk in transportation safety. As with the unusually high rate of fatalities due to air and sea travel (including submarines) in 1968, ground transportation had a greater risk. On this date in 1968, four separate bus accidents around the world would claim a total of 73 lives and injure at least 87 more:

- In Turkey, a head-on collision of two buses killed 35 people and injured 45. The buses had been traveling on the highway between İstanbul and Edirne.

- In Nigeria, 19 people were killed and 12 injured as an oil truck collided with a bus near Lagos.

- In Yugoslavia, 10 were killed and 30 injured when a bus overturned in Lazarevac, near Belgrade.

- Also in Yugoslavia, in Kraljevo south of Belgrade, nine people drowned after their bus struck a tree and toppled into the Ibar River.

March 18 (Monday)

The United States broke from its traditional adherence to the gold standard as it eliminated the requirement of backing all U.S. currency deposits with U.S. gold reserves.

The Jabidah Massacre, also called the Corregidor Massacre, took place in the Philippines as members of the armed forces executed a number of Moro Muslim soldiers who reportedly had been absent without leave after not being paid. Although some details have never been confirmed, it is believed that between 11 and 28 Moro Muslims were killed. The event was a contributing factor to the growth of the Muslim Independence Movement in the Philippines.

In Israel near the border with Jordan, two adults were killed and 28 high school students from the Herzliya Hebrew Gymnasium high school in Tel Aviv after their school bus struck and detonated a Palestinian land mine. Israeli Defense Forces responded three days later with an attack on the Jordanian village of Karameh.

On the island of Iwo Jima, Japan, the American flag was lowered for the first time since the Battle of Iwo Jima took place in February 1945. A group of American servicemen climbed to Mount Suribachi, where a U.S. flag had flown day and night since the battle, one of the bloodiest during all of World War II. Contrary to the traditional treatment of the American flag, the flag on Iwo Jima had flown day and night rather than being raised each dawn and lowered each sunset. The lowering of the American flag was symbolic of the end of American occupation of the island since the battle some 23 years before.

Mel Brooks' comedy film, *The Producers*, opened in New York City, the setting of the Broadway-themed story. The film had opened previously with a limited release in Pittsburgh in November 1967, and would be released nationally in the U.S. on November 10, 1968.

The film starred Zero Mostel and Gene Wilder. *The Producers* would win the Academy Award for Best Original Screenplay and decades later (in June 2000), it would be ranked 11th on the American Film Institute's *100 Years ... 100 Laughs* list. The film would be re-made as a successful Broadway musical in 2001 with Nathan Lane and Matthew Broderick, and again as a musical comedy film in 2005 with Lane, Broderick, Uma Thurman and Will Ferrell.

March 19 (Tuesday)

At Howard University in Washington, D.C., the first takeover of a college campus building took place, in protest of American involvement in Vietnam. Students at Howard, a traditionally black university, waged the sit-in of the school's administration building; the students were particularly concerned about the presence of Howard University's Reserve Officers' Training Corps (ROTC) program and recruitment on campus, as well as the disproportionately high percentage of black men who were being sent to Vietnam. (Although blacks comprised 11 percent of the civilian population in the U.S., they comprised 23 percent of all combat troops in Vietnam. In December 1967, NBC News aired the documentary *Same Mud, Same Blood*, describing the experiences that veteran news journalist Frank McGee (a white man) had found during a trip to Vietnam.)

In Poland, the First Secretary of the Polish United Workers' Party, Wladyslaw Gomulka, continued making negative comments about Jews. Speaking about the protests of students in Warsaw, Gomulka blamed "Zionist revisionists."

In the United Kingdom, Chancellor of the Exchequer Roy Jenkins announced a 10% increase in taxes on gasoline, oil, alcohol, tobacco, gambling, and a number of consumer goods. The intent was to increase revenue for the national budget. The general income tax rate in Britain of 41.25% remained in effect.

Crown Prince Harald of Norway announced his engagement to a "commoner" (a person outside of royal lineage), Sonja Haraldsen. Their nine-year-period of dating beforehand was kept secret because the marrying of a commoner was generally not considered acceptable. However, Harald pressured his father, King Olav V, saying that if he could not marry Sonja, that he would never marry, which would have put an end to their family's rule in Norway. The pair would be married on August 29, 1968, and become King Harald V and Queen Consort Sonja in 1991, upon the death of Harald's father. Harald V became Norway's first Norwegian-born monarch since 1343, when Magnus VII abdicated.

Died: Gladys Osborne Leonard, 85, British psychic and trance medium, died at age 85. Although some researchers had concluded that she could actually communicate with spirits, others felt that her deep trance states might be the result of dissociative identity disorder, and others thought that she was simply a fraud.

March 20 (Wednesday)

Near Berkeley, California, a domestic subversive group used explosives to bring down a Pacific Gas and Electric Company (PG & E) electrical tower. The toppling of the tower collapsed two 115,000-volt power lines, which cut the power to the Lawrence Radiation Laboratory and the University of California. Power at the radiation laboratory was quickly fixed by using emergency backup generators, and the PG & E utility restored partial service to the university by 8:00 in the morning.

Died: Carl Theodor Dreyer, Danish film director regarded by many as one of the greatest directors in film history, died in Copenhagen at age 79. His films include *The Passion of Joan of Arc* (1928), *Vampyr* (1932), and *Day of Wrath* (1943).

Died: Charles Chaplin Jr., American film actor and comedian and the son of Charlie Chaplin and Lita Grey, died in Hollywood at age 42. He acted in 14 films between 1952 and 1960, and performed as a comedian on *The Ed Sullivan Show* in 1960.

March 21 (Thursday)

The Battle of Karameh took place in Jordan, as Israel Defense Forces with 15,000 troops and tanks crossed into Jordan to act against the headquarters of the Palestine Liberation Organization (PLO). After a relatively small number of PLO forces defended the headquarters for a period, they were reinforced by tanks and artillery on the orders of King Hussein. After 10 hours of fighting, Israeli forces retreated back home across its border. The PLO and Jordan suffered combined deaths of approximately 240, with the Israelis losing 28.

New York state's Governor Nelson Rockefeller surprised those who had expected him to seek the Republican Party nomination for President against Richard Nixon. Rockefeller stated that he felt "The majority of party leaders want the candidacy of Richard Nixon," and that it would "be illogical and unreasonable that I would try to arouse their support." Rockefeller de-emphasized any campaigning, but closer to the party convention in August, he would let it be known that he was still willing to be the party's candidate.

Died: John Mosely Turner, English "supercentenarian," died in Tottenham, London, England at age 111 years, 280 days. He had been recognized as the oldest living human for more than two years, upon the death of Hannah Smith in Woodhouse, Sheffield, England at age 110 years, 3 days, in 1966. A teetotaler, Turner had worked as a silk print cutter, and had been blind since age 73.

Died: Gerhart Eisler, East German politician and former resident of Queens, New York, who in 1946 had been described as "the number one Communist spy in the United States," died at age 71 in Yerevan, Armenia in the USSR. After escaping the U.S. on a ship in 1949, Eisler became the chief of East German Radio.

March 22 (Friday)

In Czechoslovakia, following the defection of Gen. Jan Sejna, Antonín Novotný resigned from his remaining job as president of the country. It was noted that Novotny's resignation was "the first time a Communist leader had been removed by public pressure." Two months earlier, Novotný had been replaced as general secretary of the Czechoslovakian Communist Party (a more powerful position than president) by Alexander Dubček. Czechoslovakia's National Assembly overwhelmingly named Ludvík Svoboda to replace Novotný, which caused concern in other communist nations in Eastern Europe. Coming on the first full day of Spring, the event unofficially began to mark the beginning of "Prague Spring," a period that reformists would hope would lead to citizens having more rights.

One hundred fifty students occupied the faculty lounge of Paris Nanterre University (then called Paris X Nanterre) in the western suburbs of Paris. The event would later be known as the "Movement of 22 March." The protest was intended to call attention to the arrest of six Nanterre students who had protested the Vietnam War. Although the students left the building peacefully after the publication of their demands, the protest led to further events that would bring France close to revolution in May 1968.

In the U.S., President Lyndon Johnson recalled Gen. William C. Westmoreland, who had led military operations in Vietnam since 1964. The recall would be effective on July 2. Gen. Westmoreland was reassigned to the Joint Chiefs of Staff as Johnson and his leadership changed the direction of U.S. efforts in Vietnam.

In Contra Costa County in California, an aerial cable of Pacific Bell was intentionally damaged by a subversive group, disrupting telephone service to the Oakland and Berkeley areas.

Born: Javier Castillejo, Spanish boxer from 1988 to 2009, was born in Madrid. Castillejo was the World Boxing Council (WBC) light-middleweight champion from 1999 to 2001, and World Boxing Association (WBA) middleweight champion from 2006 to 2007.

Born: Euronymous (the stage name of Øystein Aarseth), Norwegian heavy metal guitarist and co-founder of the Norwegian black metal band Mayhem, was born in Egersund, Norway. (In 1993, he would be murdered by a fellow musician in Oslo.)

March 23 (Saturday)

The Communist Party leaders of six Warsaw Pact nations (the Soviet Union, Bulgaria, Czechoslovakia, East Germany, Poland, and Hungary) met at a rushed conference in Dresden, East Germany to discuss the rapid social and political changes taking place in Czechoslovakia. Without advance notice, the meeting was attended by several generals of the Soviet Red Army. Czechoslovakia's Communist Party leader, Alexander Dubček, was severely criticized by the other Warsaw Pact leaders. Despite the harsh criticisms, the meeting did not result in any plan for limiting the reforms, and Dubček later recalled that the other nations continued their promise of "non-interference in internal affairs" of Czechoslovakia.

The University of California at Los Angeles (UCLA) won the NCAA basketball championship, defeating the University of North Carolina 78-55. The 23-point final scoring difference by Coach John Wooden's UCLA Bruins was the largest in NCAA finals history at the time. The Bruins were led that season by Lou Alcindor, who would change his name to Kareem Abdul-Jabbar later in the summer during his conversion to Islam. Lucius Allen, Edgar Lacey, and Michael Warren were also on the Bruins' roster.

Born: Michael Atherton, who would become an international first-class cricketer and captain of the England cricket team from 1993 to 1998, was born in Failsworth, Lancashire, England. Following his playing days, he would become a journalist and commentator.

Born: Mitch Cullin, American novelist and short story writer, was born in Santa Fe, New Mexico. Cullin would go on to write at least seven novels and one collection of short stories. His novel *Tideland* would be made into a film directed by Terry Gilliam.

Died: Edwin O'Connor, American journalist, radio commentator, and novelist who won Pulitzer Prize for Fiction for his 1961 novel *The Edge of Sadness*, died at age 49 from a cerebral hemorrhage.

March 24 (Sunday)

Off the southeast coast of Ireland, Air Lingus Flight 712 crashed into the sea, killing all 61 passengers and crew on board. The Vicker Viscount 803 turboprop airliner was flying from Cork to London. There was no known problem until the pilot radioed a single message indicating "Twelve thousand feet, spinning rapidly." Although several theories for the crash were proposed, the official explanation from a 2002 panel was that the crash was caused by metal fatigue of the left horizontal stabilizer. Contrary to usual convention of discontinuing a flight number after a crash, Air Lingus continues to use Flight 712 as the number of its Cork-to-London Heathrow flight, although today the airline uses the newer Airbus A320 jetliner for the route.

Panamanian President Marco Aurelio Robles was removed from office after the nation's National Assembly voted unanimously (29-0) to convict him on articles of impeachment following a trial on charges of "giving direct or indirect official aid to a candidate," Finance Minister David Samudio. First Vice President Max Delvalle was administered the oath of office as president, but as Robles returned from a meeting of Western Hemisphere leaders in Uruguay, he refused to accept the legislative decision. In addition, Panama's National Guard backed Robles and refused to recognize anyone other than Robles as president. On April 5, Panama's supreme court ruled, 8 to 2, that Robles' right to a fair trial was not upheld, and that Robles was legally the President. Robles completed his term in office, which ended on October 1, 1968.

In Lebanon, the first stage of parliamentary elections began, and would continue until April 7. Under Lebanon's constitution, the 99 parliamentary seats were apportioned in such a way that a specific number of seats would be held for representatives of Lebanon's Christian and Muslim denominations. Fifty-three seats were reserved for Christian denominations (Greek Orthodox, Armenian Orthodox, Armenian Catholic, Melkite Greek Catholic, Maronite, and Protestant) and 45 seats were reserved for Muslim denominations (Druze, Shi'ite, and Sunni). One additional seat was reserved for an "independent" member.

The United Nations Security Council approved its Resolution 248, condemning Israel's March 21 attack on the Jordanian village of Karameh, saying the action was in violation of UN Charter.

Died: Alice Guy-Blaché, a pioneering French film director, screenwriter, actress and producer, died in Wayne, New Jersey, at age 94. She is believed to be the first person to direct and write narrative action films. In addition to experimenting with sound syncing, she was also involved with interracial casting, special effects, and color tinting. She began to make films in the 1890s, and in 1906 made the film *The Life of Christ*, a large-budget production for the day, as it involved 300 extras. Twelve years before marrying husband Herbert Blaché, Alice Guy was present for the world's first demonstration of film projection in March 1895.

March 25 (Monday)

On television in the U.S., the 58th and final episode of *The Monkees* aired on NBC. The first episode of the musical situation comedy had aired in September 1966. The series depicted humorous situations that always found the band of four musicians. Inspired by The Beatles' film *A Hard Day's Night*, filmmakers Bob Rafelson and Bert Schneider began developing the series by staging a major national casting campaign that drew up to 400 candidates for the roles of the four primary characters. The four young men eventually cast were Mickey Dolenz, David Jones, Peter Tork and Michael Nesmith. All four shared duties for lead vocals, and the group released a number of hit albums and singles. The series won two Emmy Awards during its run, and members of the group staged a number of tours on and off for decades afterward.

Born: Cathy Dennis, British singer and songwriter, was born. Dennis found some success at the international level as a singer, but particularly excelled as a songwriter, having written or co-written at least eight songs that would become number one in the UK and be worldwide hits, including Katy Perry's "I Kissed a Girl," Britney Spears' "Toxic," and the Spice Girls "Bumper to Bumper." Dennis wrote the *Pop Idol* theme, which is also used on *American Idol* in the U.S., and Dennis has written songs for *Idol* contestants including Kelly Clarkson and Clay Aiken.

March 26 (Tuesday)

In what would become one of the most significant behind-the-scenes meetings involving the Vietnam War, U.S. President Lyndon Johnson met with his advisers, particularly Secretary of Defense Clark Clifford—who had only held the post for 25 days—and Secretary of State Dean Rusk. Johnson's top advisers had generally supported his approach to the Vietnam War since its beginning, but on this day, most of the group told him in no uncertain terms that "an American military solution in Vietnam was no longer attainable" and that the U.S. should begin to de-escalate its involvement and eventually withdraw. Those in attendance expressed that the U.S. could no longer sustain its role in the war from a financial or human perspective. As recently as November 1967, the group had unanimously supported continuing the war effort. That was prior to the Tet Offensive and other fierce battles, the departure of Robert McNamara, Walter Cronkite's editorial, and many of the protests that had taken place in the U.S. and around the world.

Born: Kenny Chesney, American country music singer, songwriter and Country Music Association Entertainer of the Year for four consecutive years, was born in Knoxville, Tennessee. Chesney would record 20 albums, 14 of which would be certified as Gold (i.e., 500,000 copies sold) or more.

Born: James Iha, American alternative rock musician and co-founder of The Smashing Pumpkins, was born in Chicago. Iha would also perform with the groups A Perfect Circle and Tinted Windows.

March 27 (Wednesday)

About 150 members of the Students for a Democratic Society (SDS) at Columbia University in New York City waged an occupation of the administration building to protest the university's association with the Institute for Defense Analyses, a think tank for weapons research with ties to the Pentagon. The protesters ended the protest after a few hours, largely because university president Grayson L. Kirk was not present. However, protests at the university would become larger and more common during the year.

A new poll of 1,145 registered voters by Gallup, Inc. indicated that, for the first time among U.S. surveys, former vice president Richard M. Nixon was favored to win the presidency over President Lyndon Johnson and former Alabama Governor George C. Wallace in a three-way presidential race. Nixon was preferred by 41% of those polled, Johnson by 39%, and Wallace by 11%. In a presidential survey taken in October 1966, Johnson had a 51% to 34% margin over Nixon.

Near St. Louis, Missouri, Ozark Airlines Flight 965, a DC-9 passenger jet flying from Sioux Falls, South Dakota to St. Louis, collided with a small Cessna 150F aircraft as both aircraft approached Lambert-St. Louis Airport. Ozark Airlines captain Russell J. Fitch regained control of the DC-9 after the Cessna struck its right wing and caused a fuel tank rupture. According to the federal accident report, the likely cause involved multiple factors, including insufficient ground control procedures and an unusually busy control tower. Both wings of the Cessna flight-instruction plane fell off and both people on board, a flight instructor and his student, were killed when the Cessna crashed in Hazelwood, Missouri, northwest of St. Louis.

Died: Yuri Gagarin, age 34, the first human in outer space, was killed along with test pilot Vladimir Seryogin, 45, when their MiG-15UTI fighter jet crashed near Kirzhach, Russia. A Soviet commission concluded that a Sukhoi Su-15 Flagon fighter jet unknowingly (possibly due to weather), passed 10-20 meters from Gagarin and Seryogin's MiG as the Sukhoi was attempting to break the sound barrier, which "caused extensive turbulence" that sent the MiG-15 into an unrecoverable spin. Such was the level of regard that American astronauts had for Gagarin and his fellow Soviet cosmonauts that astronauts Neil Armstrong and Buzz Aldrin would leave a medal with Gagarin's likeness on the surface of the moon, and several American astronauts would participate in a memorial for Gagarin at an international scientific meeting in 1971.

March 28 (Thursday)

Norway's parliament, The Storting, voted to create the University of Trondheim (Norwegian University of Science and Technology, located in the city of Trondheim) and the University of Tromsø. The Tromsø campus, which would open in 1972, would be located north of 69°N latitude and therefore inside the Arctic Circle, making it the world's northernmost university. Some of the areas studied at Tromsø include study of Auroral light, space science, Saami culture, and fishery science.

In Memphis, Tennessee, a protest march by the striking Memphis sanitation workers down Beale Street began peacefully. Civil rights leaders Martin Luther King, Jr. and Ralph Abernathy led the march.

A new James Bond novel, *Colonel Sun* by author "Robert Markham" (a pen name for Kingsley Amis) was released. Although Amis had planned the book to be a continuation of the series begun by Ian Fleming, who had died in 1964, it turned out to be the last book in the James Bond series until the series was revived by John Gardner in 1981. Gardner's first book in the series would be *License Renewed*, and he would write 13 more Bond novels.

A partial solar eclipse occurred in the Southern Hemisphere, including much of Antarctica.

Born: Nasser Hussain, the Indian-born cricketer and captain of the England cricket team from 1999 to 2003, was born in in Madras (now Chennai), India.

Born: Iris Chang, American journalist and author, was born in Princeton, New Jersey. Chang is best known for writing the 1997 best-selling book *The Rape of Nanking*, an extensive account of the Nanking Massacre, which took place during the Second Sino-Japanese War. Chang, who suffered from depression, would commit suicide in 2004.

Died: In Rio de Janeiro, Edson Luís de Lima Souto, an 18-year-old high school student in Brazil, was shot and killed by the Military Police of Rio de Janeiro while protesting at a restaurant for cheaper meals for low-income students. Concerned that the police would try to hide Edson Luis's body, his fellow students refused to release his body to them and instead carried him to the Legislative Assembly building, where his funeral would be attended by thousands. Protests would follow, including "The March of the 100,000" on June 25.

Died: In Memphis, a 16-year-old high school student, Larry Payne, was shot and killed at close range by a police officer while marching during the Memphis sanitation strike. The officer claimed that he had stopped Payne from looting, and that Payne had threatened him with a knife; however, no stolen property nor knife was ever found. Twenty-five witnesses stated that Payne had emerged from a room empty-handed immediately before the police officer shot him.

March 29 (Friday)

In Detroit, Michigan, a group of about 500 African Americans, including a number who identified themselves as members of the Malcolm X Society, gathered at the Twenty Grand Motel to announce their plan to create a nation called the Republic of New Afrika, comprised of black Americans and located in the southeastern United States, in which there were already areas of predominantly black populations. The group would be led by activist Robert F. Williams, who had previously organized and chartered a gun club through the National Rifle Association in order to protect black citizens from members of the Ku Klux Klan. Williams lived his last years in Baldwin, Michigan, and when he died in 1996, civil rights icon Rosa Parks gave his eulogy, saying "The sacrifices he made, and what he did, should go down in history and never be forgotten."

At the University of Paris (which would change its name to Sorbonne University in 1970), administration officials asked French police to arrest students who had been peacefully demonstrating in order obtain changes.

The agreement that was signed on February 18 to create the "Federation of the Arab Emirates" from the emirates Abu Dhabi and Dubai became effective and celebrated the first day of the federation. Over the next three years, these two emirates would be joined by Ajman, Fujairah, Ras al-Khaimah, Sharjah, and Umm al-Quwain, and would become the United Arab Emirates on December 2, 1971.

Born: Lucy Lawless, New Zealand actress and musician who played the title role in the television series *Xena: Warrior Princess* (1995-2001), as well as playing in *Battlestar Galactica* (2005-09) *Parks and Recreation* (2012-14), and *Agents of S.H.I.E.L.D.* (2014-15), was born Lucille Frances Ryan in Mount Albert, Auckland, New Zealand.

March 30 (Saturday)

The agreement that was signed on February 18 to create the "Federation of the Arab Emirates" from the emirates Abu Dhabi and Dubai became effective and celebrated the first day of the federation. Over the next three years, these two emirates would be joined by Ajman, Fujairah, Ras al-Khaimah, Sharjah, and Umm al-Quwain, and would become the United Arab Emirates on December 2, 1971.

In the United Arab Republic (UAR), President Gamal Abdel Nasser announced an initiative to clean up corruption in the UAR. In addition, Nasser said that positive changes would be made in the Arab Socialist Union, the only political party in Egypt, which Nasser himself had created in 1962. The changes would represent a liberalization of the UAR's policies. (Nasser would die in September 1970 of a heart attack at age 52, and his successor, Anwar Sadat, would further liberalize policies, and would negotiate the Camp David Peace Accords with Israeli Prime Minister Menachem Begin in September 1978.)

At the Aeromarine Supply Company in Birmingham, Alabama, a 40-year-old man using the name Harvey Lowmeyer purchased a Remington Model 760 Gamemaster .30-06 rifle and a Redfield 2x-7x scope (which he asked the store to mount to the rifle), along with a box of cartridges. Investigators would later learn that the man was James Earl Ray, a Missouri prison escapee who hated minorities, especially African-Americans, and was drawn to the segregationist platform of third-party presidential candidate George C. Wallace. Two days later, Ray would use the rifle to kill Dr. Martin Luther King, Jr. in Memphis.

Born: Céline Dion, Canadian singer, was born Céline Marie Claudette Dion in Charlemagne, Quebec, Canada. Dion first gained worldwide fame as a teenager in the 1980s, for winning a gold medal for Best Song at the World Popular Song Festival, and for performing the Best Song at the 1988 Eurovision Song Contest (representing Switzerland). Dion would go on to win five Grammy awards, is the best-selling Canadian artist, and one of the best-selling artists worldwide, of all time.

Died: Bobby Driscoll, 31, American actor, died in New York City at age 31 of a heart attack. Driscoll performed in many film, television, and radio productions between 1943 and 1965, more than two-thirds of his short life. Driscoll starred in a number of Walt Disney films, and is recognized by some as being Disney's first child star. His starring roles including the live/animated feature film *Song of the South* (1946) and the live-action *Treasure Island* (1950). Driscoll also provided the voice of the title role in Disney's original animated *Peter Pan* (1953). Although Driscoll's date of death is given as March 30, he had been addicted to heroin and other drugs for at least 12 years and had become penniless, and he was found, already deceased, in an abandoned building on East 10th Street in New York City's East Village.

March 31 (Sunday)

In a nationally televised address that would have impact for decades to come, President Lyndon Johnson dropped one of the most significant bombshell announcements in American history, as he told the nation at the end of a 41-minute address that he would not run for re-election as president. Despite the gains that Kennedy, Johnson and the Democratic Party would experience in the 1960s, including civil rights and voting rights legislation, Medicare, advancement of the space program and other areas, the decision was seen by many as setting back those gains. Earlier in the speech, Johnson announced the limiting of new deployment of ground troops, announced that he had called a halt to bombing north of the 20th parallel, and publicly extended his offer of unconditional peace negotiations with North Vietnam. Johnson also stated that Americans had united to make "a stronger nation, a more just society, and a land of greater opportunity and fulfillment because of what we have all done together in these years of unparalleled achievement." Anyone who was still listening 41 minutes later was stunned when Johnson concluded the address by saying:

> With America's sons in the fields far away; with America's future under challenge right here at home; with our hopes and the world's hopes for peace in the balance every day, I do not believe that I should devote an hour or a day of my time to any personal partisan causes or to any duties other than the awesome duties of this office--the Presidency of your country. Accordingly, I shall not seek, and I will not accept, the nomination of my party for another term as your President.

The decision would close one door but open others.

April 1968

April 1 (Monday)

In West Germany, bombs exploded in two department stores in Frankfurt-am-Main. Andreas Baader and Gudrun Ensslin would later be arrested and sentenced for arson. Both were members of the anarchist Baader-Meinhof Gang, or Red Army Faction.

In southern Japan, the 1968 Hyūga-nada earthquake struck. The quake had a moment magnitude (Mw) of 7.5, with its epicenter in the Hyūga-nada Sea, and having a tsunami observed. No deaths were reported; there were 15 reported injuries.

In Japan, the Abukuma Express Line, a railway line connecting Fukushima and Tsukinoki, was opened.

The last episode of *The Andy Griffith Show* aired on CBS Television. The show had begun in 1960 as a situation comedy vehicle for actor Andy Griffith, who played Sheriff Andy Taylor in the fictional small town of Mayberry, North Carolina. Don Knotts played his deputy, Barney Fife, for the first five seasons. Other main characters included Andy's son, Opie, his Aunt Bea, his girlfriend (and later wife) Helen Crump, Floyd the barber, friends Gomer and Goober Pyle, and others.

Died: Lev Davidovich Landau, Soviet physicist and Nobel Prize laureate, died in Moscow at age 60. Landau's contributions had been made primarily in the area of theoretical physics. His death was attributed to complications from injuries sustained in a car accident in early 1962.

April 2 (Tuesday)

In Wisconsin, Richard Nixon won the state's Republican presidential primary, gaining 80% of the votes cast. California Governor Ronald Reagan was runner-up with 10%. In the Democratic primary, Sen. Eugene McCarthy won with 56% of the vote, with President Lyndon Johnson winning 35% after having dropped out of the race two days before, and Sen. Robert Kennedy, who had announced his candidacy 17 days before, won 6%.

Stanley Kubrick's classic film *2001: A Space Odyssey* opened at the Uptown Theater in Washington, D.C. During the screening, 241 people walked out of the theater, including Rock Hudson, who said, "Will someone tell me what the hell this is about?" Arthur C. Clarke, author of the companion novel, written concurrently with filming, once said, "If you understand '2001' completely, we failed. We wanted to raise far more questions than we answered." There is no dialogue in the first 25 minutes of the movie nor in the last 23 minutes (excluding end credits). This was the last major motion picture made about people on the moon before the actual 1969 landing there by Neil Armstrong and Buzz Aldrin.

April 3 (Wednesday)

President Johnson continued to incrementally reduce American air attacks in North Vietnam by restricting American bombing to targets south of the 19th Parallel.

The original *The Planet of the Apes* film was released across the United States. The film starred Charlton Heston, Roddy McDowall and Kim Hunter, with screenplay by Michael Wilson and Rod Serling. The film would later be followed by four movie sequels, two television series, a remake movie in 2001, and a series of reboot films between (2011-17).

In New York City, the 1968 National Basketball Association draft took place. The first player selected was Elvin Hayes, from the University of Houston, who was selected by the San Diego Rockets. The second player selected was Wes Unseld of the University of Louisville, by the Baltimore Bullets. Unseld would become the NBA Most Valuable Player as well as Rookie of the Year in his first professional season. In 1996, both players would be named among the league's all-time top 50 players over its first 50 years, and both would be part of the 1978 world championship Washington Bullets.

April 4 (Thursday)

In one of the most shocking and defining events of 1968, Rev. Martin Luther King, Jr., 39, leader of the civil rights movement in the United States, was shot and killed by James Earl Ray at the Lorraine Motel in Memphis, Tennessee. Ray used the rifle that he had purchased in Birmingham on March 30, firing a single shot at King as the civil rights leader stood on the balcony outside of his second-story hotel room. King had been a prominent leader in the civil rights movement since 1955, during the Montgomery Bus Boycott, during which Rosa Parks had also come into the national news. A Baptist minister, King taught messages of non-violence and equality, and advocated the use of peaceful civil disobedience to achieve equality for Americans. He received many death threats during his life. He had remarked to associates on a number of occasions that he knew he would die by violence. In Memphis to support the sanitation strike workers the night before his death, despite being very tired, he was persuaded into providing some brief comments at a rally at the Mason Temple. His remarks seemed prophetic:

Well, I don't know what will happen now. We've got some difficult days ahead. But it doesn't matter with me now. Because I've been to the mountaintop. And I don't mind. Like anybody, I would like to live a long life. Longevity has its place. But I'm not concerned about that now. I just want to do God's will. And He's allowed me to go up to the mountain. And I've looked over. And I've seen the promised land. I may not get there with you. But I want you to know tonight, that we, as a people, will get to the promised land. So, I'm happy tonight. I'm not worried about anything. I'm not fearing any man. Mine eyes have seen the glory of the coming of the Lord.

The single shot was fired at 6:01 pm Central U.S. time, striking King in the cheek, jaw, neck, and several vertebrae, severing major blood vessels. King was knocked backward and became unconscious immediately. As friends and associates of King rushed out of the hotel room to help, witnesses saw James Earl Ray fleeing across the street. Ray left his rifle and binoculars behind, and his fingerprints were on them. King was rushed to St. Joseph's Hospital, where doctors tried to keep him alive, but he never regained consciousness, and he was pronounced dead at 7:05 pm.

The news broke across the country during the evening news hour. Rioting soon began in major American cities, lasting for several days afterwards. A notable exception to the rioting would be in Indianapolis, where Sen. Robert F. Kennedy had heard the terrible news, but decided to go ahead with a planned rally. In an age before cell phones and the Internet, Kennedy knew that few in the crowd would know about King's death. When Kennedy began speaking, he immediately gave the terrible news to the crowd, which was largely comprised of African Americans whose wave of screams and audible shock reflected their feelings. Kennedy gave a short speech in which he emphasized King's belief in non-violence, and mentioned that his own brother had been killed less than five years before. Kennedy's speech in Indianapolis (available on YouTube today) is credited with drastically reduced in Indianapolis the rioting that many U.S. cities experienced that night. He quoted the Greek playwright Aeschylus, saying "Even in our sleep, pain which cannot forget falls drop by drop upon the heart until, in our own despair, against our will, comes wisdom through the awful grace of God." Kennedy went on to say:

> What we need in the United States is not division; what we need in the United States is not hatred; what we need in the United States is not violence or lawlessness, but love and wisdom, and compassion toward one another, and a feeling of justice towards those who still suffer within our country, whether they be white or whether they be black.

Project Apollo: The Apollo-Saturn mission 502 ("Apollo 6") was launched. It was the second and final unmanned test flight of the Saturn V moon launch rocket. There was little news coverage of the launch because of the assassination of Dr. Martin Luther King Jr. early that evening.

April 5 (Friday)

Following the assassination of Martin Luther King, Jr. the previous evening, the greatest instance of social unrest since the Civil War broke out, in the form of rioting, looting, and violence. In Chicago, severe rioting resulted in 11 deaths, substantial injuries and damage to property. Major riots also took place in other American cities, including Washington, DC; Trenton, New Jersey; Kansas City; Louisville, Kentucky; Pittsburgh, Pennsylvania; Cincinnati, Ohio; Wilmington, Delaware; and Detroit, Michigan. In Maryland, Gov. Spiro Agnew called up National Guard troops for state duty, as unrest in Baltimore and suburban areas near Washington, DC began. The rioting across the nation, which continued for several days, resulted in at least 45 deaths, 2,500 injured, and tens of millions of dollars in property damage.

Across the United States and expanding around the world, the manhunt for the killer—or killers—of Rev. Martin Luther King, Jr. became one of the greatest searches for a suspect in history.

In London, Flight Lieutenant Alan Pollock of the Royal Air Force (RAF) made an unauthorized flight with his Hawker Hunter jet fighter, first circling the Houses of Parliament three times, then making a high-speed pass under the top span of Tower Bridge. Pollock conducted his "stunt flying" to protest the lack of an aerial display for commemorating the 50th anniversary of the Royal Air Force four days earlier. Pollock's flight marked the first time that a jet aircraft had passed under the Tower Bridge span. Aware that this would probably be his last flight as an RAF pilot, Pollack flew off to make high-speed inverted passes at three separate RAF air fields, then landed at his home base of West Raynham, where he was arrested and soon dismissed from the RAF.

In Northern Ireland, the Ulster Transport Authority (UTA), which was charged with shutting down most of the northern Irish railway system, was closed down. Northern Ireland Railways (called Ulster Transport Railways at the time) takes over operation of railways in Northern Ireland.

April 6 (Saturday)

Rioting continued following the assassination of Martin Luther King. In Baltimore, Maryland, 300 people held a memorial service for Dr. King; the service lasted from noon until 2 pm without incident. However, later in the afternoon, a crowd gathered in East Baltimore, and by 5 pm, windows were being smashed and police were called in. The city declared a 10 pm curfew, and imposed a ban on sales of alcohol and firearms. The crowd continued to expand and move around Baltimore, and local law enforcement officials were unable to respond effectively. That evening, Governor Spiro Agnew declared a state of emergency.

In Ottawa, Canada, Pierre Trudeau was elected the leader of the Liberal Party. Trudeau won on the fourth ballot, with 51% of the delegates. He would be sworn in as prime minister on April 20. As prime minister, Trudeau would enact institutional reforms, including the implementation of official bilingualism (English and French) and establishing the Charter of Rights and Freedoms. A bachelor when he entered office, his dating while in office was frequently covered in the press, including his dating of Barbra Streisand in 1969-70. In March 1971, he married Margaret Sinclair with little public fanfare. Trudeau would serve as prime minister until 1979, then would again serve from 1980 until 1984, when he retired from politics. In November 2015, his son, Justin Trudeau, would become Canada's prime minister.

In East Germany, the national legislature Volkskammer approved a new constitution. The measure was approved by 96.4% of those voting.

Two explosions in downtown Richmond, Indiana killed 41 people, injured 150, and damaged 20 buildings beyond repair. The first explosion was caused by a leaking underground natural gas main, which had been leaking for some time, and which had begun to deteriorate due to corrosion. The second explosion was caused by a supply of gunpowder at the Marting Arms sporting goods store, which was located next to the leaking main. As a result of the gas main explosion, the National Gas Pipeline Safety Act was passed on August 12, just four months later.

HemisFair, the official 1968 World's Fair, opened in San Antonio, Texas. The fair, having the theme "The Confluence of Civilizations in the Americas," commemorated the 250th anniversary of San Antonio in 1718. The fair's character symbol, Luther the Dragon, was created by children's television producers Sid and Marty Krofft, and would later become the character H.R. Pufnstuf in a television show of the same name. The HemisFair drew 6.3 million visitors and would run through October 6, 1968.

At the Royal Albert Hall in London, the Eurovision Song Contest for 1968 took place. For the first time, the contest was televised in color. The winning song, representing Spain, was *La, la, la,* performed by Massiel, with music and lyrics by Manuel de la Calva and Ramón Arcusa. Finishing in second place, performing *Congratulations*, was Cliff Richard of the United Kingdom, who would go on to become the third-top-selling performer in UK singles chart history, behind only The Beatles and Elvis Presley.

Died: Bobby Hutton, the treasurer and first person recruited into the Black Panthers, was killed in a shootout with Oakland, California police. He was 17 years old.

April 7 (Sunday)

In a general election in Lebanon, candidates who were listed as "independent" (though many were affiliated with some bloc) won the majority of seats. The estimated voter turnout of 49.6%.

Across the United States, a national day of mourning for Martin Luther King took place.

At Brands Hatch motor racing circuit (race track) in Kent, England, Belgian driver Jacky Ickx and British driver Brian Redman won the first round of the 1968 British Sports Car Championship in a Ford GT40.

Died: In Hockenheim, West Germany, Scottish racing driver and two-time world champion Jim Clark was killed in a Formula 2 race at the Hockenheimring motor racing circuit. Clark was racing in the first heat of the 1968 Deutschland Trophäe when his Lotus 48 spun off the track and crashed into a dense group of trees, killing him almost immediately. An investigation identified a punctured tire as the probable cause. Clark was (and remains to be) considered one of the best race drivers in history. He competed in multiple types of race cars, including sports cars, touring cars, Formula cars, and he won the Indianapolis 500 driving a Ford-powered Lotus in 1965. At the time of his death, he had won more Grand Prix races and Grand Prix poll positions than any other driver. In 2009, the London-based Times rated Jim Clark as the best Formula 1 driver ever.

April 8 (Monday)

In London, a British Overseas Airways (BOAC) Boing 707, operating as Flight 712 from London to Zurich, had an engine fall off after it took off from Heathrow Airport, causing the left wing to start on fire. Although the crew was able to make a successful return landing at Heathrow, the fire spread throughout the fuselage, killing five of the 127 passengers and crew on board. Flight attendant Barbara Jane Harrison, who was killed in the fire, would posthumously receive the George Cross. In addition, a British Empire Medal was awarded to Chief Steward Nevile Davis-Gordon for gallantry, and John Davis, the air traffic controller, was awarded the Most Excellent Order of the British Empire.

The Bureau of Narcotics and Dangerous Drugs, a bureau within the United States Department of Justice, was created. In 1973, the bureau would be rolled into the U.S. Drug Enforcement Administration (DEA).

The *Golden State*, a passenger train that had run between Los Angeles and Chicago on the Rock Island Railroad since 1902, left Los Angeles for the last time.

Born: Patricia Arquette, American actress, was born in Chicago. She would make numerous appearances in films and television beginning in 1987 with *A Nightmare on Elm Street: Dream Warriors*. Notably, she would play in Richard Linklater's acclaimed *Boyhood*, which was filmed over a 12-year period from 2002 to 2014. Arquette also starred in *Holes* and *Ed Wood*, and in the television role of Allison DuBois, a psychic and author, in the series *Medium*, for which she won several awards.

April 9 (Tuesday)

In Atlanta, Georgia, the funeral services for Dr. Martin Luther King, Jr. took place. Two services were conducted, including a private service for King, held at Ebenezer Baptist Church, where King had served as pastor. The service was attended by King's associates, American and foreign dignitaries, labor leaders, and people in the field of entertainment. Following a procession to Morehouse College, a public service took place.

April 10 (Wednesday)

In New Zealand, the inter-island vehicle ferry TEV *Wahine* was making a trip from Lyttelton to Wellington when it was struck by a sudden storm caused by the worst cyclone in New Zealand history, Cyclone Giselle. The *Wahine* struck Barrett Reef at the entrance to Wellington Harbor, causing it to run aground, founder, and capsize. Fifty-three lives were lost in the disaster.

April 11 (Thursday)

In West Germany, Josef Bachmann tried to kill Rudi Dutschke, the primary spokesman of the left-wing "Extra-Parliamentary Opposition" (APO) student movement in West Germany. Dutschke survived, and Bachmann tried unsuccessfully to commit suicide after the attempted killing. In 1970, Bachmann would successfully commit suicide in prison. Dutschke, who suffered brain injuries from the attempt and would suffer from related health issues for the rest of his life, would die of those brain injuries in Denmark in 1979.

In Berlin, following the assassination attempt on Rudi Dutschke, left-wing students, who felt that Springer Press had biased coverage of the student movement, blockaded the Springer Press headquarters. A number of students were arrested. Years later, Springer Press would become the largest digital publishing company in Europe.

In Washington DC, President Lyndon B. Johnson signed the Civil Rights Act of 1968, also known as the Fair Housing Act.

The 1939 classic film *The Wizard of Oz* was shown on the NBC network for the first time; the film had previously been shown on CBS since 1956. The film would continue to be shown on NBC annually over the next eight years. In the days before home video recording, children and their families would look forward with anticipation to seeing *The Wizard* that one time of the year that it was shown.

April 12 (Friday)

In Tokyo, Japan, the 36-story Kasumigaseki Building opened. It is generally regarded as the first modern office skyscraper in Japan and was the tallest building in Tokyo until the 40-story World Trade Center building in Tokyo two years later, which in turn yielded the title to the twin-towered Keio Plaza Hotel in Shinjuku, Tokyo, a year after that.

At the Shoreham Flying School in England, the Beagle B121 Pup small training and touring aircraft is put into service for the first time.

April 13 (Saturday)

A total lunar eclipse took place across Africa, western Europe, and North and South America. It was the first of two total eclipses during the year.

The ballad "Honey" by Bobby Goldsboro became the number one song in the U.S., and remained there for five weeks.

April 14 (Sunday)

At Baikonur, Kazakhstan, the Soviet Union launched the unmanned Soyuz test spacecraft Kosmos 212. While in orbit, the spacecraft would automatically dock with the Kosmos 213 spacecraft, which was also unmanned. Both spacecraft landed successfully in the USSR on April 20.

In Maryland, Gov. Spiro Agnew called an end to the state of emergency in Baltimore, and ordered the Maryland National Guard to stand down.

April 15 (Monday)

At the Astrodome in Houston, Texas, the New York Mets and the Houston Astros played what writer John McMurray would call "almost three games in one," as the two teams played a 24-inning, 6-hour-and-6-minute baseball game that ended with the Astros winning, 1-0. Mets' starting pitcher Tom Seaver, in his second year in the major leagues, went 10 innings and gave up no runs and only two hits. Astros' starting pitcher Don Wilson went 9 innings and gave up 5 hits and no runs. The winning pitcher for the Astros was Wade Blasingame. The Astros victory came in the 24th inning with a leadoff hit by Norm Miller—the only hit of the inning—followed by a balk, an intentional walk, a groundout that moved up the runners, another intentional walk, and then a ground ball that went through the legs of the shortstop, scoring Miller. Each team had 11 hits and one error in the game.

The "secret agent buddy series" *I Spy* aired for the final time on NBC Television. The show starred Bill Cosby and Robert Culp as two American spies who used their cover of tennis amateur and trainer to execute their missions.

April 16 (Tuesday)

Died: Albert Betz, German physicist and professor, died at the age of 82. Betz was a pioneer of wind technology, and developed the swept wing for jet aircraft—revolutionary at the time—for the Messerschmidt fighter.

Died: Edna Ferber, American novelist, short story writer, and playwright, died at the age of 82. Born in Kalamazoo, Michigan in 1885 and raised in the Midwestern U.S., Ferber's stories tended to feature strong female protagonists and well-defined supporting characters. Several of Ferber's best-selling novels were made into films, including *Cimarron* (which won an Oscar), *Giant*, *Ice Palace*, *Saratoga Trunk*, and *Showboat*. Ferber was a member of the famed Algonquin Round Table in New York City, and won a Pulitzer Prize for her 1925 book *So Big*, which was made into a silent film.

April 17 (Wednesday)

The Oakland A's and the Baltimore Orioles played the first baseball game at Oakland-Alameda County Coliseum. A crowd of 50,164 watched the visiting Orioles beat their A's, 4-1. The A's were in their first year based in Oakland, having moved there from Kansas City after the 1967 season. The Oakland Raiders professional football team had played at the stadium since September 18, 1966. As of 2017, the Oakland Coliseum would be the only remaining stadium in the U.S. to be shared by professional baseball and football teams. On April 3, 2017, the A's would dedicate their new playing surface as Rickey Henderson Field, to honor the team's long-time player who is considered by some to be the best base runner in the game's history; Henderson had 1,406 stolen bases in his career to accompany his 3,055 hits. (Henderson, who was born Rickey Nelson Henley (named after singer/actor Ricky Nelson) on Christmas Day 1958, came into the world in the back seat of an Oldsmobile on the way to a Chicago hospital. Remarked Henderson later, "I was already fast. I couldn't wait.")

April 18 (Thursday)

In Sierra Leone in West Africa, John Amadu Bangura, an army officer who was also chairman of the National Interim Council, led the "Sergeants' Coup" which re-installed civilian rule in Sierra Leone after it had been led by the military. Bangura became the acting Governor-General of Sierra Leone, but not having political ambitions, he would only serve in the acting governor-general position for four days.

Arizona entrepreneur Robert Paxton McCulloch purchased the "New London Bridge," which had been designed by Scottish engineer John Rennie the Elder and had spanned London's Thames River from 1831 to 1967. The bridge would be disassembled, moved, and rebuilt at Lake Havasu City, Arizona, to reopen three years later. McCulloch's grandfather had earned a fortune installing Thomas Edison's power generation equipment around the world. After graduating from Stanford University, McCullough married Barbra Ann Briggs, whose father had co-founded Briggs & Stratton, a manufacturer of small engines. McCullough was successful in manufacturing and marketing small, single-operator chainsaws built by the company that still bears his name. In addition, his companies made both McCullough and Paxton brand superchargers, which add horsepower to car and truck engines.

April 19 (Friday)

In Belgium, construction workers struck, joining other striking workers throughout Europe.

In Boston, Massachusetts, American runner Amby Burfoot won the 72nd Boston Marathon. In his senior year in college, Burfoot had been roommates with Bill Rodgers ("Boston Billy"); Burfoot would be credited with having great influence on Rodgers, who would win the Boston Marathon four times. Burfoot would continue running the annual Boston Marathon; in 2013, he was stopped less than a mile from the finish line due to the bomb explosions at the finish area. For many years, he would write books about running and contribute to running-related magazines.

April 20 (Saturday)

Pierre Elliott Trudeau is sworn in as the 15th Prime Minister of Canada after being elected to the position earlier in the month.

In Windhoek, South-West Africa (now Namibia), South African Airways Flight 228, a Boeing 707, crashed shortly after takeoff from J. G. Strijdom International Airport (now called Hosea Kutako International Airport), killing 123 of 128 passengers and crew. The crash is still the deadliest aviation accident in Namibia's history.

In Birmingham, England, British Conservative Member of Parliament (MP) Enoch Powell made his so-called Rivers of Blood speech, which criticized immigration into the United Kingdom and cautioned against anti-discrimination legislation that was being discussed.

April 21 (Sunday)

In the United States, National Airlines stopped making use of turboprop aircraft and would begin operating only jets, flying the Douglas DC-8 and Boeing 727. (National Airlines, which had been founded in 1934, would cease operations in 1980, being acquired by Pan American World Airways ["Pan Am"], which in turn would declare bankruptcy in 1991, with assets purchased by Delta Airlines.)

The day after giving his "Rivers of Blood" speech, Enoch Powell was dismissed from opposition leader Edward Heath's Shadow Cabinet because of the speech.

April 22 (Monday)

Born: Carlos Costa Masferrer, who would become one of the best clay-court tennis players in the 1990s, was born in Barcelona, Spain.

Died: Stephen H. Sholes, RCA Victor recording executive, died in Nashville, Tennessee, at age 57. Sholes had recruited a number of prominent recording artists to RCA Victor, including Eddy Arnold, Homer & Jethro, Jim Reeves, and Hank Snow. In 1955, he signed Elvis Presley to a recording contract for RCA Victor.

April 23 (Tuesday)

In Paris, surgeons at the Hôpital de la Pitié performed Europe's first heart transplant.

In the Democratic Republic of the Congo, president and military dictator Mobutu Sese Seko released captured mercenaries. Mobuto would rename the country Zaire in 1971.

In Pennsylvania, Sen. Eugene McCarthy won the Democratic presidential primary with 71% of the vote. Sen. Robert Kennedy was runner-up with 11%. In the Republican primary, Richard Nixon won with 60% of the vote, the runner-up was New York Governor Nelson Rockefeller with 19%.

At their General Council in Dallas, Texas, the Methodist Church and the Evangelical United Brethren Church merge, to form the United Methodist Church.

In New York City, students took over the Columbia University administration building in another protest of the Vietnam War. The occupation of the building led to the shutting down the university.

Born: Timothy McVeigh was born in Lockport, New York. McVeigh would become a veteran of the 1990-91 Gulf War, and later would become the leader of an American terrorist organization that built and detonated a truck bomb in front of the Alfred P. Murrah Federal Building in Oklahoma City, Oklahoma. The explosion blew away the front of the building and brought top floors of the building down onto lower floors, resulting in the deaths of 168 people and injuring over 600 more. The Oklahoma City bombing was the deadliest terrorist act inside the United States prior to the September 11, 2001 attacks, and is still the deadliest act of domestic terrorism in U.S. history. Investigators were able to locate an identification number on the demolished truck and trace it to the truck that McVeigh had rented. McVeigh was arrested later that day during a routine traffic stop, and he later stood trial, as did a small group of accomplices. McVeigh was found guilty of murder, sentenced to death (permissible in the United States for some federal crimes) and was executed in 2001.

April 24 (Wednesday)

The Desilu-Walden film *Yours, Mine and Ours*, starring Lucille Ball and Henry Fonda, was released.

Died: Tommy Noonan, U.S. actor, died in Los Angeles of a brain tumor at age 46. Noonan had starred with Marilyn Monroe in *Gentlemen Prefer Blondes* (1953) and in the 1954 version of *A Star is Born* with Judy Garland and James Mason.

April 25 (Thursday)

The 23rd Vuelta a España (Tour of Spain) bicycle race began. The event would consist of 18 separate stages, cover 1,873 miles (3,014 km), and would conclude on May 12, with Italian Felice Gimondi of Team Salvarani winning.

The SIV-B third stage of the unmanned Apollo 6, which had been launched on April 4, re-entered the Earth's atmosphere. The Apollo 6 command module had re-entered the atmosphere 10 hours after launch, and was recovered in the North Pacific Ocean by the carrier USS *Okinawa*.

April 26 (Friday)

At the Nevada Test Site, about 65 miles (105 km) northwest of Las Vegas, Nevada, the U.S. Department of Energy and support groups detonated the nuclear weapon "Boxcar" as part of *Operation Crosstie. Operation Crosstie* was a U.S. series of 48 tests conducted in 1967-68. *Operation Crosstie* was preceded by *Operation Fishbowl* (high altitude nuclear tests), and then *Operation Storax* (47 nuclear tests), *Operation Roller Coaster* (four nuclear tests), *Operation Niblick* (41 nuclear tests), *Operation Whetstone* (46 nuclear tests), *Operation Flintlock* (47 nuclear tests), and *Operation Latchkey* (38 nuclear tests). Twenty-three more such series of nuclear tests would be carried out before the Comprehensive Test Ban Treaty by the United Nations General Assembly in September 1996.

April 27 (Saturday)

Vice President Hubert H. Humphrey of Minnesota announced his candidacy for the Democratic presidential nomination. Humphrey's announcement came one month after President Lyndon Johnson announced that he would not run for the nomination. In a public statement that would be regarded as loyalty to Johnson, Humphrey essentially agreed with Johnson's Vietnam War policy, saying that he supported sending American troops "where required by our own national security." With American participation in the war becoming increasingly unpopular, Humphrey's stance may have been significant later in the year, during the Democratic Convention in Chicago, and in the general presidential election in November.

Humphrey chose not to focus his campaigning in primary states, where Sen. Eugene McCarthy and Sen. Robert Kennedy were competing. Instead, he would focus on those states where delegates and platforms were selected by state and local leader.

In the United Kingdom, Abortion Act 1967 took effect, legalizing abortion under certain circumstances.

In Oakland, California, Jimmy Ellis from Louisville, Kentucky defeated Jerry Quarry of Bakersfield, California, to win the World Boxing Association world heavyweight title, following a vacancy in the title after the boxing associations took the title from Muhammad Ali.

April 28 (Sunday)

Near Beaumont, Texas, a Beechcraft 65 Queen Air small business airplane crashed and exploded while landing, killing five members of the Lamar State College of Technology ("Lamar Tech") track team along with their coach and pilot. The team was returning from Des Moines, Iowa, where they had participated in the Drake Relays track meet.

April 29 (Monday)

On Broadway in New York City, the musical *Hair* opened at the Biltmore Theatre (now the Samuel J. Friedman Theatre). Songs from the musical that would later become recorded hits included "Hair," "Aquarius," "Easy to be Hard," and "Good Morning Starshine."

The Royal Netherlands Navy decommissioned the HNLMS *Karel Doorman*, its last aircraft carrier. Prior to being purchased by The Netherlands, the ship was the British carrier HMS *Venerable*. After decommissioning, the carrier would be sold to Argentina and used as a carrier until the year 2000, at which time it would be stripped for parts and scrapped.

April 30 (Tuesday)

In Massachusetts, Gov. Nelson Rockefeller would win a narrow 30%-26% win over Richard Nixon in the Republican primary. It would turn out to be the last primary that Nixon would *not* win in 1968, as he clearly now appeared to have the momentum to win the party's nomination to run for president. Governor John Volpe of Massachusetts withdrew from the Republican race. Volpe had been running as a "favorite son" of Massachusetts, but was defeated this day by both Nixon and Rockefeller, with the latter being a write-in candidate. Volpe may have originally planned to stay in the race long enough to be considered as a vice presidential nominee. On the Democratic side in Massachusetts, Sen. Eugene McCarthy won with

49% of the vote, with Sen. Robert Kennedy, a Massachusetts native, second with 28%.

In Australia, Jim Cairns challenged Gough Whitlam for leadership of the Australian Labor Party; the challenge was unsuccessful. By 1968, Cairns had become a leader of the movement against Australia's involvement in the Vietnam War. Four years later, Whitlam would become prime minister of Australia and serve until 1975.

May 1968

May 1 (Wednesday)

In Australia, Prince Philip, Duke of Edinburgh, consort of Queen Elizabeth II of the United Kingdom, arrived for an official visit, particularly to open the Duke of Edinburgh Study Conference.

Died: Jack Adams, former Canadian hockey player, coach, and general manager, died in Detroit, Michigan at age 76. Adams played from 1917 to 1927, and later was the head coach and general manager of the Detroit Red Wings professional hockey team for 36 years. Adams was the winningest coach in Red Wings history, with 413 wins, until being passed by coach Mike Babcock in 2014.

May 2 (Thursday)

In Paris, the Paris University at Nanterre (the Sorbonne) closed the university after Student protests in France: the administration of the Paris University at Nanterre effectively shut down the university after fighting between students and the University authorities. The event would mark the beginning of what is still called "May 68," an outbreak of massive strikes, and occupation of factories and universities that would become so expansive that a number of political leaders were concerned about the beginning of a revolution or civil war. President Charles de Gaulle became involved in seeking a solution, and at one point on May 29, he fled France for several hours in order to reduce the possibility of bloodshed for others. The outbreak would continue until June 23.

The Israel Broadcasting Authority (IBA) made its first television broadcasts. The authority broadcast programs in black and white; it would begin broadcasting in color in 1983. The IBA ceased operations on May 13, 2017, and was replaced by the Israeli Broadcasting Corporation. The last show carried by the IBA was the Eurovision Song Contest 2017.

In Oxford, UK, the Christ Church Picture Gallery, a private gallery on the campus of Oxford University that was designed by Philip Powell and Hidalgo Moya, was opened. The gallery holds a major collection of roughly 300 Old Master paintings and almost 2,000 drawings. Drawings include those of Leonardo da Vinci, Michelangelo, Raphael, and Peter Paul Rubens.

The original film *The Odd Couple*, based on the Neil Simon play and starring Jack Lemmon and Walter Matthau, was released in theaters.

May 3 (Friday)

Near Dawson, Texas, Braniff Flight 352 crashed, killing all 80 passengers and five crew members. Braniff Flight 352 was a domestic flight from Houston to Dallas Love Field. The Lockheed L-188A Electra broke up in midair and crashed while flying through a severe thunderstorm. The accident report stated that the crash was caused by structural stress and failure of the left wing as the crew made an unusually steep turn trying to avoid the severe weather.

The first heart transplant in the United Kingdom was performed, by a team led by South African-born thoracic surgeon Donald Ross.

Students at the Sorbonne in Paris, France, protested against the closure of Paris University at Nanterre and the proposed expulsion of some students.

May 4 (Saturday)

At Churchill Downs in Louisville, Kentucky, the 94th Kentucky Derby was run. The big race was won by Dancer's Image, but later that evening, a laboratory test of urine samples of the competing horses resulted in a positive test for the pain-killer Butazolidin for one horse, which turned out to be winner Dancer's Image. Discussions took place through the following Tuesday, when the president of Churchill Downs announced the disqualification of Dancer's Image, and that the second-place finisher, Forward Pass, would be considered the winner. As of 2017, Dancer's Image remains the only horse in the 143 runnings of the Kentucky Derby to be disqualified. (In 1974, Butazolidin would be legalized by the Kentucky Racing Commission.)

In Vietnam, the second phase of the Tet Offensive, also called the May Offensive, began. Although allied intelligence reports had allowed forces to be better prepared for attack than they had been in late January, 13 Viet Cong battalions fought to reach 119 targets throughout South Vietnam, including Saigon and the Tan Son Nhut air base.

May 5 (Sunday)

A twin-engine Grumman Gulfstream II became the first business jet to cross the Atlantic Ocean nonstop.

Albert Dekker, American character actor, died in Hollywood, California, at age 62 from what was ruled accidental asphyxiation. Dekker had performed in more than 50 films and more than 15 television shows, and was particularly known as the character Dr. Thorkel in the film *Dr. Cyclops*. He had performed in a number of classic films including *Gentlemen's Agreement, East of Eden, The Sound and the Fury, Suddenly Last Summer,* and *The Wild Bunch.*

May 6 (Monday)

Student protests continued in Paris. At the Sorbonne, a march against actions by the police was staged by the Union Nationale des Étudiants de France (UNEF, the largest student union in the nation), along with the union of university teachers. Some 20,000 protesters marched towards the Sorbonne, with the police charging with batons. Students threw stones at police and created barricades, and police responded by firing tear gas.

The United States Court of Appeals for the Fifth Circuit upheld the guilty verdict from June 20, 1967, finding that boxer Muhammad Ali had violated the Selective Service Act for refusing induction into the armed service. The court ruled that Ali "had been fairly afforded due process of law without discrimination."

At the port of Ensenada in Buenos Aires, Argentina, the Argentinian oil tanker MV *Islas Orcadas* exploded and caught fire. The explosion spread burning oil which in turn caught the nearby tankers *Fray Luis Beltran* and *Cutral Co* on fire. All three tankers sank.

May 7 (Tuesday)

In Paris, an estimated 50,000 students, teachers and youth gathered at the Arc de Triomphe to protest police brutality and demand the dropping of criminal charges that had previously been brought against hundreds of arrested students. The crowd also demanded that authorities reopen Nanterre and Sorbonne universities.

In Indiana, Sen. Robert Kennedy won the Democratic presidential primary 42%-27% over Sen. Eugene McCarthy. Richard Nixon won 100% of the vote among Republicans.

Died: In Speedway, Indiana, British racing driver Mike Spence, 31, died during practice runs for the Indianapolis 500. Spence had raced in 37 Formula One races in his five years of racing. Following the death of Jim Clark in early March, Lotus team lead Colin Chapman had asked Spence to join the team and race one of the revolutionary four-wheel-drive STP Turbine cars in at Indy. On his second lap test-driving a new turbine car, Spence hit the concrete wall in Turn 1, and the right front tire/wheel was slammed back into the cockpit, where it fatally struck Spence in the helmet. Spence's teammates, Graham Hill, Art Pollard, and Joe Leonard would all continue to run their turbine cars in the race on May 30.

May 8 (Wednesday)

In Oakland, California, pitcher Jim "Catfish" Hunter of the Oakland A's pitched the ninth perfect game in major league history. The A's beat the Minnesota Twins 4-0 at Oakland-Alameda County Coliseum. Hunter struck out 11 Twins batters in the effort. The game was only the 25th in the history of the Oakland A's, who had moved to Oakland from Kansas City following the 1967 season. In addition to Hunter's pitching, he helped the cause by batting in 3 of his team's 4 runs. Hunter, who was 22 years, 30 days old on that date, remains the youngest pitcher to throw a perfect game in the modern era of the game.

May 9 (Thursday)

Born: Marie-José Pérec, French track & field (athletics) athlete who would become an Olympic champion, world champion, and

European champion in the 200-400-meter range, was born in Basse-Terre, Guadeloupe. Pérec won championships at the 1992 Barcelona Olympics (400 m), 1996 Atlanta Olympics (200 m and 400 m), 400-meter world championships at Tokyo (1991) and Gothenburg (1995), and 400-meter and 4 x 400-meter European championships in Helsinki (1994).

Died: Mercedes de Acosta, U.S. poet, playwright, novelist, costume designer, and socialite, died in New York City at age 75. In addition to a 15-year marriage to Abram Poole, De Acosta was known for having a number of open relationships with women (including some of the most famous women of the time), which was very uncommon at the time.

May 10 (Friday)

In Paris, a crowd gathered after midnight on La Rive Gauche (the Left Bank, or southern bank of the Seine River in Paris), where violence erupted again between the crowd and the police. Police attacked the crowd at 2:15 am after negotiations were unsuccessful. Protesters built as many as 60 barricades, and they captured much of the French Quarter. Protesters claimed that police used *agents provocateurs* to aggravate the situation by burning cars and throwing Molotov cocktails.

Also in Paris, the first negotiations took place between U.S. and North Vietnamese representatives to discuss an end to the war in Vietnam. The demand by North Vietnam was that the U.S. stop all bombing of North Vietnam, and the demand by the U.S. was for North Vietnam to de-escalate hostilities in South Vietnam. Disagreements about whether to recognize South Vietnam as a negotiating party led to lengthy discussions about the shape of the conference table, with the North insisting that the table be circular, to give more of an appearance of equality to the involved parties.

In the city of Akyab, Burma (now called Sittwe; the country now Myanmar), the Greek cargo ship *Gero Miklaos* ran aground and broke up in a cyclone.

May 11 (Saturday)

In Paris, hundreds of people were injured as violence continued.

The single "MacArthur Park," written by Jimmy Webb and sung by Richard Harris, made its way onto the music charts for the first time. The record would peak at number 2 in June.

The psychedelic rock band H. P. Lovecraft (named after the horror writer) performed at The Fillmore in San Francisco, California. A recording of the event was eventually released in 1991, and is called the *Live May 11, 1968* album. The album was reissued in 2000.

Born: Jeffrey Donovan, American actor who played the lead character of Michael Westen in the television series *Burn Notice*, was born in Amesbury, Massachusetts.

May 12 (Sunday)

The march of the Poor People's Campaign, led by Ralph Abernathy following the death of Rev. Martin Luther King, Jr., reached Washington DC.

In Peru, the football club Carlos A. Mannucci, based in Trujillo, Peru, won the 1968 Copa Perú (Peru Cup) football tournament.

Near Paris, AS Saint-Étienne defeated Girondins de Bordeaux in the 1967–68 Coupe de France football tournament final match.

Born: Tony Hawk, U.S. champion skateboarder and actor, was born in Carlsbad, California. Hawk is acknowledged to be one of the most influential pioneers of skateboarding,

May 13 (Monday)

In France, well over one million people marched in Paris. Prime Minister Georges Pompidou announced the release of prisoners, and stated that the Sorbonne would reopen. In addition, police were ordered to minimize their presence in order to minimize angering the crowd. However, the protests continued and even increased. The Confédération Générale du Travail (CGT, General Confederation of Labor) and the Force Ouvrière (CGT-FO, or Working Force) called for a general strike.

In the UK, Manchester City F.C. won the 1967-68 Football League First Division for the second time in the club's history with a 4-3 win at Newcastle United, while local rivals Manchester United lost 2-1 at home to Sunderland.

May 14 (Tuesday)

In New York City, the Beatles announced the creation of Apple Records, a division of Apple Corps Ltd. The group initially founded the company as a creative outlet, and to serve as a label for a group of other selected artists including Billy Preston, Badfinger, James Taylor and Mary Hopkin, but following the breakup of the Beatles in 1970, it served as a label for the four former members of the group as solo artists. The new company was announced at a press conference, coming nine months after the death manager Brian Epstein.

Near Nantes in western France, a sit-down strike began at the Sud Aviation plant. Workers locked company management out of their offices. Strikes would also begin at four Renault plants in France.

In Dublin, Ireland, King Baudouin and Queen Fabiola of Belgium arrived for a state visit. A state dinner took place that evening in their honor, at the official residence of the Irish president.

In downtown Toronto, the Toronto-Dominion Centre (TD Centre) was formally opened. Some critics compared the dual dark monolithic structures to the monolith featured in *2001: A Space Odyssey*, which premiered six weeks before.

May 15 (Wednesday)

Across the central and southern U.S., a number of severe thunderstorms arose, giving birth to tornadoes in several cities including Charles City, Iowa; Jonesboro, Arkansas; and Oelwein, Iowa. At least 46 tornadoes were produced, which resulted in the deaths of at least 72 people, 45 of whom were in Arkansas. In Iowa, two category F5 tornadoes were produced. The list of confirmed tornadoes also struck U.S. states of Minnesota, Illinois, Kansas, Missouri, Indiana, Ohio, Tennessee, and Mississippi.

In Paris, the National Theater was seized by protesters and began to be used for dialogue between parties.

The drama film *The Swimmer*, starring Burt Lancaster and based on the short story by John Cheever, was released in theaters.

May 16 (Thursday)

In Newham, East London, Ronan Point, a 21-story tower block, partly collapsed after a gas explosion. The explosion destroyed several load-bearing walls, killing five people. Ronan Tower had been completed only two months before. The tragedy served to highlight potential structural problems in buildings that had not always been considered before, and led to new building standards in the UK and other countries.

In France, it was estimated that protesting workers occupied roughly 50 factories.

May 17 (Friday)

In Catonsville, Maryland, a group of Catholic U.S. anti-war demonstrators entered the Selective Service offices, removed draft records and took them to the parking lot, where they burned them with home-made napalm. The group included Jesuit priest Daniel Berrigan, his brother, former priest Philip Berrigan, and artist Tom Lewis. The group would come to be known as the Catonsville Nine.

In France, an estimated 200,000 workers were now on strike.

May 18 (Saturday)

In France, the number of people protesting had increased to 2 million.

In Miami, Florida, Dorothy Anstett of the state of Washington won the 17th Miss USA pageant. The pageant was hosted by long-time television game show host Bob Barker.

At Pimlico Race Course in Baltimore, Maryland, Forward Pass, ridden by Ismael Valenzuela, won the 93rd running of the Preakness Stakes.

The Prisoner, an innovative, 17-episode show created by and starring Patrick McGoohan, aired its first episode in the U.S. on CBS. *The Prisoner* told the story about a British former secret agent who inexplicably resigned in the first episode. The agent returned home only to be knocked out and abducted, and when he awoke, he was imprisoned in a mysterious coastal resort, "The Village," where his captors tried to determine why he abruptly resigned. Throughout the series, we never learned the name of the primary character; he's called simply "Number Six" throughout. The show combined elements of spy thrillers, science fiction, and psychological thrillers.

May 19 (Sunday)

In the Italian general election, the Christian Democrat Party maintained a level of popularity by retaining 38% of the vote. The Communist Party had increased its popularity somewhat by increasing from 25% to 30% since the 1963 general election.

Almost one year into the Nigerian Civil War (or "Biafran War"), Nigerian forces captured Port Harcourt and surrounded Biafra, blockading food and supplies from entering. The blockade would result in a likely 1 million Biafrans dying from starvation or related problems.

In Iran, the 1968 AFC Asian Cup soccer tournament was won by the home team, Iran.

May 20 (Monday)

In France, about 4,000 students who were occupying the Sorbonne left to support the protesters who were occupying the Renault plant. The French government called an additional 10,000 police to be available. During this week, the number of French workers who were on strike was an estimated 10 million, which was about two-thirds of the French workforce. Some protesters were beginning to call for sudden changes in the government, including the removal of the French government including President de Gaulle.

In the northern Italian province of Como, the 1968 Giro d'Italia bicycle race began in the municipality of Campione d'Italia. Thirteen 10-rider teams competed over 22 stages, with the event concluding on June 12.

May 21 (Tuesday)

Prime Minister of India Indira Gandhi, who traveled widely during her tenure, began an official visit to Australia.

At Wrigley Field in Chicago, Billy Williams of the Chicago Cubs set a National League record for most consecutive games played (695). The record for the NL would later be broken by Steve Garvey (1975-83), with 1,207 consecutive games.

May 22 (Wednesday)

The U.S. Navy nuclear submarine USS *Scorpion* suffered a major failure and sank to the bottom of the Atlantic Ocean 400 nautical miles (460 miles) southwest of the Azores. The search for the *Scorpion* continued until June 5, when it became official that the submarine was lost and all 99 crew members listed as "presumed dead." During the last hours of the *Scorpion*, there were difficulties communicating with naval stations, but the last communication to come from the *Scorpion* was from Commander Francis Slattery, who said that they were closing in on a Soviet submarine. The *Scorpion* was at a depth of about 350 feet (107 m) when last known. The remains of the boat would not be located until late October 1968.

The United States' worst helicopter mishap to that date occurred as Los Angeles Airways Flight 841, a Sikorsky S-61L helicopter, crashed in Paramount, California, killing all 20 passengers and 3 crew members on board. The cause was believed to be a problem with the blade rotor system; the incident began when one of the blades struck the fuselage. The loss of 23 remained the worst helicopter-involved crash in U.S. history until a midair crash of a helicopter in the Grand Canyon—which involved a fixed-wing airplane striking a helicopter—in 1986 killed 25.

Born: Graham Linehan, who would become an Irish comedian and comedy writer, was born in Dublin, Ireland.

May 23 (Thursday)

For the first time, a surface-to-air missile destroyed an enemy aircraft, as the U.S. Navy's guided-missile cruiser USS *Long Beach* shot down a North Vietnamese MiG flying over North Vietnam. The *Long Beach* hit the MiG with a RIM-8 Talos missile 65 nautical miles away from the target.

The British comedy film *Prudence and the Pill* was released in theaters. The film, starring Deborah Kerr and David Niven, was controversial for the time as it dealt with the use of birth control pills.

May 24 (Friday)

The French government and military were preparing for a revolt by the people of France. The Paris Stock Exchange was set on fire by protesters, and 20,000 French troops were brought in to guard against further violence.

On the French Riviera, the Cannes Film Festival ended early due to the turmoil in France. Soon after the beginning of the festival, the restored version of the 1939 film *Gone with the Wind* was shown, after which Jean-Luc Godard and Claude Lelouche took the stage and announced an early end to the festival, in solidarity with students and workers who were protesting across the country. Princess Grace of Monaco, the former American actress Grace Kelly, was the host of opening and closing ceremonies.

In Quebec City, French separatists bombed the U.S. consulate.

May 25 (Saturday)

At the Ministry of Social Affairs on the Rue de Grenelle in Paris, discussions started between representatives of the Pompidou government, trade unions, and the Organisation patronale (employers' organization), leading to the Grenelle agreements, which provided a 25% increase in the minimum wage and a 10% increase in real wages. Workers rejected the agreements, and the unrest continued.

In St. Louis, Missouri, the Gateway Arch was dedicated. The structure is the tallest arch in the world, and the tallest human-made monument in the Western Hemisphere. The arch recognizes western expansion in the United States. The arch was designed by Finnish-American architect Eero Saarinen in 1947.

May 26 (Sunday)

In Paris, in the middle of turmoil throughout the country, the 1968 Federation Cup tennis tournament continued and was won by Australia, which defeated the Netherlands 3-0 in the final.

Born: Frederik, Crown Prince of Denmark, was born to Princess Margrethe and her husband, Prince Henrik, in Copenhagen. Frederik's mother would become Queen of Denmark in January 1972.

Died: Little Willie John, 30, U.S. Rhythm and Blues singer, died at the age of 30 at Washington State Penitentiary in Walla Walla, Washington, while serving time for murder. John had at least 17 hit singles on the Rhythm and Blues chart during his career, and a number of prominent artists, including The Beatles, the Beach Boys, and Fleetwood Mac performed their versions of his songs. His song "Fever" reached #1 on the R&B charts, was later covered by Peggy Lee, and it became her signature song. Little Willie John, who had been born William Edward John, was posthumously inducted into the Rock & Roll Hall of Fame in 1996.

May 27 (Monday)

In Louisville, Kentucky, a crowd of 400 protesters, mostly black, gathered in the Parkland neighborhood to protest the reinstatement of a white police officer who had beaten a black man several weeks before. As violent actions increased, Mayor Kenneth A. Schmied established a curfew and called for 700 Kentucky National Guard troops. The turmoil lasted for nearly two days, during which time two people were killed.

In Chicago, the founder, owner, and long-time head coach of football's Chicago Bears, George Halas, officially retired as Bears head coach for the fourth and final time. Halas had actually coached his last game the previous season.

May 28 (Tuesday)

In France, François Mitterrand, socialist leader from the Federation of the Democratic and Socialist Left, declared that "there is no more state," and offered to run for president if new elections were held. Mitterrand would become the president of France in 1981, the first person from the political left to hold that position under the Fifth Republic (the current republican system of government that was established by Charles de Gaulle in 1958).

In Oregon, Sen. Eugene McCarthy defeated Sen. Robert Kennedy in the state's Democratic primary, 44%-38%. In Oregon's Republican primary, Richard Nixon defeated Gov. Ronald Reagan 65%-20%.

Born: Kylie Minogue, Australian singer, actress, and dancer, was born in Melbourne. She first became well known starring in the soap opera *Neighbours* in 1986, and later turned to a musical career, in which she has released numerous singles and albums.

Died: Kees van Dongen, Dutch-French painter and member of the Fauvist movement, died in Monte Carlo, Monaco, at age 91.

May 29 (Wednesday)

In Paris, in preparation for a possible attack by demonstrators, President Charles de Gaulle canceled a meeting with his Council of Ministers and removed his personal papers from Élysée Palace. On the same day, Pierre Mendès France, a former prime minister, said that he was prepared to form a new government, and to include Communists in that government.

At Wembley Stadium in London, Manchester United F.C. became the first football (soccer) team from England to win the European Cup competition.

Ireland's President, Eamonn de Valera, opened the John F. Kennedy Memorial Park in New Ross, County Wexford. De Valera, the third president of Ireland (from 1959 to 1973) had been born as George de Valero in New York City in 1882, and was head of state in Ireland in June 1963 when Kennedy visited Ireland. Kennedy, who was proud of his Irish roots, made a special stop at County Wexford during his visit. Five months after JFK's visit to Ireland, de Valera would attend Kennedy's state funeral, and would visit Kennedy's grave with a group of 24 Irish Defense Force cadets who performed a silent drill.

May 30 (Thursday)

France's Prime Minister, Georges Pompidou, persuaded President Charles de Gaulle to conduct a new election. De Gaulle called for an election to be held on June 23, and also threatened to declare a state of emergency if necessary. Opposition parties agreed to de Gaulle's call for the June election.

After de Gaulle had confirmed that there was sufficient loyalty among military units to support him if the situation required it, he went on the radio (with the national television service being on strike) and announced that the National Assembly would be dissolved, with elections to follow on June 23. De Gaulle ordered workers to return to work, threatening a state of emergency if they did not. In order to minimize turmoil, de Gaulle had been in Baden Baden, West Germany, out of the public eye for three days.

The Indianapolis 500 was won by Bobby Unser in a turbocharged, rear-engine Offenhauser-powered car. Unser's car would be the first turbocharged car to win the race. Of the 33 cars in the race, the only front-engine car was driven by Jim Hurtubise, and his would be the last front-engine car to run at the Indy 500. Although Joe Leonard had won the pole position with a speed of 171.559 miles per hour, the STP Turbine cars finished 12th (Leonard), 13th (Art Pollard), and 19th (Graham Hill). The Indy 500 was covered live on radio, with 900 affiliate stations carrying the race across the country and around the world. The race was also shown live via closed-circuit television in roughly 175 theaters across the country. However, the race was not broadcast live on television. From 1965 to 1970, ABC Sports would tape/film the race and show highlights the following weekend on its *ABC's Wide World of Sports* show. (In 1968, the highlights would be shown two weeks later because of the funeral of Sen. Robert F. Kennedy.) From 1971 to 1985, ABC would show the race later the same day, on a tape-delay, edited somewhat for time. Since 1986, the race has been covered live from start to finish, with the exception of the local Indianapolis area. In 2016, for the first time, the race was completely sold out, and the race was shown live in Indianapolis.

Born: Zacarias Moussaoui, French-born terrorist who played a major role in planning the September 11, 2001 attacks against the

United States, was born. For his crimes, he is serving a term of life in prison without parole.

May 31 (Friday)

Actor James Stewart officially retired from the U.S. Air Force. Like a number of other Americans of his generation, Stewart's career was split into two parts: before World War II and after. He made his first stage appearance in 1932 on Broadway, made his first film in 1935, and gave his first performance on radio in 1937. Nine months before the bombing of Pearl Harbor, Stewart enlisted in the U.S. Army, where he used his piloting experience to become part of the Army Air Corps, becoming the first major Hollywood celebrity to wear the uniform during World War II. During the war, Stewart commanded a squadron of B-24 Liberator bombers on missions over Germany, and was awarded two Distinguished Flying Crosses, four Air Medals, and the French Croix de Guerre with bronze palm. Although he continued his acting career upon his return from Europe, and acted in many classic films, he continued to be active in the newly established U.S. Air Force. He remained current in newer aircraft, and rose to the rank of brigadier general. Upon his retirement, he was awarded the U.S. Air Force Distinguished Service Medal, and in 1985, he would be advanced to the rank of major general.

June 1968

June 1 (Saturday)

Following authorization by the provincial legislature, the flag of Alberta was officially adopted to represent the Canadian province. The flag's design had been widely discussed during the Alberta's preparations for the centennial of the Canadian Federation in 1967.

The Simon & Garfunkel song "Mrs. Robinson," which had been featured in the 1967 film *The Graduate*, became the number one song on the Billboard charts.

At Belmont Park in Elmont, New York, chestnut-colored State Door Johnny, owned by Greentree Stable and trained by John Gaver, won the 100th running of the Belmont Stakes.

Born: Jason Donovan, Australian actor and singer, was born in Melbourne. Donovan had initially achieved fame by starring in the soap opera *Neighbours* with Kylie Minough, with whom he recorded one of his number one hits in the UK.

Died: Helen Keller, U.S. author, political activist, and lecturer, died in Easton, Connecticut at age 87. Keller had been the first deaf-blind person to earn a bachelor of arts degree. She and her teacher, Anne Sullivan, were the subjects of the 1962 film *The Miracle Worker*, which was based on Keller's own autobiography, *The Story of My Life*. She was a pacifist and suffragette who helped found the American Civil Liberties Union in 1920.

June 2 (Sunday)

In Yugoslavia, the first mass protest since the end of World War II, some 23 years earlier, erupted. After students in Belgrade announced that they were beginning a strike for seven days, police beat some of the students and banned public gatherings. President Josip Broz Tito calmed the unrest by agreeing to some of the students' demands.

In Ecuador, a general election took place, with José María Velasco Ibarra of the Velasquista National Federation being elected to his fifth (and final) non-consecutive term as president. He received 32.8% of the vote.

In Turkey, senate elections were held. The Justice Party (AP) received 49.9% of the vote. Voters would elect 53 members to the senate: (50 members representing one-third of the senate, plus three empty seats).

June 3 (Monday)

At the art studio called The Factory in New York City, feminist Valerie Solanas shot and attempted to kill artist Andy Warhol as he entered his studio. Solanas, who had written the anti-male declaration *The SCUM Manifesto* the previous year, fired three shots, hitting Warhol once, and also slightly wounding art critic Mario Amaya. She also fired point blank at Warhol's manager, Fred Hughes, but her gun jammed. Following a five-hour operation, Warhol recovered. Solanas turned herself into police and stood trial for assault, attempted murder, and illegal possession of a firearm. She served three years including psychiatric counselling and was released, after which she resumed promoting *The SCUM Manifesto*.

At Yankee Stadium in New York City, the Yankees executed their first triple play in the history of the franchise. Their opponent, the Minnesota Twins, won the game 4-3. Twins' catcher Johnny Roseboro hit into the triple play, with the play going relief pitcher Dooley Womack to third baseman Bobby Cox to first baseman Mickey Mantle.

June 4 (Tuesday)

The Standard & Poor's 500 (S&P 500) stock market index, still considered a primary indicator of the state of the U.S. economy, closed above 100 for the first time, at 100.38.

In Punta Gorda, Florida, Category 1 Hurricane Abby, which formed on June 1 and weakened to a tropical storm before hitting the U.S., came ashore around midday. Abby continued as a tropical storm up through Florida, Georgia, and the Carolinas. Abby caused six deaths indirectly, and caused roughly $450,000 in damage (equivalent to about $3.2 million in 2017).

Died: Walter Nash, former prime minister of New Zealand, died in Wellington at age 86. Nash had been the 27th prime minister of New Zealand (1957-60), and was noted for his long service to the country, having held a government or Labour Party position since 1910, resulting in some 58 years of service.

June 5 (Wednesday)

In the ballroom of the Ambassador Hotel in Los Angeles, Sen. Robert F. Kennedy of New York gave a victory speech to cheering supporters after his major win of the California primary. Leaving the ballroom, he took a detour from the planned route, instead passing back through the kitchen, where while shaking hands, he was shot three times by Palestinian activist Sirhan Bishara Sirhan. The feeling of déjà vu—the familiar chill that what had happened before was happening again—was overwhelming and inescapable. For millions of people, including supporters of Kennedy and opponents, the memories of two other deaths were too close. Robert Kennedy's brother, John, had been shot and killed less than five years before, and Martin Luther King had been killed just 63 days earlier. In 1968, King and Robert Kennedy had to many people represented a hope of less division in the country, and now that hope was all but gone. That night in the hotel, Kennedy had gone into the kitchen against advice of bodyguards. At about 12:15 am, as Kennedy was shaking hands with busboy Juan Romero, Sirhan quickly approached Kennedy and fired his .22 caliber revolver, hitting Kennedy in the head once and in the back twice. Shots hit five others, who recovered. As Sirhan continued firing the gun wildly, football Player Rosie Greer and Olympic decathlon champion Rafer Johnson, along with authors George Plimpton and Pete Hamill, fought to take the handgun away from Sirhan and subdue him. Standing only feet away, a radio corresponded described the fight for the gun as it happened, and referring to John Kennedy's assassin in 1963, said "Get the gun, Rafer! Hold him! We don't want another Oswald!" Kennedy spoke with busboy Romero as he lay on the kitchen floor. The senator was taken to nearby Central Receiving Hospital, where doctors manually massaged his heart, and then transferred to the Hospital of the Good Samaritan for surgery, where he would remain until the following day.

June 6 (Thursday)

Died: Robert F. Kennedy, U.S. Senator from New York state and candidate for the Democratic Party nomination for U.S. president, died in Los Angeles at the age of 42, from the gunshot wounds received the previous day. He was pronounced dead at 1:44 am, about 26 hours after being shot. Kennedy is one of only two U.S. senators to be assassinated, the other being Louisiana Senator Huey Long in 1935. Kennedy was also a former U.S. attorney general, and had served as campaign manager for his brother, President John F. Kennedy.

Died: Randolph Churchill, English journalist and politician, and son of Sir Winston Churchill, died of a heart attack at age 57. Randolph Churchill was considered a skilled author, who wrote at least 20 books, including two volumes about his father, Sir Winston, when he was a child and a young adult. During the war years of 1940-45, Randolph was a member of parliament in addition to serving as a major in the 4th Queen's Own Hussars unit of the British Army.

June 7 (Friday)

At the Ford Dagenham assembly plant in the UK, sewing machinists went on strike as women workers demanded pay comparable to that of men. The strike would be a trigger for the Equal Pay Act 1970.

In New York City, the body of Sen. Robert Kennedy, which had been flown to New York from Los Angeles, lay in repose at St. Patrick's Cathedral.

Died: Dan Duryea, U.S. stage, film, and television actor, died in Los Angeles of cancer at age 61. Duryea made more than 60 films and played in a number of television series from 1952 to 1968.

June 8 (Saturday)

It was a sad weekend in the U.S. as many Americans would say goodbye to Sen. Robert F. Kennedy, who had died two days earlier. Sen. Kennedy's body would continue to lay in repose at St. Patrick's Cathedral until 10:00 am, when a high requiem mass would be held, and attended by President Johnson and his wife Lady Bird, as well as members of Johnson's cabinet and other officials. Sen. Kennedy was eulogized by his brother Edward "Ted" Kennedy—also a U.S. senator, from Massachusetts—who said about Robert: "Those of us who loved him and who take him to his rest today pray that what he was to us and what he wished for others will someday come to pass for all the world." The mass concluded with singer/actor Andy Williams singing "The Battle Hymn of the Republic."

Following the mass, in a scene unique to the 20th Century but reminiscent of President Abraham Lincoln's funeral train from Washington DC to Springfield 103 years before, a private train carried the flag-draped coffin of Sen. Kennedy and members of his family from New York City to Washington DC. Hundreds of thousands of American men, women, and children, of all backgrounds, lined the railroad tracks as the train slowly passed. Many waited outside for four hours or more as the slow train passed. The train took eight hours to travel the route that would normally take four. People saluted or waved American flags. Many held signs saying things like "Thank you" or "Goodbye Bobby." The train, which had been scheduled to arrive in the nation's capital at 4:30 pm, arrived at 9:10 pm. Upon arrival in Washington, a funeral procession took Sen. Kennedy and family members from Union Station to the New Senate Office Building, then past the Lincoln Memorial. The procession continued across the Potomac River to Arlington National Cemetery. As the vehicles in the procession arrived at almost 10:30 pm, people lining the drive to the burial spot lit candles spontaneously, to guide the senator on his last brief journey. The short service took place starting at 10:30 pm. Arlington National Cemetery officials say that the burial was the only night burial ever to take place at Arlington. In addition, the simple white wooden cross that marks his grave is the only wooden marker in the cemetery of some 400,000 graves.

At Heathrow Airport in London, James Earl Ray was arrested for the assassination of Martin Luther King, Jr. During Ray's check-in, the ticket agent noted that the name Ray used on his falsified Canadian passport, Raymond George Sneyd, was on the Royal Canadian Mounted Police watchlist. The arrest came two months after Ray killed King in Memphis, during which time the U.S. Federal Bureau of Investigation had staged its biggest manhunt in history, with the help of other law enforcement agencies around the world. After his arrest at Heathrow, Ray was extradited to the United States where he would confess to the crime on March 10, 1969, his forty-first birthday.

At a night game at Dodger Stadium in Los Angeles. LA Dodgers' pitcher Don Drysdale broke Walter Johnson's 55-year-old record for consecutive scoreless innings pitched. Drysdale broke Johnson's stretch of 55 2/3 scoreless innings, and would not give up a run until reaching the new record of 58 scoreless innings. (Drysdale's record would remain intact for 20 seasons, until Dodger Orel Hershiser pitched 59 scoreless innings in regular season games, a streak that would end in the first inning of the next season.)

At Stadio Olimpico in Rome, Yugoslavia and Italy played to a 1-1 draw in the final of the 1968 European Championship football (soccer) tournament. Because of the draw, the two teams would engage in a replay game two days later to determine the champion.

June 9 (Sunday)

Following the assassination of presidential candidate Sen. Robert F. Kennedy, President Lyndon Johnson assigned U.S. Secret Service protection to all presidential candidates, and declared a day of mourning. Congress would also change legislation to mandate Secret Service protection for presidential candidates, which had not been done before that time. Following that day, presidential candidates would be protected by the Secret Service, as revised in the U.S. Code, which now states that "major" candidates, as determined by the secretary of homeland security, will be protected.

At the Circuit de Spa-Francorchamps in Francorchamps, Belgium, New Zealand driver Bruce McLaren won the Belgian Grand Prix for Formula One cars. In addition to being a driver, McLaren also designed vehicles and created innovations for them, and founded the McLaren Racing Team, which had a number of Formula and Can Am wins, as well as wins at Le Mans, Sebring, and Indianapolis.

In Queensland, Australia, the 1968 Surfers Paradise 4-Hour endurance race for touring cars was held at Surfers Paradise International Raceway. The race was won by Australian driver John French, driving an Alfa Romeo GTV.

June 10 (Monday)

In Rome, the team from Italy defeated Yugoslavia 2–0 in the re-played final of the 1968 European Championship.

June 11 (Tuesday)

In Washington, DC, the progression of the Gun Control Act of 1968 was delayed due to a tied vote in the U.S. House Judiciary Committee. Discussion of the act had begun in late 1963 after the assassination of President Kennedy, and resumed at an accelerated pace after the deaths of Dr. Martin Luther King and Sen. Robert Kennedy in the previous 70 days. The act focused primarily on regulating the interstate sales of firearms.

June 12 (Wednesday)

The film *Rosemary's Baby*, starring Mia Farrow and directed by Roman Polanski, premiered in the U.S. The film told the story of a pregnant woman who suspects that a cult wants to use her baby in rituals. In 2014, despite—or perhaps because of—the controversial nature of the film, the Library of Congress deemed it worthy of official preservation as "culturally, historically, or aesthetically significant."

The U.S. Interstate Commerce Commission approved the proposed merger of Chicago and North Western Railway with Chicago Great Western Railroad. In 1995, the combined railway would be acquired by Union Pacific.

In Italy, the 1968 Giro d'Italia cycle race that began on May 20 concluded in Naples. The winner was Belgian Eddy Merckx, with Italian riders Vittrorio Adorni second and Felice Gimondi third.

June 13 (Thursday)

Hurricane Abby dissipated and was absorbed near the Delmarva Peninsula in Delaware.

June 14 (Friday)

Atco Records released the album *In-A-Gadda-Da-Vida* by the group Iron Butterfly. The album took its name from the group's single of the same name. The single spanned the entire B-side of the album, an extended 17-minute single that included solo parts by the band's members. Drummer Ron Bushy said that when vocalist/organist Doug Ingle wrote the song, it was called "In the Garden of Eden," but that Ingle slurred his words the first time they dried performing it, after Ingle had had consumed a large quantity of wine, and the group kept the song title as it sounded.

Born: Yasmine Bleeth, American actress best known for her role as Caroline Holden on the series *Baywatch*, was born in New York City.

Died: Salvatore Quasimodo, Italian novelist, poet, and Nobel Prize laureate, died in Naples, Italy of a cerebral hemorrhage at age 66. His 1959 Nobel Prize in Literature was awarded for Quasimodo's "lyrical poetry, which with classical fire expresses the tragic experience of life in our own times." He was also recipient of other awards, including the 1953 Etna-Taormina International Prize in Poetry, along with Dylan Thomas.

June 15 (Saturday)

In the UK, a by-election was held in order to fill the seat of Labour MP Richard Winterbottom, who had died in February. Winterbottom had represented the Sheffield Brightside parliamentary constituency. As a result of the election, the seat was retained for the party by Edward Griffiths.

In the U.S., the bubble-gum pop song "Yummy Yummy Yummy" by Ohio Express hit its peak of number four on the Billboard singles chart.

June 16 (Sunday)

In Rochester, New York, Lee Trevino won the 68th U.S. Open golf tournament. As a young boy, Trevino (whose father left when Lee was young) spent little time in school, instead working in order to earn money for his family. The Dallas, Texas native began working in cotton fields at the age of 5. Over his career, Trevino won 29 Professional Golfers Tour (PGA) events and six major championships. During the 1975 Western Open, sitting under an umbrella with fellow golfer Jerry Heard during suspended play due to a storm, both players were severely injured by lightning. Trevino's heart reportedly stopped, and he required two surgeries to repair damage to his back.

June 17 (Monday)

In Malaysia, the Communist Insurgency in Malaysia (or "Second Malayan Emergency," the first having taken place in 1960) began, with the Malayan Communist Party attacking Malaysian federal security forces. The conflict would continue into 1989. The term

168

"emergency" instead of "war" was used by the colonial government at the request of large mining and agricultural businesses, because Lloyd's insurers would not have insured their property if the event was called a "war."

Died: Cassandre (born Adolphe Jean-Marie Mouron), French commercial artist, died by suicide in Paris at age 67. Cassandre was inspired by surrealism and cubism as a young man, and he would later design art deco posters. He was also commissioned by *Harper's Bazaar* to design magazine covers.

June 18 (Tuesday)

The 37th Air Division of the U.S. Air Force, an air defense command group in North America, was deactivated. In the process, the U.S. Air Force and affiliated Strategic Air Command abandoned Hopedale Air Station in Newfoundland and Labrador, Canada. The air station had been used to monitor potential Soviet nuclear bombers that might have attacked Canada or the United States from polar routes, and to work with USAF interceptor aircraft.

June 19 (Wednesday)

The Vietnam-themed film *The Green Berets* opened in theaters in the U.S. The film, starring John Wayne, David Janssen, Jim Hutton, and George Takei, would be panned by critics and some media as "unrealistic," but applauded by those who still supported the war.

The first version of the heist film *The Thomas Crown Affair*, starring Steve McQueen and Faye Dunaway, was released in theaters.

At the Teatro Municipal in Lima, Perú, the Miss Perú 1968 pageant was held. It was won by María Esther Brambilla, representing the Amazonas region of northern Perú.

June 20 (Thursday)

In Washington, DC, discussions on the 1968 Gun Control Bill resumed, as the House Judiciary Committee withdrew concerns it had expressed earlier.

In Caledon, County Tyrone in Northern Ireland, Stormont MP Austin Currie, Father Tom Savage and others began squatting (occupying property owned by another), to bring attention to housing discrimination based on religion. The event is recognized as an early catalyst of the Northern Ireland civil rights movement.

In Cleveland, Ohio, Temptations singer David Ruffin missed a performance with the group in order to attend a performance by his new girlfriend, Gail Martin, a daughter of singer/actor Dean Martin. Ill feelings between Ruffin and the other members had already begun to develop, likely because of a cocaine addiction he had developed. Ruffin had provided the primary vocal for many of the Temptations' biggest hits, including "My Girl," "Ain't Too Proud to Beg," "Since I Lost My Baby," "I Wish It Would Rain," and "(I Know) I'm Losing You." A week after the Cleveland concert, Motown Records would fire Ruffin from the Temptations, though he still had a solo contract with Berry Gordy's Detroit-based recording company.

Born: Robert Rodriguez, American filmmaker, screenwriter, and musician, was born in San Antonio, Texas. Most of his films are shot in Mexico or his home state of Texas. His films include *Sin City*, which starred Jessica Alba, Bruce Willis, and Elijah Wood, and

Once Upon a Time in Mexico, which starred Salma Hayek, Antonio Banderas, Johnny Depp, Willem Dafoe, Eva Mendes, and others.

June 21 (Friday)

In West Berlin, the 18th Berlin International Film Festival opened. The festival ran through July 2.

June 22 (Saturday)

Near Manzanillo, Colima, Mexico, Tropical Storm Annette dissipated. Maximum winds of Annette had been recorded at 50 miles per hour (85 km/h) with no record of damage. (On October 23, 2015, Hurricane Patricia would strike Manzanillo. Patricia was a Category 5 hurricane with 200-mile-per-hour (320 km/h) winds, becoming the most powerful cyclone ever recorded in the Western Hemisphere. Hurricane Patricia killed eight people directly and five indirectly, and caused at least $460 million [U.S.] in damage. Due to the magnitude of the hurricane, the name Patricia has been retired from future use.)

The ballad "This Guy's in Love with You" by Herb Alpert became the number one song in the U.S.; it would remain there for four weeks.

June 23 (Sunday)

At Estadio Monumental in Buenos Aires, Argentina, following a football match between the city's Boca Juniors and Club Atlético River Plate, a fan stampede broke out, causing 74 deaths and 150 injuries. Most of the dead were teenagers and young adults, with an average age of 19. A three-year government investigation was unable to determine an exact cause, though some fans had testified that burning flags were thrown between groups in attendance. The government was not able to determine guilt, and nobody was charged with the deaths or injuries. The event is commonly referred to as the Puerta 12 tragedy.

In France, following the public turmoil of May 1968, the first voting in the French legislative election took place.

June 24 (Monday)

Near Rimini, Italy, Bolognese engineer Giorgio Rosa declared the independence of the Republic of Rose Island, an artificial island designed and built by Rosa. The "micronation" consisted of a 400-square-meter (4,300 sq. ft.) platform supported by pylons, similar to an offshore oil platform. The complex was equipped with a restaurant, bar, nightclub, shop and post office. Rosa "officially" named the island by the Esperanto *Insulo de la Rozoj*. Although no currency was known to have been developed, stamps were issued. Italian police later took possession of the micronation, and in early 1969 the Italian Navy would use explosives to destroy it.

In Montreal, Quebec, riots attributed to Quebecois separatists broke out in Montreal during a visit by new Prime Minister Pierre Trudeau. June 24 is St-Jean-Baptiste Day, which is celebrated by French Canadians in Canada and the U.S. Trudeau refused to leave the city despite threats against him. Members of a crowd threw bottles at Trudeau, but instead of seeking cover, he refused to leave, saying that he was a fellow Quebecois. Camera crews captured the exchange, which was shown later on network news. The act by Trudeau was perceived as courageous.

At Cleveland Stadium in Cleveland, Ohio, Detroit Tigers outfielder Jim Northrup hit grand slams on consecutive at-bats in the 5th and 6th innings, leading the Tigers' hitting attack against the Indians and helping the Tigers to win 14-3. The feat made Northrup just the sixth player to hit two grand slams in one game, and the second player to hit grand slams in consecutive at-bats. Five days later, Northrup hit another grand slam at home against the White Sox. He would have another grand slam in Game 6 of the World Series, and in Game 7 would also have the key hit of the series-winning game against Bob Gibson, lofting a triple over the head of center fielder Curt Flood, to score the game's first two runs with two outs in the 7th inning.

June 25 (Tuesday)

Across Canada, federal elections took place to elect members to the Canadian House of Commons. New Prime Minister Pierre Trudeau's Liberal Party of Canada won a majority of seats, with some commentators attributing his victory in part to standing up to the crowd the previous day.

Died: Tony Hancock, 44, English comedian and actor, died of suicide at age 44 in his flat (apartment) in Bellevue Hill, New South Wales. Hancock had been a successful comedic performer on radio before taking his humor to television. In a 2002 British Broadcasting Corporation poll, radio listeners would vote Hancock as their favorite British comedian. Critics would say that many later-generation British comedians owed much of their success to copying (intentionally or unintentionally) aspects of Hancock's humor.

June 26 (Wednesday)

In Rio de Janeiro, Brazil, the "March of the One Hundred Thousand" took place, marked by rioting against Brazil's military government.

In the South Pacific, 620 miles (1,000 km) due south of Tokyo, the Bonin Islands (also called the Ogasawara Islands) were returned to Japan after being occupied by the United States Navy for the 23 years since the end of World War II. Japanese citizens were allowed to return to the archipelago of about 30 subtropical islands, which remain inhabited by relatively few people.

Born: Shannon Sharpe, former American football tight end (Denver Broncos and Baltimore Ravens) who has been a television analyst for the sport since 2004, was born in Chicago. Sharpe finished his career as the National Football League's all-time leader in receptions (815), receiving yards (10,060), and receiving touchdowns by a tight end (62), until each of those records was broken by Tony Gonzalez. Sharpe was the first tight end to gain over 10,000 receiving yards.

June 27 (Thursday)

Motown Records fired popular Temptations singer David Ruffin due to his unpredictable behavior. Ruffin was replaced by Dennis Edwards of the Detroit-based Contours. Despite Ruffin being fired and not rehearsing with the group, he would later sometimes show up unannounced at Temptations concerts, and when the group was scheduled to sing hits on which Ruffin had originally sung vocals, he would come up on stage, take the microphone from Edwards, and begin singing. Though his group members didn't appreciate some of these surprise performances, the audience usually loved them. Although the group considered taking Ruffin back to continue with his "cameo" performances, they finalized their decision to keep Edwards and not allow Ruffin to rejoin the group.

In Prague, the *Two Thousand Words* Manifesto by Ludvik Vaculik was published. The manifesto was signed by a number of artists, writers, intellectuals and scholars in Czechoslovakia, and became a key documented description of the hopes of the Prague Spring.

At Bloomfield Stadium in Tel Aviv, Israel, the 5th Israel Super Cup took place. Maccabi Tel Aviv F.C. defeated Bnei Yehuda Tel Aviv F.C. by a score of 2-1.

June 28 (Friday)

Born: Chayanne (born Elmer Figueroa Arce), Latin pop singer, composer, and actor, was born in Rio Piedras, Puerto Rico.

Born: Adam Woodyatt, British actor best known for playing the character Ian Beale in the BBC soap opera *EastEnders*, was born in London. Woodyatt is also an award-winning photographer, having taken up the hobby at age 13.

June 29 (Saturday)

At Hyde Park, London, the "Midsummer High Weekend" rock concert took place. The event was the first major free concert in the UK. Acts performing included Pink Floyd, T-Rex, Jethro Tull, and Roy Harper. The concert was scheduled to be held in parallel with the release of Pink Floyd's second album, *A Saucerful of Secrets*.

June 30 (Sunday)

Across France, in the second round of the French legislative election, Prime Minister Georges Pompidou's UDR party ("Union for the Defense of the Republic") gained sufficient support to control the National Assembly. The UDR won 354 seats, with François Mitterrand's FGDS party (Federation of Democratic and Socialist Left) winning 57 seats.

In Marietta, Georgia, U.S., a prototype Lockheed C-5A Galaxy military transport aircraft made its first flight. The first Galaxy flight was piloted by Lockheed Chief Engineering Test Pilot Leo J. Sullivan, along with test pilot Walter E. Hensleigh and flight engineers Jerome H. Edwards, and E. Mittendorf. The C5A is still in use by the U.S. military and remains one of the largest aircraft in the world; its cargo hold is one foot (.3 meter) longer than the distance flown during the first successful flight of the Wright Flyer on December 17, 1903.

July 1968

July 1 (Monday)

In Moscow, the international Treaty on the Non-Proliferation of Nuclear Weapons was signed by the Soviet Union and the United States. The treaty remains a major control intended to limit the worldwide spread of nuclear weapons. The treaty was signed by Soviet Foreign Minister Andrei Gromyko and U.S. Ambassador Llewellyn Thompson.

On the same day, over the Soviet-controlled Kuril Islands north of Japan, Seaboard World Airlines Flight 253A, a Douglas DC-8 chartered by the U.S. armed forces, was intercepted by two Soviet MiG-17 fighters and forced to land after the DC-8 accidentally flew into Soviet airspace. Flight 253A was carrying 214 American soldiers on their way to South Vietnam via Yokota Air Base in Japan. Because the DC8 was on its maiden flight, it was carrying an operations crew of 24, including a check pilot and engineer, in addition to standard crew and the 214 soldiers. The flight was detained in the Kuril Islands for two days while top-level negotiations took place between Soviet Premier Alexei Kosygin and U.S. Ambassador Llewellyn Thompson, under the direction of President Johnson. (Ironically, the incident took place on the same day that the Soviet Union and United States signed the Treaty on the Non-Proliferation of Nuclear Weapons in Moscow.) Upon landing at the Soviet interceptor airbase in the Kurils, the American soldiers and crew were allowed off the plane, but instructed to stay within a 100-meter radius of the aircraft. After the flight's food ran out, the Soviets provided military rations. On the second night of their stay, female flight attendants were allowed to sleep in a nearby maintenance building. After the U.S. issued a note of apology, the flight was permitted to leave.

Near the airfield at Uli, Anambra, Nigeria, a Lockheed L-1049 Super Constellation carrying medical supplies to Biafra from the International Red Cross crashed short of the runway, killing all four people on board, and destroying 10.5 tons of medicines. Bad weather was cited as the cause.

The "Phoenix Program" was initiated by the U.S. Central Intelligence Agency. The program was developed to identify and "neutralize" actions of the Viet Cong, by means including capture, infiltration, counter-terrorism, interrogation, or even assassination.

In the U.S., the merger of the Chicago Great Western Railway with the Chicago Great Western Railway, which had been approved by U.S. officials on June 12, took place.

At Tokyo's Central Post Office, Japan's new postal code system was initiated. (In the U.S., the Zone Improvement Plan [ZIP] system with ZIP Codes was implemented exactly five years earlier.)

At Dodger Stadium in Los Angeles, the streak for consecutive scoreless innings pitched by St. Louis Cardinals pitcher Bob Gibson ended at 47 2/3 innings when Gibson allowed a run in the first inning. Gibson's streak came in the same season that Los Angeles Dodgers pitcher Don Drysdale broke Walter Johnson's 55-year-old record. Coincidentally, while Gibson would be the winning pitcher on this day, Drysdale would take the loss, as the Cardinals won the game 5-1. In this "Year of the Pitcher," Gibson was also in the middle of an 11-game streak of complete games, during which he allowed 3 runs in 99 innings, for an earned run average of 0.27 over the span. Gibson's 1.12 ERA for the entire season remains the record in modern Major League Baseball; Gibson also pitched 28 complete games and 13 shutouts that year.

Also, on one day in July 1968—though the parties involved don't remember the specific date, or whether it took place at Cass Elliot's house or Joni Mitchell's—David Crosby and Stephen Stills sang Stills' newly written song "You Don't Have to Cry" together, and Graham Nash then asked them to sing it again, adding his own third part to the mix. Wherever it was, and whatever day in July it took place, the three singers and others in attendance agreed that their combined harmonies were unique, and the three formed the group Crosby, Stills, and Nash, and would later add Neil Young's distinctive voice to theirs.

July 2 (Tuesday)

In Yugoslavia, student protests broke out in the cities of Belgrade, Zagreb, and Sarajevo.

In West Berlin, the 18th Berlin International Film Festival ended. The festival's highest prize, the Golden Bear, was awarded to the black-and-white Swedish film *Ole Dole Doff* (*Who Saw Him Die?*) directed by Jan Troell.

Died: Francis John Joseph Brennan, American Cardinal in the Roman Catholic Church, died in Philadelphia at age 74 of a heart attack. At the time of his death, the Cardinal held the highest post in the church ever held by an American.

July 3 (Wednesday)

At Heathrow Airport in London, six people, along with eight racehorses belonging to English businessman William Hill, were killed when a BKS Air Transport flight arriving from Deauville, France crashed during landing. There were two survivors aboard the BKS flight, even though the aircraft had cartwheeled into two parked Trident airplanes and then into Heathrow's Terminal 1, which was still under construction. Investigators attributed the crash to metal fatigue of a rod used to operate the flaps, which resulted in imbalanced lift.

At Cleveland Stadium in Cleveland, Ohio, Indians pitcher Luis Tiant struck out 19 Minnesota Twins batters as the home team won, 1-0, in a 10-inning game, setting a league record for strikeouts in games of that length. Twins pitcher Jim Merritt gave up only one run and four hits over nine innings. Coming into 1968 after a shoulder injury, Tiant changed his pitching motion so that he began the motion by turning away from home plate, looking back at second base and the outfield. The result was evidently effective, even in this "Year of the Pitcher": Tiant led the American League in earned run average (1.60) and strikeouts per nine innings (9.22), and pitched nine shutouts (including four consecutive shutouts). Over the season, opposing hitters had a batting average of a paltry .168 off Tiant, a major league record.

Cleveland had a high temperature of 41 degrees the day of Tiant's 19-strikeout game, the coldest daytime high ever recorded for Cleveland in the month of July.

July 4 (Thursday)

At Southsea, Portsmouth, UK, hundreds of thousands of cheering fans welcomed local store owner Alec Rose as he arrived from across the sea to complete a 354-day circumnavigation of the globe. The British nursery owner and fruit seller had begun his voyage on July 16, 1967. Rose, a self-described loner as a youth who was described by others as a quiet, humble seaman, spent the trip aboard his 36-foot ketch *The Lively Lady*, which remains on display in Portsmouth.

In Florida, Explorer 38 was launched to monitor low-frequency cosmic radio noise. Explorer was a series of unmanned satellites that would have different equipment for different purposes. Explorer 1 was launched in January 1958, and the last satellite to have the name, Explorer 58, was launched in 1981.

July 5 (Friday)

The day after completing his solo voyage around the world, Alec Rose was knighted by Queen Elizabeth II in recognition of his achievement.

Born: Susan Wojcicki was born in Santa Clara County, Florida. In 2014, she would become the chief executive officer (CEO) of YouTube.

July 6 (Saturday)

At the All England Club in Wimbledon, American tennis player Billie-Jean King defeated Australian Judy Tegart in the final, 9–7, 7–5, to win her third ladies' championship. King won £750 in prize money for the win. 1968 was the first year that Wimbledon offered prize money to players. King had won two previous singles championships at Wimbledon as an amateur.

Born: American journalist John Dickerson was born in Washington DC to businessman C. Wyatt Dickerson and to Nancy Dickerson. Nancy had been a pioneering news journalist on television and radio. In 2015, John would become the moderator of the CBS Sunday morning news program *Face the Nation*.

July 7 (Sunday)

At Luton College of Technology in Bedfordshire, England, the British rhythm & blues group The Yardbirds played their final concert. The core group was comprised of Jeff Beck, Jimmy Page, Chris Dreja, Keith Relf, and Jim McCarty. In the mid-1960s, the group had a number of hits including "For Your Love" and "Heart Full of Soul." The members would go on to form other groups, with Page co-founding a group that would at first be called "The New Yardbirds," but beginning on October 19, would be called Led Zeppelin.

At Wimbledon, tennis player Rod Laver defeated fellow Australian Tony Roche in the men's final, 6-3, 6-4, 6-2. Laver was the number one ranked player in the world from 1964 to 1970. He won £2000 in prize money for the men's championship.

Died: Leo Sowerby, American musician and composer of church music, died in Port Clinton, Ohio, at age 73. Sowerby, who had been born in Grand Rapids, Michigan in 1895, was regarded as the "Dean of American Church Music" during his career.

July 8 (Monday)

A Saudi Arabian Airlines Convair CV-340 crashed at Dhahran International Airport in Saudi Arabia, killing all 11 on board. The crash occurred after the crew aborted the airplane's third approach due to visibility problems created by blowing dust. The airport is now called King Abdulaziz Air Base.

Born: Billy Crudup, American stage, film, and television actor, was born in Manhasset, New York. Crudup has performed in at least 15 productions on Broadway, as well as a number of films including

Almost Famous, *Big Fish*, *Mission: Impossible III*, *Eat Pray Love*, and *Justice League*.

Born: Michael Weatherly, American actor best known for playing Logan Cale on *Dark Angel* (2000-02), Anthony DiNozzo on *NCIS* (2003-16), and Jason Bull on *Bull* (beginning in 2016) was born in New York City.

July 9 (Tuesday)

At the Astrodome in Houston, Texas, the National League defeated the American League 1-0 in baseball's All-Star Game. The game's only run came in the first inning when Willie Mays of the San Francisco Giants got on base with a single, and came home on a double-play ball after failed pickoff attempt and a wild pitch. The game remains the only All-Star game ever played without a run batted in (RBI). In addition, the game, played in the enclosed Astrodome, was the first All-Star game ever to be played indoors, and the first one to be played at night since 1944. Willie Mays was selected as the most valuable player for the game, making him the first player to win a second MVP for the All-Star Game (he had won his first for the 1963 game).

In Columbus, Mississippi, 15.68 inches (39.83 cm) of rain fell in 24 hours. It was a record amount for the state in a 24-hour period.

July 10 (Wednesday)

Maurice Couve de Murville became the prime minister of France, succeeding Georges Pompidou.

In El Segundo, California, toy manufacturer Mattel Inc. introduced Hot Wheels cars. Mattel's Hot Wheels cars are small-scale die cast cars, frequently made in bright colors with bright finishes, and frequently depicting actual vehicles, sometimes with special markings. A number of auto manufacturers have licensed Mattel to make scale Hot Wheels models of their vehicles, often providing the use of original blueprints and other details. A primary competitor to Hot Wheels was Matchbox cars, until Mattel acquired Tyco Toys (then the manufacturer of Matchbox cars) in 1997. Generally, Matchbox cars were intended to represent everyday production vehicles, while Hot Wheels were more modified versions. In recent auctions, rare Hot Wheels vehicles have sold for as much as $70,000 each.

Mattel, named after company founders Matt Matson and Elliot Handler, also sold other toys such as the Chatty Cathy doll, the See 'n Say talking toy line, Monogram Models, Barbie, Fisher-Price, Masters of the Universe, and American Girl. The company licenses many superhero figures. During its history, Mattel, Inc. also purchased the real-life Ringling Bros. and Barnum & Bailey Circus, and Holiday on Ice.

In the U.S., Major League Baseball officially announced that beginning with the following season, which would be the 100th season of professional baseball, the American and National leagues would each be divided into two divisions, which would require post-season playoffs in addition to the World Series between the two league champions.

July 11 (Thursday)

At Memorial Stadium in Baltimore, Maryland, Earl Weaver won his first game as Baltimore Orioles' manager, having replaced Hank

Bauer the previous day. The Orioles beat the Washington Senators, 2-0, in front of 6,499 fans. The Orioles would finish the rest of the season with a 48-34 record under Weaver and finish second place in the American League, 12 games behind the Tigers. For the next 14 seasons under Weaver, the Orioles would win more major league games than any other team, winning six division titles, four American League pennants, and one World Series championship. The Orioles went to the World Series in 1969, being defeated by the "Miracle" Mets in five games, then came back to win the World Series against the Cincinnati Reds in 1970.

July 12 (Friday)

In Paris, new French Prime Minister Maurice Couve de Murville formed his new government.

July 13 (Saturday)

While approaching Lagos Airport in Nigeria, a Belgian Sabena Airlines Boeing 707 cargo plane struck trees and crashed, killing all seven on board. Investigators were not able to determine why the airplane was flying low enough (300 feet, or 91 meters above sea level) to strike the trees.

At Carnoustie Golf Links in Scotland, the 1968 Open Championship golf tournament was won by South Africa's Gary Player. The win was the second of three Open titles that Player would win in his career.

At the Miami Beach Auditorium in Miami Beach, Florida, Martha Vasconcellos of Brazil won the 17th Miss Universe pageant.

Television game show host Bob Barker, who had hosted the Miss USA pageant in May, also hosted this pageant.

Born: Robert Gant, American actor, was born in Tampa, Florida. In addition to appearing in television shows including *Melrose Place, Caroline in the City, Ellen, Friends*, and *Nip/Tuck*, he played Supergirl's father Jor-El in the CBS (and later The CW Network) superhero show *Supergirl*.

Died: Westbrook Van Voorhis, American narrator famed for doing voice-overs on The March of Time radio and newsreel series, died in New Milford, Connecticut, at age 64.

July 14 (Sunday)

The 1968 Northern 300 NASCAR motor race was run at Trenton Speedway in Trenton, New Jersey. The race was won by LeeRoy Yarbrough, driving a Ford.

At Atlanta Stadium in Atlanta, Georgia, Henry "Hank" Aaron of the Atlanta Braves hit the 500th home run of his career, off San Francisco Giants pitcher Mike McCormick. In April 1974, Aaron would go on to tie and then break Babe Ruth's major league record of 714 career home runs. Aaron would hold the record for 33 years. Aaron also hit at least 24 home runs every season from 1955 to 1973, and is consistently rated one of the greatest baseball players of all time.

July 15 (Monday)

Commercial air travel between the USSR and the U.S. began as Aeroflot and Pan American airlines began to fly routes between

Moscow and JFK airports. The first flight was a Pan Am 707 that flew from JFK Airport to Denmark, completing its flight to Moscow the following day.

At Crosley Field in Cincinnati, Ohio, Houston Astros pitcher Don Wilson struck out 18 Cincinnati Reds in a complete game performance, as the Astros defeated the Reds 6-1. The mark was a team record for strikeouts. (Wilson had thrown a no-hitter against the Atlanta Braves the previous season, and would pitch another against the Reds the following season.)

The New Jersey Americans basketball team, which had been established the previous year as one of the teams in the upstart American Basketball Association (ABA), changed its name to the New York Nets. After the ABA merged with the larger, established National Basketball Association in 1976, the team would change its name to the New Jersey Nets in 1977, and then to the Brooklyn Nets in 2012. The Brooklyn Nets play their home games at the Barclays Center in Brooklyn, New York.

July 16 (Tuesday)

Born: Larry Sanger, American Internet developer, entrepreneur, and co-founder of Wikipedia, was born in Bellevue, Washington. Sanger, who earned Bachelor and Doctor of Arts degrees in Philosophy, was previously involved with online encyclopedias, and developed Wikipedia as a means of a free online source of reliable information for all, and to which all could contribute.

Born: Barry Sanders, American football player, was born in Wichita, Kansas. Sanders would go on to win the 1998 Heisman Trophy as the season's best U.S. college football player. That year, Sanders would rush for 2,850 yards and score 42 touchdowns in 12 games for the Oklahoma State Cowboys. The following year, he would begin a 10-year tenure with the Detroit Lions in the National Football League, being selected an All-Pro all 10 seasons that he played. Sanders was the NFL Rookie of the Year in 1989, and in 1997 he would become the third player to rush for more than 2,000 yards in a season. He was also named the league's most valuable player that season. He has been selected by the NFL Network as the most elusive runner in NFL history, and also the best player never to play in the Super Bowl.

Born: Dhanraj Pillay, Indian field hockey player and team manager, was born in in Khadki, Maharashtra, India. Pillay played in four Olympic games as well as World Cups and other championships.

July 17 (Wednesday)

In Iraq, the 17 July Revolution took place. The revolution was a bloodless coup that brought the Arab Socialist Ba'ath Party into power. Saddam Hussein (who would later be president of Iraq) consolidated power over time. Iran's Ba'ath Party would hold power from this date until it was removed from power by the invasion by American and British troops in 2003.

The Beatles' animated musical fantasy film *Yellow Submarine* was released in the UK. Although speaking parts in the animated film were voiced by other actors, the Beatles performed their own music including vocals, and the group participated in the closing scene.

July 18 (Thursday)

In Mountain View, California, semiconductor manufacturing company Intel was founded by Gordon E. Moore and Robert Noyce.

As of December 2017, Intel is the second-largest computer chip manufacturer in the world, having been surpassed by Samsung in July 2017.

Died: Corneille Heymans, Belgian physiologist, died of a stroke at age 76 in Knokke, Flanders, Belgium. In 1938, Heymans won the Nobel Prize for Physiology or Medicine for discovering how blood pressure and oxygen level are detected by the body and sent as a message to the brain.

July 19 (Friday)

The Filipino cargo ship SS *Magsaysay* caught fire in the South China Sea off South Korea and was abandoned. The ship was towed into Busan but was subsequently scrapped. (Note that the name "Busan" officially replaced the spelling "Pusan" in the year 2000.)

Born: LeRoy Butler, American professional football player, was born in Jacksonville, Florida. Playing with the Green Bay Packers, Butler would win a Super Bowl, be selected as an All-Pro four times, and become the first defensive back to record at least 20 interceptions and 20 quarterback sacks in a season. Butler is credited with creating the Lambeau Leap, a celebration move in which a Green Bay player who scores a touchdown leaps above the end zone stands into the arms of fans during home games at Green Bay's Lambeau Field.

July 20 (Saturday)

At Soldier Field in Chicago, the first Special Olympics games began. The games were founded by Eunice Kennedy Shriver, a younger sister of President John F. Kennedy, as a major sports activity for children and adults with intellectual disabilities. One thousand competitors participated in the first games.

On the live television show Dee Time in the UK, Jane Asher announced that she and the Beatles' Paul McCartney no longer planned to be married; the two had been in a close relationship since 1963 and had planned for years to be married.

July 21 (Sunday)

Near Sufi-Kurgan in the Kirghiz Soviet Socialist Republic, an Aeroflot Antonov An-2R crashed into a steep slope on a 4000-meter (13,000 foot) mountain, killing all passengers and crew. Flying in poor weather, the crew had strayed 10 km (6.2 miles) off course, into the mountain.

In Paris, the 1968 Tour de France ended, with Jan Janssen of the Netherlands the winner. He was the first Dutch rider to win the race, which in 1968 covered 4,492 km (2,791 mi) over 22 stages.

In San Antonio, Texas, American golfer Julius Boros won the 1968 PGA Championship, held at Pecan Valley Golf Club. Boros finished one stroke ahead of runners-up Bob Charles and Arnold Palmer. Winning the '68 PGA championship at the age of 48, he became and remains (in late 2017) the oldest golfer to ever win a major championship. Boros, born in Fairfield, Connecticut, played baseball in college and did not become a professional golfer until the age of 29.

In Cincinnati, Ohio, Carol Mann from Buffalo, New York, won the LPGA Buckeye Savings Golf Invitational.

Died: Ruth St. Denis, American dance pioneer and choreographer, noted for her "oriental" and Egyptian dances, died in Los Angeles at age 89.

July 22 (Monday)

Died: Giovannino Guareschi, Italian cartoonist, journalist, and humorist who created the character of priest Don Camillo, died in Cervia, Italy at age 60.

July 23 (Tuesday)

During its flight from London to Rome, El Al Flight 426 was hijacked, in the first such event to be carried out by the Popular Front for the Liberation of Palestine (PFLP). The Boeing 707, with a final destination of Lod Airport in Israel, was diverted to Algiers. Negotiations for release were conducted by the Israeli and Algerian governments. The last of the passengers were released five weeks later, making the hijacking, according to the BBC, the longest hijacking of a commercial airliner. Additional hijackings of other flights worldwide would be carried out in the future.

In the Glenville area of Cleveland, Ohio, police exchanged gunfire with a black power group called the "Black Nationalists of New Libya." The exchange lasted four hours, and three policemen, three suspects and a bystander were killed and 15 people injured.

July 24 (Wednesday)

In Algiers, the 26 non-Israeli passengers who were on El Al Flight 426 were released by the Palestinian hijackers.

At White Sox Park in Chicago, White Sox pitcher Hoyt Wilhelm broke Cy Young's 57-year-old record (which ended in September 1911) of pitching in 906 games. Wilhelm set the record despite the fact that he didn't play in his first major league game until the age of 29. Wilhelm would continue pitching in the major leagues until just days short of his 50th birthday.

Born: Kristen Chenoweth, American singer and actress who originated the role of Glinda in the musical *Wicked*, was born in Broken Arrow, Oklahoma. Chenoweth also played on *The West Wing* and *Pushing Daisies*.

July 25 (Thursday)

Pope Paul VI reaffirmed the Roman Catholic Church's position on birth control by issuing the papal encyclical *Humanae vitae: On the Regulation of Birth*. The church continued to prohibit all forms of contraception.

July 26 (Friday)

Lilian Harvey, Anglo-German singer and dancer, and star of the 1931 film *Congress Dances*, died in Juan-les-Pins, France at age 62.

July 27 (Saturday)

In continuing violence across the U.S., a race riot broke out in Gary, Indiana, near Chicago.

Born: Jorge Salinas, Mexican television and film actor, was born in Zacatecas, Mexico. He is primarily known for performing in telenovelas. His film career began with the 1983 film *Viva El Chubasco*.

July 28 (Sunday)

In Brazil, a U.S. Air Force C-124C Globemaster II cargo plane crashed into mountain about 50 miles (80 km) from Recife while preparing to land at Guararapes International Airport. All 10 people on board perished.

England's Court of Appeal reversed a guilty verdict against the publishers of Hubert Selby, Jr.'s descriptive novel *Last Exit to Brooklyn*. A lower court had previously found the book to violate England's Obscene Publications Act. Author, screenwriter, and barrister John Mortimer argued on behalf of the publishers. The case represented a defining moment for England beginning to change its obscenity laws.

Died: Charles William Mayo, prominent American surgeon and son of Mayo Clinic founder Charles Horace Mayo, died in an auto accident on his 70th birthday near Rochester, Minnesota.

Died: Otto Hahn, the German chemist who won the 1944 Nobel Prize in Chemistry for discovering the radiochemical confirmation of nuclear fission, died in Göttingen, West Germany at age 89.

July 29 (Monday)

At 7:30 am, in the mountains of Costa Rica, Arenal Volcano erupted violently and without warning, and would continue to erupt over several days. The eruption caused the deaths of 87 people and many animals, and destroyed three small villages that were in its path. The eruption came as a surprise to the local residents, as Arenal had not erupted in at least 400 years and was thought by many to be extinct. The volcano continued to be very active until 2010.

The night before the American band The Byrds were scheduled to leave for a musical tour of South Africa, then-Byrds member Gram Parsons and Keith Richards of the Rolling Stones began to discuss apartheid rule in South Africa. They agreed not to join the tour, and Parsons left the group.

At Connie Mack Stadium in Philadelphia, George Culver of the Cincinnati Reds pitched a no-hitter against the Phillies, winning 6-1 in the first game of a doubleheader. The Reds would also win the second game that evening, 7-6, with the teams collecting a total of 25 hits in the second game (the Phillies had 13 of the hits).

July 30 (Tuesday)

Near Red Bluff, California, a U.S. Air Force Boeing KC-135 Stratotanker military refueling aircraft crashed during a training exercise after its vertical stabilizer separated from the aircraft while doing a sharp turn as part of a practice emergency descent. The crash killed all nine people on board. It was the second crash of a KC-135 tanker in 1968.

In London, Thames Television broadcast for the first time, to London and vicinity. The company would continue broadcasting until New Year's Eve 1992.

The final passenger train ran on the Grand Canyon Railway, with only three passengers. The railway would reopen in 1989.

At Cleveland Stadium in Ohio, Shortstop Ron Hansen of the Washington Senators had an unassisted triple play against the Cleveland Indians. It was the first unassisted triple play in the major leagues in 41 years, and the only one executed in the majors between 1927 and 1992. (Despite the very rare play, Cleveland won the game 10-1). On the offensive side, Hansen followed his feat by striking out six consecutive times, then hitting a grand slam on August 1. On August 2, he was traded to the Chicago White Sox.

Born: Terry Crews, American professional football player and actor, was born in Flint, Michigan.

Died: Jón Leifs, Icelandic composer, pianist, and conductor, died of lung cancer in Reykjavik at age 69. In the 1920s, Leifs had conducted symphony orchestras in Czechoslovakia, Denmark, Germany, and Norway. He remains one of the most successful Icelandic conductors at the international level.

July 31 (Wednesday)

The Clint Eastwood western film *Hang 'Em High* was released in theaters. The film also starred Inger Stevens, Ed Begley, and Pat Hingle.

Died: Jack Pizzey, the premier of Queensland, died while in office in Brisbane, Queensland Australia of a heart attack at age 57. Pizzey had only been premier since January 17 of that year, when he replaced Frank Nicklin, who had retired. He was succeeded by Deputy Premier Gordon Chalk, who only acted as premier for one week, while a new premier was elected. The newly elected premier, Joh Bjelke-Petersen, would serve for 19 years.

August 1968

August 1 (Thursday)

In Brunei Town (now called Bandar Seri Begawan) in the Sultanate of Brunei, Hassanal Bolkiah was crowned the Sultan of Brunei. The Sultan remains in office as of late 2017, and he is also the first and current prime minister of Brunei. The Sultan is among the wealthiest people in the world, and with his worth of an estimated $20 billion, the wealthiest monarch in the world.

Canada began replacing silver in its coins with nickel. The U.S. had done a similar move in 1964.

August 2 (Friday)

In Quezon, the Philippines (now in the province of Aurora), Casiguran earthquake struck, killing at least 207 people and injuring 261. The quake had a magnitude of the 7.6 Mw.

At Soldier Field in Chicago, the 35th Chicago Charities College All-Star Game took place. In the game that was held annually in the preseason for professional and college football, the National Football League (NFL) professional champion Green Bay Packers defeated the college All-Stars, 34-17, in front of 69,917 fans. The win by the professional team gave the NFL a record of 24 wins, 9 losses, and two ties since the first such game was played in 1934. The NFL vs. college contest was last held in 1976.

Married: In the Philippines, economics professor and politician Gloria Macapagal married attorney and businessman Jose Miguel Arroyo. Macapagal-Arroyo, daughter of 9th president of the

Philippines Diosdada Macapagal, herself would be elected the 14th president of the Philippines, serving from 2001 to 2010.

August 3 (Saturday)

The rock single "Hello, I Love You" by The Doors hit number one on the U.S. charts and remained there for two weeks.

In Hendersonville, Tennessee, guitarist Luther Perkins collapsed after a fire broke out inside his newly built home. Perkins had evidently fallen asleep while smoking a cigarette. Perkins was the guitarist for the Tennessee Three, the band that backed up singer Johnny Cash. Perkins, born in Como, Mississippi, is credited as being an early pioneer of rockabilly music, and for helping to develop Cash's "boom-chicka-boom" rhythmic style.

Died: Konstantin Rokossovsky, former vice premier of Poland (1952-56) died in Moscow at age 71. Born in Poland, Rokossovsky became a Soviet military officer who was among the top Red Army commanders during World War II, and had served as Poland's defense minister.

August 4 (Sunday)

In Costa Mesa, California, the Newport Pop Festival was held. The event was the first music concert ever to have more than 100,000 paid attendees. Performers included the Grateful Dead, Jefferson Airplane, Eric Burdon & The Animals, Canned Heat, Iron Butterfly, Country Joe & The Fish, and Blue Cheer.

Born: Daniel Dae Kim, Korean American actor known for his roles in the television series *Lost* and the 2010 reboot *Hawaii Five-O*, was born in Busan, South Korea.

August 5 (Monday)

In Miami Beach, Florida, the Republican National Convention began; the convention would continue through August 8. With Democrat Lyndon Johnson no longer in the race, Nixon and the Republican Party would develop a "Southern strategy" to take advantage of the sentiment by many Southerners against liberal policies of the Johnson administration, which included the Civil Rights Act of 1964 and the Voting Rights Act of 1965.

Born: Marine Le Pen, French politician and leader of the conservative National Front, was born in Neuilly-sur-Seine, France.

Born: John Olerud, first baseman with the Toronto Blue Jays, New York Mets and other teams, was born in Seattle, Washington. Olerud was the American League batting champion with the Blue Jays in 1993 (with a .363 average), and National League batting average runner-up with the Mets in 1998, hitting .354.

Died: Guitarist Luther Perkins, who was badly injured in a fire at his home two days before, died in Nashville, Tennessee at age 40.

August 6 (Tuesday)

In Miami Beach, the Republican National Convention continued. In 1968, the three major television networks (ABC, CBS, and NBC) covered much of the evening activities of both major parties' conventions, including the voting for presidential and vice-presidential nominees and the acceptance speech by the winning nominee.

Married: Children's author, illustrator, poet, and book publisher Dr. Seuss (Theodor Seuss Geisel) married Audrey Stone Dimond. It was the second marriage for both.

August 7 (Wednesday)

Richard M. Nixon won the Republican Party's nomination to run as president. Nixon won the vote on the first ballot with 692 votes, with Gov. Nelson Rockefeller getting 277 votes and Gov. Ronald Reagan receiving 182.

The comedy film *With Six You Get Eggroll*, with Doris Day, Brian Keith, Barbara Hershey, George Carlin, and Pat Carroll, was released in theaters. It was the last film in which Doris Day performed, Day having started as a featured performer in films in 1948.

August 8 (Thursday)

Republican Richard Nixon gave his acceptance speech at the Republican National Convention in Miami Beach, Florida. In his speech, Nixon said that he could unite America as he had united the Republican Party. He mentioned Vietnam and other divisive issues across the country. Nixon selected Maryland Governor Spiro T. Agnew as his running mate. Nixon's former running mate in 1952 and 1956, President Dwight Eisenhower, could not attend the convention due to ill health. Eisenhower would die seven months later, in March 1969, from congestive heart failure.

In Montreal, Canada, Mayor Jean Drapeau approved the use of Jarry Park Stadium as an interim baseball stadium for the expansion Montreal Expos, which would begin play in the Major League

Baseball's National League beginning in 1969. The team was named after the 1967 World's Fair, Expo 67, which was held in Montreal the previous year. Over the next nine years, Montreal and Canada would build Olympic Stadium in preparation for the 1976 Olympic Games in Montreal. The Expos would begin playing at Olympic Stadium in 1977. (In 2004, the Expos would move to Washington DC and become the Washington Nationals.)

August 9 (Friday)

In Prague, Czechoslovakia, Yugoslav President Marshal Tito paid a state visit in support of the increased freedoms in Czechoslovakia. The visit may have been seen by the Soviet leadership as the last straw in regard to their pledge of non-interference with the freedoms known as Prague Spring, and intervention would take place later in the summer.

Born: Gillian Anderson, best known for her role of FBI agent Dana Scully on the science series *The X-Files*, was born in Chicago.

August 10 (Saturday)

Across the U.S., race riots broke out in Little Rock, Arkansas; Miami, Florida; and Chicago.

Born: In Minsk, Belarusian hockey player Alex Andrievski was born. Anrievski played right wing for a number of professional and semi-professional teams over his career from 1984 to 2003, including the professional Chicago Blackhawks. He played on the Belarus Olympic team in 1998.

August 11 (Sunday)

The last steam passenger train service ran in Britain. A selection of British Railways steam locomotives made the 120-mile journey from Liverpool to Carlisle and returned to Liverpool – the journey is known as the Fifteen Guinea Special.

Leroy "Satchel Paige," 62-year old American professional baseball pitcher, was signed to a contract with the Atlanta Braves. Paige had thrown his last pitch in organized baseball in 1966, but Braves owner William Bartholomay hired Paige as pitching coach and "pitcher" so he could gain the few additional days needed to qualify for a major league pension. Paige began pitching in 1926, but played in the Negro Leagues because segregation rules kept him from playing on a major league team. Paige played for some of the best Negro League teams of his day, and his pitching abilities became legendary, with millions of baseball fans wondering what Paige could do against the best white players in the game. Paige also pitched for teams in Cuba, Mexico, and the Dominican Republic. Following the integration of Major League Baseball in 1947, Paige was signed by the MLB Cleveland Indians in July 1948.

Born: Anna Gunn, American actress noted for her role in the television series *Breaking Bad*, was born in Santa Fe, New Mexico.

August 12 (Monday)

Died: Esther Forbes, American historian, author, and children's writer, died at age 76 in Worcester, Massachusetts. Forbes wrote the novel *Johnny Tremain* and other works, won a Pulitzer Prize and Newbery Medal.

August 13 (Tuesday)

Near Varkiza, Greece, Alexandros Panagoulis, Greek politician and poet, carried out an unsuccessful assassination attempt against Greek dictator Georgios Papadopoulos. Panagoulis and his collaborators would be put on trial by military court starting on November 3.

August 14 (Wednesday)

In Montreal, after obtaining funding for the new team, the Expos officially became a member of baseball's National League. Investor Charles Bronfman was named chairman of the Expos, with Jim Fanning the first general manager.

Born: Catherine Bell, Iranian-American actress known for her roles in the military crime procedural *JAG* and for the series *Army Wives*, was born in London.

August 15 (Thursday)

In Prague, Romanian President Nicolae Ceauşescu paid a state visit.

Born: Debra Messing, who played the character of Grace Adler on the situation comedy *Will & Grace* (1998-2006) was born in Brooklyn, New York.

August 16 (Friday)

Singer and actor Frank Sinatra and his wife, actress Mia Farrow, were divorced after two years of marriage. After Farrow reportedly refused Sinatra's demand that she quit making the film *Rosemary's*

Baby in order to work in his film *The Detective*, Sinatra had Farrow
served with divorce papers while she was making her film.

August 17 (Saturday)

The Rascals' single "People Got to Be Free" became number one in
the U.S. and remained there for five weeks.

August 18 (Sunday)

In Gifu Prefecture, Japan, two charter buses driving on National
Highway Route 41 were pushed into the Hida River on National
Highway Route 41 by a mudslide caused by torrential rains. The
tragedy claimed 104 lives.

At Ramey Air Force Base in Puerto Rico, Sgt. Thomas Carulli and
approximately 15 other security policemen reportedly saw a spheroid
unidentified flying object rising out of the ocean near the beach, and
after it hovered for a short while, it very quickly took off into the
sky, "almost indistinguishable from the other stars." Sgt. Carulli
submitted a written report on the event. This sighting was one of
hundreds that were reported on a fairly regular basis around the
world at the time.

In St. Louis, Missouri, Kathy Whitworth won the Ladies
Professional Golf Association (LPGA) Holiday Inn Golf Classic. In
1981, Whitworth would become the first woman to reach $1 million
in career earnings on the LPGA Tour.

August 19 (Monday)

At the Kennedy Space Center in Florida, the Apollo crew of Frank Borman, Jim Lovell, and Bill Anders was informed that instead of planning their upcoming mission as an earth-orbit flight to test the Lunar Module (LM) in earth orbit, that they should plan to go to the moon in December, orbit it several times, and then return to the earth. The designation of the flight would be Apollo 8. The possibility of a lunar orbit mission had first been discussed with the crew nine days before. The final decision on whether to plan on a lunar orbit mission or an earth orbit mission (without a real LM) would be made following the Apollo 7 mission coming up in October. The potential lunar orbit flight was proposed because, following two months of testing the Lunar Module that had started in June, NASA management determined that the LM would still not be ready for its first trip into space in December. Additional pressure for a lunar orbit flight would come in September, when NASA management was provided with intelligence suggesting that Americans' primary opponent in the space race, the Soviet Union, planned to send their own cosmonauts around the moon before the end of 1968. The Apollo 8 crew of Borman, Lovell, and Anders began in earnest their training and preparations for flying around the moon. The proposed lunar mission would not yet be disclosed to the American public and the world.

August 20 (Tuesday)

In Czechoslovakia, the advancements of Prague Spring came to an abrupt halt as 250,000 Soviet and Warsaw Pact troops with 2,000 tanks and 800 aircraft invaded the country, beginning at 11:00 pm on August 20. The Soviet Union and other invading nations (Bulgaria, Hungary, and Poland), following the Brezhnev Doctrine, ended Alexander Dubček's steps to ease oppression and expand freedoms.

Romania and Albania refrained from participating, and most East German troops were ordered not to cross the border into Poland. One hundred thirty-seven Czechoslovakian citizens were killed, and more than 500 severely injured. By the time the invasion was completed the following day, 500,000 invading troops would be in Czechoslovakia. Seventy thousand citizens fled to Western Europe immediately, with an eventual number of 300,000. Dubček and other Czechoslovakian leaders were arrested, flown to Moscow, and interrogated. When the Warsaw Pact leadership realized the potential negative impact of a citizen uprising in Czechoslovakia, they returned Dubček and the other leaders to Prague, but they were no longer able to implement additional freedoms.

August 21 (Wednesday)

Shortly before 1:00 am, Radio Prague publicly broadcast the Soviet-led Warsaw Pact invasion. Warsaw Pact troops continued the invasion they had begun the previous evening. The invasion was the largest military operation in Europe since the end of World War II.

After five years of allowing the Voice of America to broadcast to Eastern European nations, the Soviet Union resumed blocking the broadcast signal.

High over California, pilot Bill Dana flew the experimental X-15 rocket plane on its last high-altitude flight (above 50 miles, or 80,000 meters). The flights of NASA's two X-15 rocket planes began in June 1959 to test the ability of humans and machines to fly much higher and faster than any other airplanes in existence. The X-15 was capable of speeds between four and seven times the speed of sound. The super-fast X-15 was piloted by some of the best test pilots at the time, including Joe Walker, Scott Crossfield, Bob White, and Neil Armstrong.

August 22 (Thursday)

In Bogota, Colombia, Pope Paul VI began the first-ever visit by a pope to Latin America. The Pope discussed birth control along with his related encyclical from July, *Humanae Vitae*, which banned any artificial birth control among Roman Catholics.

At Tiger Stadium in Detroit, after Chicago White Sox pitcher Tommy John threw two consecutive pitches at or behind Tigers' second baseman Dick McAuliffe, McAuliffe charged the mound. With both teams rushing out onto the field, McAuliffe and John swung at each other and John's shoulder was separated. He missed the remainder of the season. McAuliffe was fined $250.

Cynthia Lennon filed divorce proceedings against her husband, John Lennon, on the grounds of adultery.

Born: Rich Lowry, author and conservative commentator who would become editor of *The National Review*, was born in Arlington County, Virginia.

August 23 (Friday)

Drummer Ringo Starr left the Beatles after tensions that had built up while recording the group's double-disk album *The Beatles* (usually called the *White Album*). Starr didn't feel productive, and he felt left out of the group—a sentiment, it turned out, that other members expressed about themselves, as well. Some of Starr's parts (for example, on "Back in the U.S.S.R.") were performed by other members, but Starr returned when differences were straightened out.

At Yankee Stadium in New York City, in the second game of a double-header, the visiting Detroit Tigers and New York Yankees played 19 innings of a second game that was suspended shortly after 1:00 the next morning due to a curfew. The game ended in a 3-3 tie.

August 24 (Saturday)

France exploded its first hydrogen bomb. The 2.6-megaton test device was exploded at Fangataufa Island in the South Pacific. The detonation made France the fifth thermonuclear power in the world. France had exploded its first atomic bomb in February 1960.

In Northern Ireland, the country's first civil rights march took place, to protest discrimination against Catholics and Irish nationalists.

August 25 (Sunday)

The U.S. Open tennis tournament began on the outdoor grass courts in Forest Hills, New York. It would be the first year of the event as the U.S. Open; it was previously called the U.S. National Championships. The tournament would run through September 8.

Born: Rachael Ray, American television host, cook, businesswoman and author, was born in Glens Falls, New York.

August 26 (Monday)

The Democratic National Convention began in Chicago. The convention began with the backdrop of the Vietnam War, the assassinations of Dr. Martin Luther King, Jr. and Sen. Robert

Kennedy, unrest around the world, and major rioting that had occurred throughout the United States. Although all of these conditions also existed when the Republican held their convention earlier in the month, the Democrats held the White House and both houses of Congress, so the Democrats were now looking much more injured and split than the Republicans. (The Republicans had lost the presidency in 1960 with Nixon, and again by a landslide with Sen. Barry Goldwater of Arizona in 1964.) There was further confusion because there were competing sets of delegates from some of the Southern states: Alabama, Georgia, Mississippi, North Carolina, and Texas, with some slates being more racially integrated than others.

The baseball game between the visiting Detroit Tigers and the Chicago White Sox was played at County Stadium in Milwaukee, Wisconsin instead of Chicago. The game had been relocated due to the violence around the Democratic National Convention in Chicago.

The single "Hey Jude" by the Beatles was released. Written by Paul McCartney, the ballad was the first to be released on the group's new Apple label. The far more boisterous "Revolution" was the B-side of the record. With a run time of 7 minutes, 11 seconds, it was the longest single to top British charts up to that time. "Hey Jude" also became a number one record in the U.S., and stayed there for nine weeks, making it the longest streak of any Beatles single. In 2013, Billboard would name "Hey Jude" the 10th biggest song of all time. McCartney wrote the song as a message to John's son, Julian, during his parents' (John and Cynthia Lennon's) divorce. Ironically, Julian said that he didn't know the song was written about him for 20 years. Julian has commented "It's very strange to think that someone has written a song about you. It still touches me."

August 27 (Tuesday)

Princess Marina of Greece and Denmark died at Kensington Palace in London at age 61 from a brain tumor. Her family relationships were an example of the marriages between royal families across Europe. Princess Marina was born in Athens in 1906, the daughter of Prince Nicholas of Greece and Denmark and Grand Duchess Elena Vladimirovna of Russia. In 1934, she was married to Prince George, Duke of Kent. From that point, she also was known as the Duchess of Kent.

August 28 (Wednesday)

In Chicago, while nominating speeches were underway on at the International Amphitheater, 10,000 protesters at Grant Park began to protest the Democratic Party's selection process, as well as the Vietnam War. The crowd began to throw bottles and rocks, and the Chicago police began to fire tear gas. As the crowd spread to other areas, part of the group moved near the Hilton Hotel, where tear gas fired by police seeped into the building, affecting eventual nominee Hubert Humphrey while he was taking a shower. When the police began to beat protesters as well as use teargas, the crowd began chanting "The world is watching." Inside the convention hall, the news of the violence spread. While nominating Sen. George McGovern, Sen. Abraham Ribicoff of Connecticut criticized Mayor Richard J. Daley's management of the violence, saying "With George McGovern as President of the United States, we wouldn't have to have Gestapo tactics in the streets of Chicago!" to which Daley responded from the audience with what some observers said was an anti-Semitic comment. Later, Daley would attempt to defend his police force but inadvertently did so with a slip of the tongue: "The policeman is not here to <u>create</u> disorder. The policeman is here to <u>preserve</u> disorder."

There were even fisticuffs inside the convention center. When CBS News correspondent Dan Rather tried to talk to one Georgia delegate who was being escorted outside, Rather was grabbed and punched by security guards. Rather, wearing a microphone and headset, explained to anchor Walter Cronkite and the television audience that "We got violently pushed out of the way...I'm sorry to be out of breath, but somebody belted me in the stomach during that. The security people...put me on the deck. I didn't do very well." Cronkite responded by saying "I think we've got a bunch of thugs here, Dan."

Subsequent investigations of the rioting would conclude that the violence in Chicago during the convention was a "police riot," an instance where on multiple occasions, law enforcement officers got out of hand, in a systemic manner. However, eight of the protesters, who would come to be known as the Chicago Eight, would stand trial for conspiracy and incitement to riot. Members of the group, which included Abbie Hoffman, Tom Hayden, Rennie Davis, Jerry Rubin, and Bobby Seale, would be convicted of incitement to riot, but not of conspiracy. Those convicted would be sentenced, but their convictions were overturned on appeal.

Vice President Hubert Humphrey came out of the convention as the nominee, with Maine Senator Edmund S. Muskie as his vice-presidential running mate. This came despite the fact that Humphrey had not entered (or won) any of the 13 state contests that involved primaries, and that 80% of the votes cast during the state primaries were for anti-war candidates. The Democrats came into the convention damaged and split, and would leave Chicago in even worse shape, to conduct a presidential campaign against Richard Nixon and Spiro Agnew. Some pundits said that Nixon won the presidency that night of rioting in the streets of Chicago.

In a separate event, John Gordon Mein, the U.S. Ambassador to Guatemala, was assassinated by rebels near the U.S. consulate in Guatemala City. Mein was the first U.S. ambassador to be assassinated while in office. Five other U.S. ambassadors have been assassinated since (as of December 2017).

August 29 (Thursday)

In Chicago, Hubert Humphrey gave his acceptance speech for the Democratic Party's nomination for president. With his party and his nation so badly divided, it would be an uphill battle to win the presidency against Richard M. Nixon, with Gov. George Wallace also in the race.

Married: In Oslo, Crown Prince Harald of Norway married Sonja Haraldsen, the commoner he had dated for nine years. They would become king and queen of Norway in January 1991.

Died: Ulysses S. Grant III, U.S. Army officer and grandson of President Ulysses S. Grant, died in Clinton, New York at age 87. Born in Chicago in 1881, Grant would graduate from West Point in 1903 and serve as an aide to President Theodore Roosevelt in 1904. Grant served in the Philippines, Cuba, and in the Poncho Villa Expedition into Mexico in 1916 as well as World Wars I and II.

August 30 (Friday)

John Lennon and Yoko Ono led a fund-raising concert at Madison Square Garden in New York City. Other performers included Roberta Flack, Sha-Na-Na, and Stevie Wonder.

William Talman, American film and television actor, died of lung cancer in Encino, California at age 53. Between 1957 and 1966, Talman had played Los Angeles District Attorney Hamilton Burger to Raymond Burr's title role in *Perry Mason*. Talman had performed in 212 episodes of the CBS courtroom and detective drama. As a youth, Talman founded the drama club at the private preparatory school Cranbrook in Bloomfield Hills, Michigan, which would also be attended by Sen. Alan Simpson, Massachusetts Governor Mitt Romney, and actress Selma Blair. A few months before his death, Talman, a heavy smoker for decades, was diagnosed with lung cancer. Following the diagnosis, Talman became the first actor in Hollywood to film antismoking public service announcements. He requested that the filmed announcements not be shown until after his death, to make them more effective. Talman ended announcements with the message "If you don't smoke, don't start. If you do smoke, quit." Talman died a month after recording his second public service announcement.

August 31 (Saturday)

In the Khorasan Province of Iran, 15,000 people died and 60,000 buildings were destroyed as a magnitude 7.4 (on the moment magnitude scale) earthquake struck. Major aftershocks continued into the following day.

Hideo Nomo, baseball pitcher in Japan and the U.S., was born in Osaka, Japan. Nomo would pitch for the Kintetsu Buffaloes in Nippon Professional Baseball, and then 13 seasons (1995 to 2008) for eight different Major League Baseball teams in the U.S. Nomo would twice lead the league in strikeouts, and he threw two no-hitters, becoming the first Japanese-born MLB pitcher to do so, in addition to becoming the first Japanese-born pitcher to permanently relocate to the U.S. (Other players from Japan had temporarily moved to the U.S. as their seasons required.)

September 1968

September 1 (Sunday)

A strong aftershock (measuring 6.4 on the moment magnitude scale) from the previous day's Khorasan quake destroyed the town of Ferdows. More than 175 towns and villages were badly damaged or destroyed by the September 1st aftershock.

Born: Mohamed Atta, primary planner among the terrorists who hijacked the commercial airliners involved in the September 11, 2001 attacks, was born in Egypt. On 9/11, Atta took over the controls of American Airlines Flight 11, which crashed into the North Tower of the World Trade Center in New York City. Flight 11 was a Boeing 767 flying from Boston to Los Angeles. All 92 people on board the flight were killed, as well as an unknown number of people directly when the aircraft struck the North Tower, and an additional number when the tower collapsed.

Born: Atsuko Yuya, Japanese voice actress, was born in Nagasaki, Japan. Yuya is a member of the Theatre Company Subaru based in Tokyo, and is the officially designated actress in Japan who does voice over-dubs for U.S. actress Angelina Jolie and Canadian actress Natasha Henstridge.

September 2 (Monday)

Nigerian troops began invading the Biafran city of Aba after bombing the city with artillery. Nigerian ground troops met heavy Biafran fire. Three battalions followed in an amphibious assault. Nigeria would suffer more than 21,000 casualties, and Biafra an unknown number, in an operation that continued until October 15.

September 2 was Labor Day in the U.S. and Canada. The third annual Muscular Dystrophy telethon was hosted by Jerry Lewis, and for the first time, television stations outside of the New York City market carried the event. The 1968 telethon brought in $1.4 million in donations. The telethon would peak in 2011, the first year that Lewis did not host, collecting $61.4 million to fight the disease.

At Darlington Speedway in Darlington, South Carolina, the NASCAR Southern 500 stock car race was held. Driver Cale Yarborough won, driving a 1968 Mercury. Yarborough led for 169 of the 364 laps, with an average speed of 126.132 miles per hour (203 km/hr). David Pearson finished second, driving a '68 Ford. Dodge, Plymouth, and Chevrolet also had vehicles entered in the 44-car field.

Born: Cynthia Watros, American actress, was born in Lake Orion, Michigan. Watros would star in ongoing roles in the television series *The Guiding Light*, *The Drew Carey Show*, *Lost*, *House*, and *The Young and the Restless*.

September 3 (Tuesday)

At D.C. Stadium in Washington DC, the Chicago White Sox set an American League record for number of 1-run losses in a season, losing 2-1 to the Washington Senators. Over the season, the White Sox would lose a major league record 44 games by a single run.

Born: English actor Raymond Coulthard was born in Chester, Cheshire in England. Coulthard would perform in the films *Hotel Babylon*, *Emmerdale*, *The English Patient* and *The Muppet Christmas Carol*, as well as television series *Mr. Selfridge*, *Emma*, and *Extras*.

Died: Juan José Castro, Argentine composer and conductor, died in Buenos Aires at age 73. In his career, Castro conducted the Havana Philharmonic, the Melbourne Symphony Orchestra, the National Symphony in Buenos Aires, and was director of the Conservatory of Music of Puerto Rico.

Died: Isabel Withers, American actress, died in Hollywood, California, at the age of 72. She had 92 stage, film, and acting credits in her career. After starring in a Chicago stage production of *Little Women*, she was selected for her first Broadway role, in *The Tavern*, by George M. Cohan.

September 4 (Wednesday)

Born: Carlette Guidry, American sprinter and long jumper, was born in Houston, Texas. Guidry was a member of the U.S. women's gold-medal winning 4x100-meter relay team in the 1992 Olympic Games in Barcelona, the 1996 Olympic Games in Atlanta, and the 1995 World Championships in Gothenburg, Sweden.

Born: Mike Piazza, American baseball player, was born in Norristown, Pennsylvania. Piazza played 16 major league seasons as a baseball catcher, mostly for the New York Mets and Los Angeles Dodgers. Piazza is regarded as one of the best-hitting catchers ever; he was a 12-time All-Star who logged 427 home runs, including a record 396 as catcher.

Born: John DiMaggio, American voice actor and comedian, was born in North Plainfield, New Jersey. DiMaggio has performed the voice of the robot Bender in *Futurama* and also performed the voice of Rico in *The Penguins of Madagascar*.

Born: Phill Lewis, American actor, comedian, and director, was born in Uganda. Lewis performed in the Disney series *The Suite Life of Zack & Cody*, as well as *Friends*, *Scrubs*, and *Lizzie Maguire*.

September 5 (Thursday)

At the Semipalitinsk test site in Eastern Kazakhstan, the USSR detonated a 32-kiloton atomic weapon underground. The device was one of 23 detonated by the Soviet Union in 1968, and one of 1,000 detonated by the Soviet Union between 1949 and 1990, after which the country would ratify the Comprehensive Nuclear Test Ban Treaty.

Born: Thomas Levet, French golfer, was born in Paris. Levet would win the 2004 Scottish Open and was a member of the winning 2004 European Ryder Cup team.

September 6 (Friday)

In southern Africa, Swaziland became independent of Great Britain.

In San Diego, California, the Cincinnati Bengals would play their first regular-season professional football game. The Bengals' first game ended in a 29-13 loss to the San Diego Chargers. The Bengals were an expansion team whose first head coach was Paul Brown, who had established a 115-49-6 record as long-time coach of the Cleveland Browns.

In London, George Harrison's good friend Eric Clapton used George's Gibson Les Paul guitar "Lucy" to record tracks for the song "While My Guitar Gently Weeps" for the Beatles' *White Album*. Clapton would join Harrison on stage a number of times to perform the song, including at the 1971 Concert for Bangladesh and during their 1991 tour of Japan.

September 7 (Saturday)

In Atlantic City, New Jersey, about 400 women who identified themselves as feminists protested the Miss America pageant as being exploitive of women. The protest was organized by author and activist Robin Morgan. The demonstration was one of the first large pageants to call media attention to what they perceived to be the sexualization and exploitation of women. The women generally protested on the boardwalk outside the Atlantic City Convention Center, where the pageant was being held. Four protesters bought tickets to the event and unfurled a "Women's Liberation" sign while shouting "Women's Liberation" and "No more Miss America" while the outgoing Miss America was giving her farewell comments. The protesters in the convention center were quickly arrested.

At the women's final of the U.S. Open tennis tournament, Britain's Virginia Wade defeated the defending champion, American Billie Jean King. Wade won the women's first prize of $6,000.

September 8 (Sunday)

At the U.S. Open in Forest Hills, New York, American Arthur Ashe defeated Tom Okker of the Netherlands in the men's final. It was the first win by an African American at the tournament. Although Ashe won a $14,000 winner's prize, he was still an amateur and a lieutenant in the U.S. Army, and he had to decline the prize, which then went to runner-up Okker.

Born: Louise Minchin, British journalist and news presenter, was born in British Hong Kong.

September 9 (Monday)

Two new PBS stations began operating as WGIQ TV channel 43 in Louisville, Alabama and WVPT TV channel 51 in Staunton, Virginia opened for business.

Born: Julia Sawalha, English actress known for portraying the Saffron Monsoon on the BBC program *Absolutely Fabulous,* was born in London.

September 10 (Tuesday)

Born: Big Daddy Kane, American hip-hop artist and actor, was born as Antonio Hardy in Brooklyn, New York. In addition to being a Grammy winner, Kane had his first acting role in Mario Van Peebles' film *Posse,* and has performed in at least six other films

Born: Guy Ritchie, British film director known for crime films such as *Sherlock Holmes* (2009), *Lock, Stock, and Two Smoking Barrels* (1998), and *The Man from U.N.C.L.E.* film (2015), was born in Hatfield, Herfordshire, in the UK.

September 11 (Wednesday)

In Hamburg, Germany, the International Association of Classification Societies (IACS) is founded. The objective of the group is to maintain the marine classification system, which involves "promoting the safety of life, property, and the environment ... primarily through engineering standards for the design, construction and life-cycle maintenance of ships, offshore units and other marine-related facilities."

September 12 (Thursday)

Air France 1611, a Sud Aviation SE-210 Caravelle jetliner flying from Corsica to Nice, France, crashed into the Mediterranean Sea, killing all 95 passengers and crew. The investigation indicated that the cause was likely a fire that began in the rear of the cabin, though there was speculation that a missile or bomb might have downed the plane. Among those killed on Air France 1611 was René Cogny, who was a French general during World War II, a member of the French Resistance, and a survivor of the Buchenwald and Mauthausen concentration camps. Cogny later commanded French troops in the Tonkin area of Vietnam.

Born: Kay Hanley, American musician who was a member of the group Letters to Cleo, was born in Boston, Massachusetts.

Born: Tetsuo Kurata, Japanese actor, was born in Tokyo.

Died: Tommy Armour, Scottish golfer, died in Larchmont, New York at age 71. Armour won three major golf championships: the 1927 U.S. Open, the 1930 PGA Championship, and the 1931 Open Championship.

September 13 (Friday)

Albania, which had increasingly shifted toward Chinese communism from Soviet communism, officially left the Warsaw Pact. The

Soviet-led Warsaw Pact invasion of Czechoslovakia factored into the split, though Albania had already stopped actively participating in Warsaw Pact activity in 1962.

English Electric, which was known for building military aircraft, merged with General Electric Company. The merger resulted in the largest industrial merger in the UK up to that date, with a total of 250,000 employees.

Born: Bernie Williams, major league baseball player who would play with the New York Yankees for 16 years (1991-2006) was born in San Juan, Puerto Rico. Williams played on four world champion Yankees teams and was a five-time All-Star.

Born: Laura Cutina, Romanian artistic gymnast, was born in Bucharest, Romania. Cutina won a gold medal in team competition at the 1984 Olympics in Los Angeles, and one silver medal each for team competition at the world championships in Budapest (1983) and Montreal (1985).

Died: In Loc Ninh, Vietnam, U.S. Army Maj. Gen. Keith L. Ware was killed when his helicopter was shot down. Ware had been awarded a Medal of Honor in World War II. He was posthumously awarded the Distinguished Service Cross.

September 14 (Saturday)

At Tiger Stadium in Detroit, Michigan, a crowd of 33,688, along with a national television audience on NBC Television's Game of the Week, watched as Detroit Tigers pitcher Denny McLain became the first major league baseball pitcher to win 30 games in a season since 1934. The last pitcher to perform the feat, the St. Louis Cardinals' Dizzy Dean, was on hand. McLain remains the last to accomplish the feat. McLain would have one more win that season. On this Saturday afternoon, the Tigers would be playing the Athletics (A's). As would be the case in many Tigers games in this world championship season, the team was behind going into the bottom of the 9th inning. Today, the late rally would come from the Tigers' outfielders. With the A's leading 4-3, veteran right fielder Al Kaline started the rally as he came in to pinch hit for McLain. Drawing a walk, Kaline was then moved to third base on a single by center fielder Mickey Stanley. With Kaline on third and Stanley on first, Jim Northrup, playing in right field instead of Kaline today, would hit a grounder to move Stanley to third, and scoring Kaline to tie the game 4-4. Next up to the plate was Willie Horton, who hit a single over the head of the drawn-in left fielder to win the game.

In Stockholm, Sweden, Jimmy Ellis defeated Floyd Patterson in a controversial split decision to retain the World Boxing Association world heavyweight title that Ellis had won on April 27th by defeating Jerry Quarry.

The Archie Show and *The Bugs Bunny/Road Runner Hour* premiered on the CBS Saturday Morning lineup.

Born: Actor Dan Cortese was born in Sewickley, Pennsylvania. Cortese would be known for roles in *Veronica's Closet*, *What I Like About You*, and the 1993 sequel of the 1960s television series *Route 66*.

September 15 (Sunday)

In Cincinnati, Ohio, the Cincinnati Bengals football team would play its first home game, at Nippert Stadium. The Bengals won the game against the Denver Broncos, 34-23.

The CBS television network broadcast the musical special program *A Happening in Central Park*, which was recorded by singer/actress Barbra Streisand in June 1968 with a live audience of 135,000 at New York's Central Park. The live album that was released after the concert sold 500,000 copies.

Born: Danny Nucci, Austrian-born American actor, was born in Klagenfurt, Austria. Nucci had supporting roles in the films *Crimson Tide*, *Titanic*, and *The Rock*, as well a number of appearances on television series.

September 16 (Monday)

Married: Sally Field, American actress known for starring in the television series *Gidget* and *The Flying Nun*, and the films *Smokey and the Bandit* and *Norma Rae*, married Steven Craig.

Born: Marc Anthony, American actor and singer, was born in New York City. Anthony is recognized as the top-selling tropical/salsa artist in recording history.

September 17 (Tuesday)

In an incident that would come to be known as the D'Oliveira affair, South Africans canceled play against the English Marylebone Cricket Club in South Africa because Basil D'Oliveira, a mixed-race "Cape Coloured" player, had been selected to play on the Marylebone team. The incident eventually led to the South African Cricket Board of Control beginning to remove racial barriers from the sport in South Africa.

Julia, an American situation comedy which featured an African American woman in the title role, first aired on NBC Television. The main character, Diahann Carroll, played a nurse in the doctor's office at an aerospace company. In addition, she was a single mother of a young boy; her character was widowed when her husband was shot down in Vietnam. The series ran through March 1971.

At Tiger Stadium in Detroit, Michigan, Tigers' third baseman Don Wert, whose hitting had declined substantially after he was hit in the head by a pitch in June, had a single to knock in the winning run with two out and bases loaded in the bottom of the 9th inning. The single scored Al Kaline to break the 1-1 tie and win the American League pennant for the Tigers. The win sent the Tigers to their first World Series since 1945.

At Candlestick Park in San Francisco, California, Giants pitcher Gaylord Perry pitched a perfect game against the eventual National League champions, the St. Louis Cardinals. The losing pitcher in the 1-0 ballgame was Bob Gibson, who gave up only four hits, and just one run, on a home run to Ron Hunt (who only had two home runs that entire season). Giants pitcher Perry would later become the first pitcher to win a Cy Young Award in each league, winning one with the Cleveland Indians (American League) in 1972, and another with the San Diego Padres (National League) in 1978. Along with his brother Jim, the Perry brothers would become the second most successful major league pitching brothers in history, the most successful being Phil and Joe Niekro, both of whom noted for throwing effective knuckleballs late in their careers, and who had 539 wins between them.

September 18 (Wednesday)

Appearing for just six seconds on NBC's comedy variety show *Rowan & Martin's Laugh-In,* Republican presidential candidate Richard Nixon turned to look into the camera and said to the audience "Sock it to ME?" The brief appearance is credited with helping to soften the public's view of Nixon, who had lost his last two political contests (to John F. Kennedy for president in 1960 and to Edmund "Pat" Brown for governor of California in 1962). Democratic opponent Hubert Humphrey declined an invitation to make a similar appearance on the show (as did American Independent Party candidate George Wallace), and years later, Nixon and Humphrey both credited Nixon's appearance with winning the close election for Nixon.

Zond 5, an unmanned Soviet capsule based on the Soyuz 7K-L1 manned lunar flyby spacecraft (which would never actually be launched) became the first spacecraft to orbit the moon that would later safely return to Earth.

The romantic musical-comedy film *Funny Girl,* loosely based on the life of comedian Fanny Brice, was released in theaters. The film starred Barbra Streisand and Omar Sharif.

The St. Louis Cardinals, who had been no-hit the previous evening by Gaylord Perry and the San Francisco Giants, returned the favor as Cardinals' pitcher Ray Washburn pitched a no-hitter against the Giants at Candlestick Park. The back-to-back no-hitter games by Perry and Washburn marked the first time in major league history that two no-hitters were thrown in the same series. Washburn's no-hitter was also the first thrown by a St. Louis Cardinals pitcher since Lon Warneke in 1941.

Born: Toni Kukoč, Croatian basketball player, was born in Split, Croation SSR, Yugoslavia. Kukoč would play basketball in the

EuroLeague, and starting in 1993 would become one of the first European basketball players to become very successful in the U.S.

September 19 (Thursday)

At Tiger Stadium in Detroit, Tigers' pitcher Denny McLain won his 31st game of the season, in what would be his last win of the year. The Tigers beat the Yankees 6-2. McLain's 31 wins remains tied with the modern "live ball" record for most wins in a season, with Jim Bagby, Sr. (1920) and Lefty Grove (1931). McLain would have two more starts in the regular season, and only gave up a total of two earned runs in those games, but the Tigers lost both games in 1-run decisions, turning back McLain's hopes for a record 32nd win. Later in the same game, with the Tigers leading 6-1 in the 8th inning, Yankees veteran Mickey Mantle came to the plate. Mantle was playing in his last major league season. He'd have only nine games left in his great career, and was tied with Jimmie Foxx (who had played from 1925 to 1945) for third most home runs in a career with 534. McLain, an admirer of Mantle, communicated to Mantle through his catcher, Jim Price, that he was going to throw Mantle a fastball over the plate so Mantle could hit it. Mantle thought McLain was trying to fool him, and didn't swing at that first pitch: a fastball over the plate. By now, Mantle knew that McLain wasn't joking, and he hit McLain's second pitch for a home run, putting Mantle solely in third place for most career home runs. (Mantle would hit one more home run the following day against Jim Lonborg of the Boston Red Sox, for a career total of 536.)

In England, censorship of theater productions based on obscenity officially ended.

Died: Red Foley, American country music singer, musician, and radio performer, died in Fort Wayne, Indiana. Foley sold more than 25 million records, and is known for his gospel songs such as "Peace in the Valley."

September 20 (Friday)

The police drama *Hawaii Five-O* premiered on CBS Television. The show followed a fictional special state police task force, led by Detective Captain Steve McGarrett, played by actor Jack Lord. The team's name, Five-O, was a reference to Hawaii being the 50th state (Hawaii became a state just nine years earlier). The series was shot on location in Hawaii. The show would run 12 seasons, until April 1980, becoming what would be the longest-running police/crime show in television history, until *Law & Order* in 2003. A reboot of the original series, also called *Hawaii Five-O*, premiered in September 2010.

At Yankee Stadium in New York City, Yankees outfielder and first baseman Mickey Mantle, still recognized as one of baseball's all-time greats, hit the last home run of his career, number 536, off Boston Red Sox pitcher Jim Lonborg.

The musical *Hair* opened in Stockholm, Sweden.

Born: American drag racer Darrell Russell was born. Russell would become the National Hot Rod Association Rookie of the Year in 2001, and had six event wins to his credit. His death on the drag strip in 2004, when his racing slick rear tire exploded, led to an upgrade of tires across the industry.

Born: Philippa Forrester, British TV presenter and author, was born in Winchester, Hampshire, England. Forrester has presented on shows such as *Robot Wars* and *Tomorrow's World*, and made a number of television programs about wildlife with her husband.

Born: Leah Pinsent, Canadian actress, was born in Toronto. Pinsent has starred in the comedy-drama series *Made in Canada* as well as films including *April Fool's Day* and *The Bay Boy*.

September 21 (Saturday)

The Soviet's Zond 5 unmanned lunar flyby mission returned to Earth, with its biological payload of tortoises, mealworms, plants, and other life forms, intact.

The police drama *Adam-12* premiered on NBC Television. The show, created by Jack Webb (who had previously created and starred in *Dragnet*), followed two Los Angeles police officers, Pete Malloy (played by Martin Milner) and Jim Reed (played by Kent McCord). The name of the show came from the number assigned to the vehicle of the main characters. The show ran until May 1975.

Inside the Vehicle Assembly Building at the Kennedy Space Center, the Apollo 8 Command/Service Modules (CSM) and a test article representing the same weight as a Lunar Module, was placed atop a Saturn V rocket.

Born: Ricki Lake, American actress, producer, and television presenter, was born in Hastings-on-Hudson, New York. Lake would host her own talk show from 1993 to 2004. When she started the series, she was 24 years old, making her the youngest ever to host a syndicated talk show at that time.

Born: Lisa Angell, French singer, was born in Paris. Angell represented France in the Eurovision Song Contest 2015.

September 22 (Sunday)

The Irwin Allen science fiction series *Land of the Giants* aired on television for the first time. Set fifteen years in the future—1983—the series premise was that a crew of a spacecraft in suborbit encountered a "magnetic space storm" that propelled it through a wormhole to another, strange planet where everything is twelve times the size as on Earth. The series ran until March 1970. Series creator Irwin Allen had previously brought the science fiction series *Voyage to the Bottom of the Sea* (1964-68), *Lost in Space* (1965-68), and *The Time Tunnel* (1966-67) to television.

At Metropolitan Stadium in Minneapolis, Minnesota, versatile fielder César Tovar became just the second player in major league history to play all nine positions in a single game. While on the mound, Tovar pitched a scoreless first inning against the Oakland A's; the first batter he faced was Bert Campaneris, coincidentally the first player in major league history to play all nine positions in a game.

Born: Megan Hollingshead, American voice actress, was born in New York City. Hollingshead is especially known for voicing roles in video games and anime, including the voice of Nurse Joy in *Pokémon.*

Born: Mihai Răzvan Ungureanu, 62nd Prime Minister of Romania, was born in Iaşi, Romania. Ungureanu served as prime minister for three months in 2012, and has held other national office including director of foreign intelligence and minister of foreign affairs.

September 23 (Monday)

In South Vietnam, the Tet Offensive, which had begun on January 3, ended.

The new Lucille Ball television vehicle, *Here's Lucy*, aired for the first time. It replaced Ball's previous situation comedy, *The Lucy Show*, which had run since 1962. Ball's long-time friend Gale Gordon played her boss (and frequently the foil of her schemes), while her real-life children, Lucie Arnaz and Desi Arnaz, Jr., played her kids.

Born: Yvette Fielding, English television presenter, was born in Manchester, England. Fielding hosted the series *Most Haunted* and others.

Born: Michelle Thomas, American actress, was born in Boston. Thomas played in *The Cosby Show* and *Family Matters*. (Thomas would die of cancer in 1998 of cancer, at age 30.)

September 24 (Tuesday)

The CBS newsmagazine *60 Minutes* aired its first episode. The show had a different format than most television news programs in that it featured reporter-centered segments rather than being anchored by a centralized individual. The show has perennially been in the top of the ratings, and based on U.S. ratings, the show is the most successful television program in history. The show is still on the air as of 2017.

The situation comedy *The Doris Day Show* premiered on CBS, and the counterculture police drama *The Mod Squad*, with young actors Peggy Lipton, Michael Cole, and Clarence Williams III, premiered on ABC. Both shows ran until 1973.

In Kentucky, eight new Public Television stations began broadcasting for the first time, with stations located in Ashland, Bowling Green, Lexington, Madisonville, Morehead, Owenton, Somerset, and Elizabethtown.

September 25 (Wednesday)

New York Mets manager and former Brooklyn Dodgers first baseman Gil Hodges, age 44, suffered a mild heart attack. He would miss the remainder of the season with the Mets, but would return the following season to manage the "Amazing Mets" to their first world championship. Just four years later, Hodges would die of a heart attack while returning to his room after playing 27 holes of golf.

Born: Will Smith, American rapper and actor, was born in Philadelphia. Smith attained national exposure while rapping under the name of Fresh Prince, and would go on to star in a situation comedy *The Fresh Prince of Bel-Air*. He would become the first (and to date, only) actor to have eight consecutive films gross $100 million in the domestic market. Forbes has ranked Smith as the number one actor in the world for earning power based on the success of his films.

September 26 (Thursday)

The motion picture musical *Oliver!* opened in London.

Born: Jim Caviezel, American actor, was born in Mt. Vernon, Washington. Caviezel's acting credits include the portrayal of Jesus Christ in the 2004 film *The Passion of the Christ*, as well as *The Thin Red Line*, *Frequency*, and *Person of Interest*.

Born: Ben Shenkman, American television, film and stage actor, was born in New York City. Shenkman played in *Angels in America* and *Royal Pains*.

Born: Tricia O'Kelley, American actress, was born in Melrose, Massachusetts. Her credits include *The New Adventures of Old Christine* and *Gilmore Girls*.

September 27 (Friday)

In Portugal, Marcelo Caetano became the country's prime minister. He would serve in that position until April 1974.

In St. Louis, Bob Gibson pitched his last regular-season game of the 1968 season, with a complete game shutout against the Houston Astros. Gibson struck out 11 batters. The shutout would lower Gibson's earned run average to 1.12 over the season, a modern baseball record.

The musical *Hair* opened in London.

Born: Mari Kiviniemi, a Finnish politician who was the 41st prime minister of Finland, was born in Seinäjoki, Finland. Kiviniemi was the second woman to serve in the position. Since 2014, she has also been the deputy secretary-general of the Organization for Economic Cooperation and Development (OECD).

September 28 (Saturday)

Alberto Giolani of Italy roller skated a record 23.133 miles (37.23 km) in one hour.

Blues/rock singer Janis Joplin announced that she was leaving her original backup band, Big Brother and the Holding Company. Joplin completed the split three months later, in December, at which time she had already formed a new band, The Kozmic Blues Band.

Born: Naomi Watts, English-born Australian actress who starred in *Mulholland Drive* and *The Ring*, was born in Shoreham, Kent in the UK.

Born: Mika Häkkinen, Finnish double Formula One world champion, was born in Vantaa, Finland.

September 29 (Sunday)

A referendum in Greece gave more power to the military junta.

September 29 was the last day of the regular baseball season. In "The Year of the Pitcher," batting statistics were below normal levels. Carl Yastrzemski of the Boston Red Sox, who the year before had won a rare triple crown (leading the league in batting average, home runs, and runs batted in), finished the '68 season with a .3005 batting average. It was the lowest for an AL batting champion since 1900, with runner-up Danny Cater of Oakland hitting .290. Frank Howard of the Washington Senators led the league in home runs with 44, and Ken Harrelson of the Boston Red Sox led the league in runs batted in with 109. In the National League, Pete Rose of the Cincinnati Reds led the league in batting average, hitting .335. Willie McCovey of the San Francisco Giants had 36 home runs, and also led in runs batted in with 105.

Born: Patrick Burns, American paranormal investigator and television personality, was born in Highland Park, Illinois.

Born: Alex Skolnick, American jazz/heavy metal guitarist, was born in Berkeley, California. Skolnick has been named one of the best and fastest guitarists in the world by readers of *Guitar World* magazine. Skolnick was formerly a member of Testament and the Alex Skolnick Trio, and has played with the Trans-Siberian Orchestra.

Born: Samir Soni, Indian film and TV actor, was born in New Delhi, India.

September 30 (Monday)

At Paine Field, near Everett, Washington, Boeing rolled one of the most historic aircraft in history out of its enormous hangar, revealing the Boeing 747 to the public and the media for the first time. A tractor slowly towed the aircraft out of the hangar, and many in attendance had never seen an aircraft so large. The U.S. secretary of commerce was on hand to speak, and Boeing's chief executive officer, Bill Allen, said that the project was one of the biggest in history. Washington's governor and both of its U.S. senators were in attendance. The 747 remains in service as of this writing, but is being phased out by some airlines. An immense aircraft, the original "Jumbo Jet" can be identified by the "hump" upper deck near the front of the aircraft. In a single-class layout, the airline is capable of carrying up to 660 passengers, though the more common configuration of the 747-400 can carry between 416 and 524 passengers. According to Boeing literature, 1,536 Boeing 747s had been built as of September 2017, with 17 aircraft remaining on order. The two aircraft normally used to transport the president of the United States ("Air Force One") continue to be Boeing VC-25 aircraft, the military version of the 747.

Motown Records released the single "Love Child" by Diana Ross & The Supremes. It was the group's 11th single to reach number one on the U.S. charts.

Sharon Miller won the LPGA Seven Lakes Golf Invitational in Palm Springs, California. While in college at Western Michigan, the 5-foot, 3.5-inch Miller won letters in five sports: golf, tennis, field hockey, basketball, and volleyball.

October 1968

October 1 (Tuesday)

George A. Romero's cult horror film *Night of the Living Dead* was released in theaters. The film was shot on a budget of $114,000 U.S., and grossed $12 million domestically and $18 million globally. (Romero died in July 2017.)

Mark Durden-Smith, British television presenter, was born in Soho, London. Durden-Smith would host shows including *This Morning Summer*, *The Match*, and *Double or Nothing*.

Jay Underwood, American actor, was born in Oceanside, California. Underwood would perform in films including *Uncle Buck*, *The Invisible Kid*, and *The Boy Who Could Fly*.

October 2 (Wednesday)

The western film *Coogan's Bluff*, with Clint Eastwood, Lee J. Cobb, and Susan Clark, was released in theaters.

The 1968 World Series between the Detroit Tigers and the St. Louis Cardinals began in St. Louis. The starting pitcher for the Cardinals was National League MVP, Cy Young and Gold Glove winner Bob Gibson, who had an astounding 1.12 Earned Run Average for the season. The starting pitcher for the Tigers was American League MVP and Cy Young winner Denny McLain, whose 31 wins for the season made him the first Major League pitcher since 1934 (and the only one since) to win at least 30 games in a season. The Cardinals finished the regular season with a 97-65 win-loss record and, in addition to Gibson, were led by Tim McCarver, Lou Brock, Curt

Flood, and Roger Maris. The team was managed by Red Schoendienst. The Tigers had finished the regular season with a 103-59 record, and in addition to McLain were led by Bill Freehan, Willie Horton, Jim Northrup, Norm Cash, and Gates Brown. The Tigers were managed by Mayo Smith. The series was played entirely during daytime hours, before the advent of night World Series games in 1971. People in offices, bars, and schools frequently arranged to watch the Series on a television set (usually black and white) that would be brought in for the occasion. The Cardinals would win Game 1, 4-0, thanks largely to Bob Gibson's World Series record 17 Tiger batters struck out, and only five hits scattered.

Born: Czech tennis player Jana Novotná was born in Brno, Czechoslovakia. She won Wimbledon in 1998 and won 12 Grand Slam women's doubles titles. She won three Olympic medals in tennis, including two silvers and one bronze. She would die of cancer in November 2017 at age 49.

October 3 (Thursday)

A military coup took place in Peru, overthrowing President Fernando Belaúnde Terry and the constitutional government that had been in place since 1933.

Europe's first satellite, ESRO 1A, was launched. The satellite examined the planet's auroral zones with regard to solar and geometric activity.

On Broadway, the play *The Great White Hope*, about heavyweight boxer Jack Johnson and his wife Etta Terry Durya, started its run. It was the first time that an entire regional production (the play started at Arena Stage in Washington, DC) was brought to Broadway. Leads

James Earl Jones and Jane Alexander both won Tony Awards for their performances, and the play won a Pulitzer Prize.

In St. Louis, the Detroit Tigers defeated the Cardinals 8-1 in Game 2 of the World Series. Mickey Lolich was the winning pitcher, with Nelson Briles getting the loss. Lolich also helped the cause at the plate by hitting the only home run of his major league career.

Born: Paul Crichton, English goalkeeper, was born in Pontefract, England. Crichton played for a number of teams between 1986 and 2011.

October 4 (Friday)

In Northern Ireland, a civil rights association's delegation met with the Derry march leaders in an attempt to cancel the upcoming civil rights march. The decision was to continue planning the march.

October 5 (Saturday)

In Northern Ireland, the march planned for Derry was halted by officials. Resulting violence escalated into riots; this event is frequently considered to be the beginning of the Northern Ireland period called "The Troubles," which would last until 1998 (i.e., 30 years). More than 3,600 people were killed and thousands injured during this period.

In Detroit, the Cardinals beat the Tigers 7-3 in Game 3 of the World Series. Ray Washburn was the winning pitcher, Earl Wilson was the loser.

Married: Action film star Charles Bronson married actress Jill Ireland.

October 6 (Sunday)

The weekly one-hour comedy and variety show *The Smothers Brothers Comedy Hour* featured the Beatles singing "Hey Jude."

The second total lunar eclipse of 1968 was visible from all of earth's continents.

Prior to the start of Game 4 of the World Series in Detroit, the national anthem was sung by 23-year-old Jose Feliciano, who delivered an "unconventional" slow, meaningful rendition of the Star-Spangled Banner. Feliciano's soulful rendition of the American national anthem, which did not strictly adhere to the traditional melody and tempo of the version normally played by bands and orchestras, was uncommon for the day, and drew boos and angry letters from some. The Cardinals would defeat the Tigers 10-1, with a second win for Gibson and a second loss for McLain.

Died: Mathematician Phyllis Lockett Nicolson died in Sheffield, England, of cancer at age 51. Nicolson had graduated with bachelor's, master's, and doctorate degrees in physics from the University of Manchester.

October 7 (Monday)

The Motion Picture Association of America (MPAA) adopted the voluntary ratings system, which was the predecessor to the system that remains in place today. Prior to the ratings system, the industry followed the Hays Code, which simply listed what was acceptable and what wasn't, by standards that were in place.

In Detroit, the Tigers came into Game 5 with a 3-games-to-1 deficit, and needed a win to stay alive against the Cardinals. The team scored three runs in the 7th inning to come from behind, and defeat the Cardinals 5-3.

Born: Luminița Anghel, Romanian dance/pop recording artist, songwriter, television personality and politician, was born in Bucharest. Anghel represented Romania in the Eurovision Song Contest 2005. In 2008, she made an unsuccessful bid for a seat in the Chamber of Deputies on the Social Democratic Party ticket.

Born: Thom Yorke, British singer-songwriter, was born in Wellingborough, Northamptonshire, England. Yorke would become the lead singer and primary songwriter for the band Radiohead.

October 8 (Tuesday)

Presidential candidate Richard M. Nixon appeared in an interview on the CBS newsmagazine *60 Minutes*, saying that he "hoped to restore respect for the presidency at all levels."

The Netherlands sold the aircraft carrier Karel Doorman, which the Dutch Navy had decommissioned in April, to Argentina. Argentina renamed the carrier ARA *Veinticinco de Mayo,* in recognition of the 5th of May, the anniversary of Argentina's revolution in 1810.

Born: Daniela Castelo, Argentine journalist, was born in Buenos Aires. Castelo developed and acted as journalist on several television and radio news programs.

Born: Emily Procter, American actress, was born in Raleigh, North Carolina. Procter played major parts in the television series *The West Wing* and *White Collar.*

October 9 (Wednesday)

Apollo 8, sitting atop the enormous Saturn V rocket, with a combined height of 363 feet (111 meters) made the three-mile trip from the Vehicle Assembly Building. The rocket was carried on the huge, tracked crawler-transporter and its launch tower, to Launch Complex 39A, from where it would be launched to the moon in December. In order to meet launch schedules, NASA ordered two of the crawler-transporters, which were designed and built by Marion Power Shovel Company. Each of the crawlers has a top deck surface of 131 ft. x 114 ft. feet (40m x 35m), and weighs 6 million lbs. (2,721 tonnes). Following the moon launches that ended in December 1972, the crawler-transport units were used for the Apollo-Soyuz and space shuttle programs. The two units, now nicknamed "Hans" and "Franz," will be used for America's new Space Launch System that is expected to take humans out of earth orbit again, and eventually to Mars.

In Belfast, 2,000 students from Queen's University tried to march to Belfast City Hall to protest against what they perceived as police brutality. The marching protesters were stopped by loyalists. The confrontation led to the formation of People's Democracy, a student civil rights group.

Back in St. Louis for Game 6 of the World Series, the Tigers trailed the Cardinals 3 games to 2 and still needed a win to stay alive. A 10-run third inning, featuring a Jim Northrup grand slam, ensured that a Game 7 would be needed. The Tigers won 13-1, giving Denny McLain a win.

Born: Pete Docter, American animator and director, was born in Bloomington, Minnesota. Docter became highly involved with Pixar Animation Studios; he was the director of *Monsters, Inc., Inside Out*, and others.

October 10 (Thursday)

The Detroit Tigers came back from their 3-to-1 game deficit to defeat the St. Louis Cardinals in Game 7 of the World Series, to win the Tigers' first world championship since 1945. The Most Valuable Player of the series was Mickey Lolich, who won three games for the Tigers. To date, Lolich remains the last pitcher in Major League Baseball to win three complete games in a World Series. Just days before the World Series, manager Mayo Smith moved outfielder Mickey Stanley to shortstop in order to improve the team's overall hitting, and to allow veteran Al Kaline back into the outfield (along with Jim Northrup and Willie Horton) after Kaline's return from injury. ESPN baseball staff later selected Smith's decision to move Stanley to shortstop as the third "gutsiest call" in sports history.

Following the 1968 season, the American and National leagues would be divided into separate divisions.

Born: Bart Brentjens, Dutch mountainbiker, was born in Haelen, the Netherlands. Brentjens would win the Olympic gold medal for mountain biking at the 1996 Olympic Games, the first Olympic Games to recognize cross-country mountain biking as an event.

October 11 (Friday)

At the Kennedy Space Center in Florida, Apollo 7 was launched on an 11-day earth orbit mission. Apollo 7 was the first manned Apollo spacecraft, and the first American manned launch in 21 months, since a flash fire during launch rehearsals killed the crew of the Apollo One on January 27, 1967. The crew killed in the fire was Gus Grissom (America's second person in space), Ed White (America's first spacewalker), and rookie astronaut Roger Chaffee. Following an investigation, numerous safety improvements were made to the spacecraft.

The Apollo 7 mission would not only be the first manned launch of the Apollo spacecraft, but it would also be the last launch before Apollo 8 launch in late December to orbit the moon. The mission would also involve the only launch using a Saturn IB to put a crew into space, as well as the first live television transmission from space. The Apollo 7 mission was commanded by Project Mercury and Project Gemini veteran Walter "Wally" Schirra, with a crew of pilot/navigator Donn Eisele, and systems engineer Walter "Walt" Cunningham. Because a functioning Lunar Module would not be available until 1969, the main purpose of the flight was to thoroughly test the Command and Service Module package systems for life support, propulsion, control and guidance in preparation for lunar flights. The spacecraft was scheduled to orbit the earth and reenter and splash down nearly 11 full days later.

Born: Jane Krakowski, American actress and singer, was born in Parsippany-Troy Hills, New Jersey. Krakowski played roles in the television series *30 Rock*, *Ally McBeal*, and *Unbreakable Kimmy Schmidt*.

October 12 (Saturday)

In Mexico City, the Games of the XIX Olympiad began. The Mexico City games were the first Olympic games to be held in a Latin American country, and in a Spanish-speaking nation. In track & field (athletics), an all-weather track would be used for the first time instead of the traditional cinder track. These would be the first summer games to be significantly affected by the altitude of the host city (7,350 feet, or 2,240 meters above sea level). The thinner air had a negative impact on endurance sports, but a positive impact on any events involving jumping or throwing, as well as any short-distance running events. Mexican hurdler Enriqueta Basilio was the first woman in history to light the Olympic Torch.

Born: Hugh Jackman, Australian actor, singer, and producer, was born in Sydney, New South Wales, Australia. Jackman has starred in a number of major motion pictures, including the *X-Men* film series as the character Wolverine. Other films have included *Les Miserables*, *Kate & Leopold*, *Van Helsing*, and *The Greatest Showman*.

October 13 (Sunday)

In Brooklyn, Michigan, the first ever race was held at Michigan International Speedway (MIS). The winner of the first race, the USAC 250-mile Championship Car Race, was Ronnie Bucknum, who in 1964 had been the first driver to race a Honda-powered car in a Formula One race. MIS is regarded by many as the fastest track in NASCAR racing, and one of the fastest tracks in the world, because of its wide turns, long straightaways, and highly banked corners among NASCAR tracks.

Born: Tisha Campbell-Martin, American actress and singer, was born in Oklahoma City, Oklahoma. She has been in a number of television shows including *Captain Kangaroo*, *Big Blue Marble*, and *Everybody Hates Chris*.

Died: Actress Bea Benaderet died of lung cancer in Los Angeles at age 62. She had just finished filming the first three episodes of season five of the CBS situation comedy *Petticoat Junction*, in which she played the main character, Kate Bradley. Benaderet had been weakened by cancer for some time, and her absence from the show was addressed by saying that she was traveling. Benaderet was a veteran of television and radio, having been credited with more than 1,000 television and radio appearances. She performed on network radio for the first time working for Orson Welles on his *Mercury Radio Theatre* program, and performed many voice roles, in addition to being a guest on television's *The Beverly Hillbillies* and *The George Burns and Gracie Allen Show*. Benaderet was the original voice of Betty Rubble on *The Flintstones* (112 episodes).

October 14 (Monday)

The crew of Apollo 7 transmitted the first live television pictures from space. The crew described what they were doing, and showed the audience humorous cue cards, saying things such as "Keep Those Cards and Letters Coming In, Folks," and "Hello from the Lovely Apollo Room High atop Everything."

In Meckering, Australia, a magnitude 6.9 (Richter scale) earthquake struck at 10:59 am, essentially destroying the town. The quake lasted for approximately 45 seconds and was felt for a radius of about 430 miles (700 km). It was one of the most powerful earthquakes in Australian history.

The men's 100-meter final in track & field was won by American Jim Hines with a time of 9.95 seconds (electronic). The win earned Hines the informal title of "World's Fastest Human."

October 15 (Tuesday)

The women's 100-meter final in track & field was won by American Wyomia Tyus with a time of 11.1 seconds (hand-timed). Tyus would become the first person to defend a 100-meter championship; subsequent sprinters successfully defending a 100-meter title included Carl Lewis, Gail Devers, Shelly-Ann Fraser, and Usain Bolt.

LOOK Magazine published its 13th Annual Automotive Preview edition, showing the 1969 cars. Newly introduced cars included the Ford Boss Mustang 429, Mercury Capri, Honda 1300, Mitsubishi Galant, Nissan Skyline GT-R, Porsche 914, and Triumph TR6.

Born: Vanessa Marcil, American actress, was born in Indio, California. Marcil has had roles in the television series *General Hospital, Beverly Hills, 90210*, and *Las Vegas*.

October 16 (Wednesday)

The men's 200-meter final was won by American Tommie Smith, with a time of 19.83 seconds. Peter Norman of Australia was second, with American John Carlos third. In one of the most memorable moments in Olympic history, on the podium for the medal ceremony after the race, Smith and Carlos, each wearing one black glove, raised their gloved hand upward and kept it raised during the playing of the American National Anthem. In a gesture intended to reflect the January 1st United Nations declaration that 1968 would be "International Human Rights Year," Smith later said that the silent salute was a "human rights salute" rather than a "Black Power salute." Australian silver-medalist Norman, who was told about the silent gesture before the ceremony, wore a Human Rights badge on his pocket, as did Smith and Carlos. In response to the salute, International Olympic Committee chair Avery Brundage (from the U.S.) said that the gesture was inappropriate and political, and banned Smith and Carlos from the Olympic Village. Smith and Carlos were largely ostracized in the U.S., as was Peter Norman when he returned to Australia. Norman would not be selected to represent his country in the following Olympic games in 1972, despite the fact that he qualified for the games 13 times. (Australia did not send any male athletes to the '72 games to run the in the sprint events.) However, all three athletes later won awards for courage. A statue capturing the moment of the salute stands on the grounds of San Jose State University in California, where Smith and Carlos both participated in college. When Peter Norman died in 2006, Smith and Carlos traveled to Australia, where they gave eulogies and were pallbearers for Norman.

At the Milwaukee Arena in Milwaukee, Wisconsin, the new Milwaukee Bucks basketball team played the first game in franchise history, losing to the Chicago Bulls, 89-84.

October 17 (Thursday)

The police drama film *Bullitt*, starring Steve McQueen, Robert Vaughn, and Jacqueline Bissett, was released in theaters. The film features a high-speed car chase on the hilly streets of San Francisco that spans nearly 10 minutes without dialog. The scene is thought by many film experts to be one of the best car chase scenes in the history of cinema.

Born: Ziggy Marley, Jamaican musician and oldest son of Bob Marley, was born in Kingston, Jamaica. In 1979, Marley and his siblings formed the group Melody Makers.

October 18 (Friday)

Sports Illustrated magazine would call it "one of the five greatest sports moments of the 20th Century": American Bob Beamon won the long jump on his first jump, but instead of breaking the world record by a few inches, or by a fraction of an inch, Beamon obliterated the existing world record by 21 ¾ inches (55 cm). Because the announcer called out the distance of Beamon's jump in meters—which American Beamon was not familiar with—he didn't realize for some time what he had done. When Beamon's coach came over and told him the magnitude of his performance, Beamon collapsed from the emotional impact. Beamon's world record would stand for 23 years before being broken by fellow American Mike Powell, who broke Beamon's mark by slightly less than two inches.

Within an hour of Bob Beamon shattering the world record in the long jump, Lee Evans won the men's 400 meters in world record time of 43.86 seconds.

In Las Vegas, Nevada, the $15 million hotel and casino Circus Circus opened.

October 19 (Saturday)

In Northern Ireland, Derry Citizens' Action Committee (DCAC), formed on October 9, staged a sit-down at Guildhall Square as part of large civil disobedience campaign.

The New York Daily News reported that former first lady Jacqueline Kennedy would marry her long-time friend, Aristotle Onassis.

American Bill Toomey won the two-day, 10-event men's decathlon at the Olympic Games. Toomey would later be named ABC *Wide World of Sports* Athlete of the Year for 1968.

October 20 (Sunday)

Married: On the private island of Skorpios near Greece, former U.S. first lady Jacqueline Kennedy married her long-time friend, shipping magnate Aristotle Onassis. Family members said that Jacqueline Kennedy was concerned with the safety of her children, and she felt that Onassis could offer physical security on the private island, as well as financial security. With the marriage, she lost her right to ongoing Secret Service protection that is normally afforded widows of U.S. presidents.

Dick Fosbury of the U.S. won the men's high jump at the Olympic Games. Fosbury developed a revolutionary technique of clearing the bar with his back toward the bar (i.e., his body facing upward) as opposed to the roll technique that had been used for decades, whereby the jumper cleared the bar facing downward. Fosbury's technique, called the Fosbury flop, was more mechanically efficient in that it allowed the body's center of gravity to clear a higher point. Since the early 1970s, nearly all world-class competitors have used the Fosbury flop.

Mamo Wolde of Ethiopia won the men's Olympic marathon in a time of 2 hours, 20 minutes, 26 seconds. Seventy-five runners from 41 countries ran in the race, with 18 not finishing in the thinner Mexico City air. The first-ever women's Olympic games would not be held for 16 more years, when American Joan Benoit would win the race at the 1984 games in Los Angeles.

Kipchoge "Kip" Keino of Kenya won the men's 1500 meters at the Olympic Games. His win by almost 3 full seconds over the runner-up, world record holder Jim Ryun of the U.S., may have been partly attributed to Ryun's inability to adjust to the altitude of Mexico City.

Born: Damien Timmer, British managing director and television producer, was born in Chelsea, London. He was the executive producer on *Lost in Austen*, the 2009 television series *Wuthering Heights*, and a number of other productions.

October 21 (Monday)

The U.S. won the men's 4x200-meter swimming relay gold medal with the team of John Nelson, Stephen Rerych, Mark Spitz, and Don Schollander. It would be one of only two gold medals won by Spitz, both for relay team victories. Prior to the games, Spitz, who held 10 world records, predicted that he would win six gold medals. His total individual medal count for the games was one silver and one bronze. However, the experience would better prepare him for the 1972 Olympic Games, at which he would win an unprecedented seven gold medals.

Born: Francois Gravel, hockey goaltender and player for Team France in 1998, was born in Sherbrooke, Quebec.

October 22 (Tuesday)

In the North Atlantic Ocean, the Apollo 7 spacecraft and crew splashed down and were recovered by the USS *Essex*. After orbiting the earth for 11 days, Apollo 7 splashed down 8 miles (13 km) from the *Essex*.

Born: Shaggy, Jamaican singer, DJ, and musician, was born in Kingston, Jamaica. Shaggy performed on the 2004 album *True Love*, which won a Grammy Award for Best Reggae Album.

October 23 (Wednesday)

Born: Kendall Gammon, American football player, was born in Rose Hill, Kansas. Gammon would be the first long snapper (putting the football in play for field goals, punts, and/or 1-point conversions) to be selected for the National Football League's Pro Bowl game specifically for long snapping.

October 24 (Thursday)

At the University of Surrey in Bittersea, England, the group that had performed under the name The New Yardbirds for several weeks performed for the first time under their new name, Led Zeppelin. The group consisted of lead vocalist Robert Plant, guitarist Jimmy Page, bass guitar player and keyboard player John Paul Jones, and drummer John Bonham. Their music drew on rock, blues, and had occasional references to J.R.R. Tolkien's *Lord of the Rings* book series. Led Zeppelin remains one of the most successful and influential groups in rock history.

Over the California desert, Pilot Bill Dana flew the X-15 rocket plane on its 199th and final flight. Dana piloted the final flight to Mach 5.38, or about 5,980 miles per hour (9,624 km/hour).

Born: Mark Walton, American story artist and voice actor, was born in Salt Lake City, Utah. Walton became a storyboard artist and voice actor at Walt Disney Animation Studios, where his work included *Return to Neverland*, *Chicken Little*, *Bolt*, and *Meet the Robinsons*.

October 25 (Friday)

In gymnastics at the Olympic Games, the women's floor exercise appeared to have been won by Věra Čáslavská of Czechoslovakia, who had been outspoken about the Soviet invasion of her home country before and during the games. However, the judges inexplicably revised Čáslavská's Soviet opponent's score upward, allowing the Soviet competitor to win the gold medal. At the medal ceremony afterward, silver medalist Čáslavská turned her face down and away from the Soviet flag during the playing of the USSR national anthem, in silent protest. Čáslavská was *persona non grata* for many years back home in Czechoslovakia due to her action. However, in later years after her country's policies changed, she was awarded a number of medals for courage, in her native country and around the world.

The science fiction film *Barbarella*, starring Jane Fonda, was released in theaters.

October 26 (Saturday)

In Baikonur, Kazakhstan, the Soviet Union launched the Soyuz 3 spacecraft, manned by cosmonaut Georgy Beregovoy. The primary purpose of the mission was to rendezvous and dock with the unmanned Soyuz 2, which had been launched the previous day. Although Beregovoy was able to successfully rendezvous with the unmanned spacecraft, it was not able to successfully dock, partly because Beregovoy switched off automatic docking systems in order to manually dock, and consumed too much fuel in his first attempt.

In Mexico City, American boxer George Foreman defeated Soviet Ionas Chepulis to win the Olympic heavyweight boxing gold medal.

October 27 (Sunday)

The closing ceremonies at the XIX Olympic Games took place. It was the first time that closing ceremonies were televised globally in color, in addition to the athletic contests.

Born: Alain Auderset, Swiss Christian writer of comics, was born in Grenchen, Switzerland. His series of comics have included Marcel, ROBI, and Willy Grunch.

Died: Lise Meitner, Austrian-Swedish physicist, died in Cambridge, England at the age of 89. In the late 1930s, Meitner and Otto Hahn led a small group in discovering nuclear fission of uranium. The work of Meitner and the group formed the basis of all atomic reactors and atomic weapons. Meitner had begun keeping a scientific diary at the age of 8.

October 28 (Monday)

Born: Juan Orlando Hernández, 55th President of Honduras, was born in Gracias, Honduras.

Born: Caitlin Cary, American alternative country musician, was born in Seville, Ohio. In 1993, Cary and Ryan Adams would form the band Whiskeytown.

October 29 (Tuesday)

Born: Johann Olav Koss, Norwegian speed skater, was born in Drammen, Norway. Koss would later win a total of four Olympic gold medals in speed skating, including three at the 1994 Lillehammer Winter Olympics in his home country.

Born: Tsunku, Japanese singer, music producer and song composer, was born. He would become the fifth best-selling lyricist in Japan.

October 30 (Wednesday)

In London, Irish Prime Minister Jack Lynch met with British Prime Minister Harold Wilson, asking that partition in Ireland be ended, in order to end the civil disturbances in Northern Ireland.

The Nobel Prize in Chemistry was awarded to Norwegian-born American physical and theoretical physicist Lars Onsager. The prize was awarded for Onsager's work on the effects of diffusion on temperature gradients.

Soyuz 3, with cosmonaut Georgy Beregovoy aboard, landed safely near its land target in the Soviet Union.

Died: Conrad Richter, American novelist, died in Pottsville, Pennsylvania at age 78. Richter's novels included *The Town* and *The Sea of Grass*. His novel *The Awakening Land*, about life on the Ohio frontier, won the 1951 Pulitzer Prize for Fiction.

October 31 (Thursday)

In an address to the U.S. five days before the general election, President Lyndon B. Johnson announced that because of developments in the Paris peace negotiations, he had ordered the complete cessation of "all air, naval, and artillery bombardment of North Vietnam." Accordingly, effective November 1, the U.S. Air Force called a halt to the air raids on North Vietnam, known as Operation Rolling Thunder. The President further disclosed that Hanoi had agreed to allow the South Vietnamese government to participate in the peace talks. Johnson said that the United States would consent to a role for the National Liberation Front, but that it "in no way involves recognition of the National Liberation Front in any form." The announcement was positive for Humbert Humphrey in the presidential race. While Humphrey had been loyal to Johnson and his policies since the beginning, as October progressed, Humphrey had begun to distance himself from Johnson, and publicly supported the end to the bombing. Humphrey had also begun to take support away from George Wallace, who had gained blue collar and union votes until his campaign faltered, in part because running mate Curtis LeMay had begun to strongly suggest the use of nuclear weapons in Vietnam. As a result, Humphrey's double-digit deficit in approval at the end of the convention in Chicago had now become a very close race.

Linda Eastman permanently moved to the UK along with her daughter, Heather. Eastman would marry Paul McCartney on March 12, 1969, and Paul would formally adopt Heather as his daughter.

In Milwaukee, Wisconsin, the Milwaukee Bucks won their first game in franchise history, beating the Detroit Pistons 138-118. It was the Bucks' sixth game of the season. The Bucks had been awarded a National Basketball Association franchise in January 1968, and a contest was held to name the team. The winning team name, the Bucks, referred to the white-tailed deer, Wisconsin's official wild animal.

November 1968

November 1 (Friday)

Detroit Tigers pitcher Denny McLain unanimously won the Cy Young Award. One year later, McLain and Baltimore Orioles pitcher Mike Cuellar would be co-winners of the award. (Following the 1969 season, *Sports Illustrated* and *Penthouse* magazines each published articles detailing McLain's involvement with illegal gambling operations. He was suspended for the first three months of the 1970 season, and though McLain returned to pitch, his career never recovered.)

Died: Georgios Papandreou, who had served as prime minister of Greece for three non-consecutive terms, died in Athens at age 80.

November 2 (Saturday)

In Derry, Northern Ireland, the banned march by the Derry Citizens' Action Committee was joined by thousands of additional protesters. Because of the number of protesters, the Royal Ulster Constabulary was unable to stop it.

November 3 (Sunday)

In Greece, Alexandros Panagoulis and other members of the National Resistance were put on trial for the attempted assassination of dictator Georgios Papadopoulos.

British race driver Graham Hill won the Formula One World Drivers' Championship.

Former Greek Prime Minister Georgios Papandreou was buried. 300,000 protesters came to demonstrate against the fascist junta.

At Shea Stadium in New York City, New York Jets kicker Jim Turner kicked six field goals, accounting for 18 points as the Jets defeated the Buffalo Bills, 25-21.

November 4 (Monday)

The Jordanian army attacked the fedayeen group Al-Nasr ("victory") after the group had attacked Jordanian police.

Capitol Records released singer/guitarist Glen Campbell's twelfth album, *Wichita Lineman*, named after the single of the same name. The album would become the number-one country album of the year. Campbell had also won the award the year before, for his album *By the Time I Get to Phoenix*, which also won the Grammy Award for Album of the Year.

November 5 (Tuesday)

In general elections held across the U.S., the Republican challenger, former Vice President Richard M. Nixon was elected the 37th president of the United States in a relatively close election. Maryland Gov. Spiro Agnew was elected vice president. Nixon defeated the Democrat, incumbent Vice President Hubert H. Humphrey, and the American Independent Party candidate, former Alabama Governor George C. Wallace. Voters acted on Nixon's promise to be a "law and order" president, and to restore leadership via U.S. actions related to the Vietnam War. The 1968 election reflected a major realignment of the voting map in the U.S. The more conservative South, which had primarily voted toward Democrats for decades, was now decidedly trending Republican. Wallace, who had publicly supported segregation for many years, also carried five states in the Deep South.

Luis A. Ferré of Puerto Rico's newly created New Progressive Party was elected the third governor of Puerto Rico. Ferré became the first Puerto Rico governor to support statehood for the island. Prior to being elected, Ferré had been an engineer, industrialist, and philanthropist.

Pitcher Denny McLain was unanimously selected the American League's Most Valuable Player for the 1968 season, becoming the first AL pitcher ever to do so. McLain's teammate, catcher Bill Freehan, was second in the voting.

Born: Sam Rockwell, American actor, was born in Daly City, California. Rockwell's work includes *Confessions of a Dangerous Mind*, *The Hitchhiker's Guide to the Galaxy*, *The Green Mile*, *Galaxy Quest*, *Cowboys and Aliens*, and *The Assassination of Jesse James*.

November 6 (Wednesday)

Following extremely close voting in several states, the major news services finally projected Richard Nixon as the winner of the presidential race, and Vice President Hubert Humphrey conceded the presidential election to Nixon. Although Nixon would win 301 electoral votes to Humphrey's 191, three large states—California, Ohio, and Illinois—had hung in the balance on close margins, and Nixon wound up winning all three of them by three percentage points or less. Nixon won the popular vote by only 512,000 votes. Humphrey sent Nixon a telegram, then announced to a gathering, "I've done my best. I have lost. Mr. Nixon has won." Nixon, who had lost a close election to John F. Kennedy in 1960, responded "I know exactly how he felt. I know how it feels to lose a close one."

The Monkees' satirical musical film *Head* was released in theaters. The movie depicted all four members of the group experiencing changes, with the feeling that they had little control over them. Although the movie was not well attended in theaters, it included music written by Carole King and Gerry Goffin (including the theme, "Porpoise Song"), Harry Nilsson, and Jack Nicholson, as well as the Monkees themselves. The cast included Teri Garr, Annette Funicello, Frank Zappa, boxer Sonny Liston, and football player Ray Nitschke.

Died: Charles Munch, French Alsacian symphony conductor and violinist, died at age 77. Munch was known for his knowledge of the French orchestral repertoire, and as leading the Strasbourg and Boston Symphony Orchestras. During World War II, he remained in France during the occupation by Germany, thinking that his presence would help national morale. He was known to protect members of his orchestra from the Gestapo, and for supporting the French Resistance.

November 7 (Thursday)

Died: Alexander Gelfond, Soviet mathematician after whom Gelfond's theorem is named, died in Moscow at age 62.

November 8 (Friday)

Cynthia Lennon was granted a divorce from John Lennon.

Born: Parker Posey, American actress, was born in Baltimore, Maryland. Posey performed in the films *Dazed and Confused*, *Best in Show*, *A Mighty Wind*, and *You've Got Mail*. Her television credits include *Will & Grace*, *The Good Wife*, *Boston Legal*, *Louie*, and *Parks and Recreation*.

Died: Wendell Corey, U.S. actor, died in Woodland Hills, California, at age 54 from cirrhosis of the liver. Corey's credits include a number of theater performances, films, and television series between 1938 and 1968, including *Rear Window*, *The Caine Mutiny Court Martial*, and *The Rainmaker*. Corey was president of the Academy of Motion Picture Arts and Sciences (1961-63) and a board member of the Screen Actors Guild.

November 9 (Saturday)

Married: In West Bromwich, West Midlands, England, Maureen Wilson married Led Zeppelin lead singer Robert Plant.

Died: Swedish jazz musician Jan Johansson died in a car accident at age 37. His recordings are the best-selling jazz records in Swedish history. The recordings incorporated traditional Swedish melodies. Johansson also composed the theme to the popular Swedish television series *Pippi Longstocking*.

November 10 (Sunday)

The Soviet Union launched the Zond 6 unmanned probe from a satellite already in earth orbit. The Zond 6 was launched to perform a lunar fly-by with photographic and radiation-measuring instruments in order to prepare for a possible manned Soviet fly-by of the moon in December 1968. Although the probe successfully navigated around the moon and returned to earth reentry, the probe crashed due to the failure of the parachute to open.

Born: Tracy Morgan, who would become a comedian and cast member of *Saturday Night Live* and *30 Rock*, was born in New York City.

November 11 (Monday)

In Vietnam, despite President Lyndon Johnson's announced end of bombing, a covert U.S. Air Force and Navy operation called Operation Commando Hunt was initiated to halt the movement of communist troops and supplies into South Vietnam. By the time the operation ended in March 1972, more than 3 million tons of bombs had been dropped on Laos. The operation reduced but did not seriously disrupt the efforts of the North Vietnamese.

In the Maldives, following an overwhelming national referendum in March, a new (second) republic was declared, ending an 853-year-old monarchy.

In Leicester, UK, British runner Ron Hill set a world record in the 10-mile run with a time of 46 minutes, 44 seconds. During his career, he also set world records for 25 km and 15 miles, and in 1970 would become the first British runner to win the Boston Marathon.

November 12 (Tuesday)

NASA made its official decision that the Apollo 8 mission, planned for December, would be a lunar orbital mission, taking humans much farther from earth than they had ever been before, and conducting the first manned test of the powerful Saturn V launch vehicle, a vehicle that still had some issues, including violent vibrations during launch.

The first mention was made to the public that Apollo 8 mission would involve orbiting the moon.

The U.S. Supreme Court ruled 9-0, in the case of Epperson v. State of Arkansas, that an Arkansas law banning the teaching of evolution in public schools violated the establishment clause of the First Amendment.

Born: Sammy Sosa, major league baseball player, was born in San Pedro de Macoris, Dominican Republic. Sosa would become the only major league player in history to hit 60 or more home runs in a season three times. Sosa's 609 home runs makes him currently the 9th highest on the career home run list, and his 66 home runs hit in 1998 remains the third highest for a season, behind Barry Bonds and Mark McGwire.

November 13 (Wednesday)

In Derry, Northern Ireland, Home Affairs Minister William Craig banned all marches, with the exception of so-called "customary" parades in Derry. The ban would have the effect of allowing Loyalist (or pro-UK) parades but banning civil rights marches.

St. Louis Cardinals pitcher Bob Gibson edged Cincinnati Reds hitter Pete Rose in voting for the National League's Most Valuable Player.

November 14 (Thursday)

Yale University announced that it would begin to admit women.

November 15 (Friday)

In Greece, a referendum overwhelmingly approved a new constitution prepared by the regime.

In the U.S., the film adaptation of Morris West's novel *The Shoes of the Fisherman* arrived in theaters. The story described a simple religious man who is released from a Soviet labor camp, to unexpectedly be elected Pope upon the death of the incumbent pontiff.

"National Turn in Your Draft Card Day" encouraged young men in the U.S. to turn in their draft cards for burning, an activity in violation of the Selective Service Act.

New York Yankees pitcher Jim Bouton began making daily entries for his best-selling but controversial book *Ball Four*, which detailed the on-field and off-field exploits of his Yankees team from early off-season through the end of the 1969 season. Detroit Tigers catcher Bill Freehan began writing a similar book, *Behind the Mask: An Inside Baseball Diary* soon after the end of the 1968 World Series.

November 16 (Saturday)

In Derry, Northern Ireland, the Derry Citizens' Action Committee defied the recent ban on "non-traditional" marches by marching in the city's Diamond area. An estimated 15,000 people took part.

In Boston, rock guitarist Jimi Hendrix completed his transition from opening act (for the Monkees) to being a major rock star, as he played the Boston Garden as the main act. With the Boston booking, Hendrix became the first rock performer from the "Fillmore circuit" to play at the home arena for the basketball Boston Celtics and the hockey Boston Bruins. The McCoys and Cat Mother were the opening acts for Hendrix's group, The Jimi Hendrix Experience, with Jimi singing and playing his Fender Stratocaster, Mitch Mitchell on drums and Noel Redding on bass. Hendrix played mostly music that he had written, but also put his own distinctive psychedelic sound on rock classics such as "Johnny B. Goode." The set list at the Boston Garden consisted of "Fire," "Voodoo Chile (Slight Return)," "Foxy Lady," "Red House," and "Purple Haze." His career was still very much on the rise, with national and international recognition by many new fans. In just nine months, Hendrix would be the much-anticipated closing act at the Woodstock music festival. In less than two years, he would be dead from a drug overdose in London. Despite his relatively short career as the lead performer of his own band, Rolling Stone would name him the greatest rock guitarist of all time.

November 17 (Sunday)

In Greece, Alexandros Panagoulis and other members of the National Resistance were found guilty and sentenced to death for the attempted assassination of dictator Georgios Papadopoulos. The group was then transported to the island of Aegina to be executed. International pressure kept the government from carrying out the executions, but the prisoners were tortured and mistreated. After democracy was restored, Panagoulis successfully ran to be a Member of Parliament.

In the U.S., the NBC television network made a decision it would regret when network executives decided to break away from its coverage of the Oakland Raiders-New York Jets football game to show a new, made-for-television version of Heidi that was scheduled to begin promptly at 7 pm Eastern U.S. time. With 1:05 still left on the game clock when the network switched to its coverage of Heidi, the Jets led the Raiders 32-29. However, after the network had broken away from the game to start coverage of Heidi, the Raiders scored two late touchdowns to take the lead and win the game 43-32. Viewer responses were negative, and many phone calls were made to the network complaining. NBC President Julian Goodman apologized. As a result of "the Heidi Game," new dedicated telephone lines and communication networks were installed so sports broadcasting crews could communicate directly with the network.

November 18 (Monday)

In the Soviet Union, the unmanned Zond 6 spacecraft was recovered after it crash-landed due to a parachute malfunction.

Born: Owen Wilson, American actor, was born in Dallas, Texas. Wilson's acting credits would include nearly 60 films, including *Bottle Rocket*, *The Cable Guy*, *Starsky & Hutch*, and *The Wedding Crashers*.

Born: Gary Sheffield, American Major League Baseball player, was born in Tampa, Florida. Sheffield would play for eight major league teams, and by the end of his career, he ranked among active players as third in runs, fourth in runs batted in, and fifth in hits and home runs.

November 19 (Tuesday)

In Mali, Moussa Traoré led a bloodless coup that overthrew President Modibo Keïta and his regime and then imprisoned Keïta.

New York Yankees relief pitcher Stan Bahnsen was named American League Rookie of the Year. In the National League,

Johnny Bench was named Rookie of the Year, narrowly beating New York Mets pitcher Jerry Koosman.

November 20 (Wednesday)

In Farmington, West Virginia, 78 men were killed in a mining disaster. At 5:30 am, a large explosion took place underground that could be felt 12 miles away. Ninety-nine miners were underground at the time. Twenty-one were able to escape from the opening, but the rest were never able to get out. Because of the explosion, new laws were enacted to protect miners. Although the cause of the explosion wasn't confirmed, a lawsuit filed in 2014 on behalf of the miners' families alleged that an electrician had disabled a ventilation fan, the suit alleged that the lack of ventilation contributed to the explosion.

The Country Music Association Awards, which were presented in October, were broadcasts on NBC. The previous year (1967), the awards were not televised at all, and beginning the following year, all CMA Awards would be broadcast live. Winners were Glen Campbell (Entertainer of the Year and Male Vocalist), Tammy Wynette (Female Vocalist), Bobby Russell's "Honey" (song of the year), and *Johnny Cash at Folsom Prison* (Album of the Year).

November 21 (Thursday)

Motown Records released the single "I'm Gonna Make You Love Me" by The Supremes and The Temptations, two of the label's biggest groups.

Born: English musician Alex James was born in Boscombe, Bournemouth, England. James may be best known as the bassist for the band Blur.

November 22 (Friday)

Near San Francisco, Japan Airlines Flight 2, a DC-8 flying from Tokyo to San Francisco, landed in the Pacific Ocean 2.5 miles from the San Francisco Airport after Captain Kohei Asoh, lost in fog and weather, thought he was landing at the airport. Once the aircraft came to a halt, it settled on the bay floor, in an area where the water was only seven feet deep; experts said that passengers and crew were fortunate that it was a high tide, as the normal depth of only four feet may have resulted in damage to the aircraft. In a landing similar to the one that would be performed by pilot Chesley "Sully" Sullenberger in the Hudson River in January 2009, all 96 passengers and 11 crew members were rescued without injury. The rescue was performed using lifeboats that were towed by police and Coast Guard boats coming out of the harbor. According to the National Transportation Safety Board, the ditching was the first such successful landing in the history of jet service.

The Beatles released their album *The Beatles*, popularly known as the *White Album*.

On NBC Television, the *Star Trek* episode "Plato's Stepchildren" aired, featuring the first interracial kiss on U.S. national television. The kiss, between Nichelle Nichols' Lieutenant Uhura character and William Shatner's character of Captain James T. Kirk, was very uncommon in the atmosphere of the 1960s.

Married: Barbara Anne Eisenhower, 19, granddaughter of former president Dwight Eisenhower, married Fernando Echavarria-Uribe, a

Columbian insurance executive. As of late 2017, Barbara Anne Eisenhower was a well-known New York designer.

November 23 (Saturday)

In U.S. college football, number-one ranked University of Southern California (USC) and number-two ranked Ohio State both came into the weekend undefeated, and would remain so. However, after Ohio State defeated Michigan 50-14 and USC defeated University of California at Los Angeles by a narrower 28-16 margin, Coach Woody Hayes' Buckeyes slipped ahead of USC in the national polls. The Buckeyes would become the eventual national champions following the Rose Bowl.

At Harvard Stadium in Boston, the Yale Bulldogs and the Harvard Crimson played to a 29-29 tie in college football. Both teams entered with perfect 8-0 records. Harvard fell behind Yale after three quarters, 22-13, and Harvard scored 16 points in the final 42 seconds to tie the final score. The game was the subject of the 2008 Kevin Rafferty documentary, *Harvard Beats Yale, 29-29*. Yale quarterback Brian Dowling would later be depicted as the character B.D. in the cartoon Doonesbury. Harvard lineman Tommy Lee Jones, a future actor, was roommates with future senator Al Gore Jr.

November 24 (Sunday)

Four men hijacked Pan Am Flight 281 (a scheduled flight from New York to San Juan, Puerto Rico) to Havana, Cuba. A group of U.S. jet fighters accompanied the Boeing 707 until it safely reached Cuban airspace. No passengers were seriously harmed. Two of the hijackers were captured in the 1970s, and another returned to the U.S. and surrendered.

Todd Beamer was born in Flint, Michigan. On September 11, 2001, Beamer and a small group of passengers on United Airlines Flight 93 would attempt to reclaim control of the aircraft after the 9/11 hijackers had killed crew members and taken over the plane. Although the terrorists crashed the airplane into a field near Shanksville, Pennsylvania, the passengers' actions likely kept the hijackers from crashing the airplane into another important target, thought to be either the U.S. Capitol Building or the White House.

November 25 (Monday)

Born: Jill Hennessy, Canadian actress and musician, was born in Edmonton, Alberta, Canada. Hennessy played on *Law & Order* for three seasons and *Crossing Jordan* for six.

Died: Paul Siple, Antarctic Explorer, died at the Army Research Center in Arlington, Virginia. Representing the Boy Scouts of America as an Eagle Scout, Siple accompanied six Antarctic expeditions, including all five expeditions conducted by Admiral Richard Byrd. Between 1928 and the 1940s, the polar regions were still a seldom-visited frontier. Along with Charles F. Passel, Siple developed the wind chill factor, and Siple coined the term. Siple also wrote five books about the expeditions.

November 26 (Tuesday)

In South Vietnam, a six-man U.S. Army Special Forces team that was pinned down between two heavily fortified enemy positions was rescued by helicopter pilot James P. Fleming, who made multiple attempts to set down his Bell UH-1 Huey helicopter. Amidst heavy Viet Cong fire, Fleming rescued the group. Fleming was awarded the Medal of Honor for his actions.

At the Royal Albert Hall in London, the "supergroup" Cream played the last concert of its farewell tour and its original run. The group of Eric Clapton, Jack Bruce, and Ginger Baker combined blues and rock in songs including "Sunshine of Your Love," "Crossroads," and "White Room."

November 27 (Wednesday)

In Lake Villa, Illinois, the first National Women's Liberation Conference took place for three days.

President-elect Richard Nixon appointed Henry Kissinger as his national security advisor. Kissinger would work with Nixon to develop a new Vietnam policy.

Born: Michael Vartan, French American actor known for playing Michael Vaughn on the ABC Television action drama *Alias*, was born in Boulogne-Billancourt, France.

November 28 (Thursday)

November 28 was Thanksgiving in the U.S. In National Football League games, Dallas shut out Detroit and the Washington Redskins defeated the Philadelphia Eagles. In the American Football League, the Kansas City Chiefs defeated the Oakland Raiders, and the Buffalo Bills and Houston Oilers played to a 10-10 tie.

In Philadelphia, the oldest Thanksgiving parade in the U.S. (since 1920), the Gimbels Thanksgiving Day Parade, was televised, as were Macy's Thanksgiving Parade in New York City and the J.L. Hudson Thanksgiving Day Parade, both of which started in 1924.

Dawn Robinson, American singer, was born in New London, Connecticut. Robinson would establish the R&B/pop group En Vogue.

November 29 (Friday)

At the Vietnam peace negotiations in Paris, North Vietnam publicly re-stated its claim that it would only negotiate with the U.S., and not with South Vietnam.

The John Lennon-Yoko Ono album Two Virgins was released in the UK. The album cover showed a nude picture of both performers.

November 30 (Saturday)

The single "Love Child" by Diana Ross & the Supremes became number one on the U.S. charts and remained there for two weeks.

In U.S. college football, in the regular season rivalry called the Iron Bowl, Paul "Bear" Bryant's Alabama Crimson Tide defeated Ralph Jordan's Auburn Tigers, 24-16 at Birmingham. The #2 ranked University of Southern California were tied by visiting and #9 ranked Notre Dame, 21-21. After this, the final week of college football, the final rankings at the end of the regular season were, from #1 to #5, Ohio State, USC, Penn State, Georgia, and Texas.

December 1968

December 1 (Sunday)

The Broadway musical *Promises, Promises* premiered at the Shubert Theatre on Broadway. The production starred Jerry Orbach and Jill O'Hara in a musical version of the 1960 film *The Apartment* with Jack Lemmon and Shirley MacLaine. The musical, with music by Burt Bacharach and Hal David, ran for 1,281 performances. The original cast album won a Grammy Award for best cast album, and singer Dionne Warwick recorded a hit single of the musical's song "I'll Never Fall in Love Again."

December 2 (Monday)

Daytime and nighttime talk shows frequently featured entertainment as well as discussions with guests. In Philadelphia, *The Mike Douglas Show* starred host Mike Douglas who would have a celebrity "co-host" on his show for the entire week, and he would usually begin the show by singing, then would engage his co-host and guests in civil discussions. Mike's host for the week of December 2 was Pat Paulsen, a comedian from *The Smothers Brothers Comedy Hour* who had waged a fake and humorous campaign for the presidency. Mike's guests for the week included CBS news anchor Walter Cronkite and NBC news anchor Chet Huntley.

Born: Lucy Liu, American actress, voice actress, director, singer, and artist, was born in Queens, New York. Liu played in *Ally McBeal* (1998-2002), the films *Charlie's Angels* and *Kill Bill*, the film musical *Chicago*, and the Holmes & Watson-themed crime-solving drama *Elementary*.

Died: Estonian painter Adamson-Eric (born Erich Adamson) died in Tallinn, Estonia, at age 66.

December 3 (Tuesday)

The television special *Elvis* was aired on NBC Television. The special had been taped in front of a live audience, and because Presley had not performed in a live concert since March 1961, the special has frequently been called the *'68 Comeback Special*. Presley, age 33 and dressed in black leather, performed a number of his past hits in the round, to a relatively small studio audience. In between songs, he talked and joked with the audience, and showed the personality that had made him so big in rock-and-roll a decade before.

To help hitters after the "Year of the Pitcher," Major League Baseball lowered the pitcher's mound from 15 inches to 10 inches and decreased the size of the strike zone, with the new zone being from the top of the batters' knees to the batters' armpits.

Born: Brendan Fraser, Canadian-American actor who played the title roles in the comedy films *George of the Jungle* (1997) and *Dudley Do-Right* (1999), and who played in *The Mummy* film series, was born in Indianapolis, Indiana.

December 4 (Wednesday)

In Dungannon, North Ireland, following the beginning of a civil rights march, violence broke out between civil rights demonstrators and loyalists. Jack Hassard, the Labour Party councillor in Dungannon, was physically attacked, and death threats were sent to his home, which led to Hassard resigning.

Born: Olympic swimming champion Mike Barrowman was born in Asunción, Paraguay. Barrowman would set the world record and win the gold medal in the men's 200-meter breaststroke. Swimming for the University of Michigan, Barrowman was named the Big Ten Conference Athlete of the Year (for all sports) in 1991, and *Swimming World* World Swimmer of the Year for 1989-1990.

December 5 (Thursday)

Born: Margaret Cho, American comedian and actress, was born in San Francisco. Cho is also a songwriter and fashion designer. She would star in *Face/Off* and *Drop Dead Diva*.

Died: Fred Clark, American film and television character actor, died of hepatitis in Santa Monica, California, at age 54. Following service in Europe as a pilot in both the U.S. Navy and U.S. Army Air Corps, Clark performed in almost 70 films, including *Sunset Boulevard*, *Auntie Mame* and *Visit to a Small Planet*. In television, he played on many shows including *I Love Lucy*, *The Beverly Hillbillies*, *I Dream of Jeannie* and *The Dick Van Dyke Show*.

December 6 (Friday)

LIFE Magazine published an issue entitled "Corruption of Chicago Police: Where Discipline Broke Down." One article in the issue was called "The Police Rioted at the Democratic Convention." The issue included both investigative and editorial material in describing the events in Chicago in August. In the days well before the Internet, digital books and magazines and cell phones, many people looked forward to magazines to update them on the status of the world and the country. Despite having morning and evening news broadcasts (but nothing approaching 24-hour news channels), it somehow made news more real when a reader held a paper copy in their hands. *LIFE* was one of the most-read magazines, selling 13.5 million copies per week at one point. Articles about entertainment, sports, science, and many other subjects were included, as well as excellent photography. Some of the most-viewed photographs in history were in the magazine, including Alfred Eisenstaedt's photo of a sailor embracing a nurse during the celebration when World War II ended. The memoirs of many notable people were serialized in its pages. In addition to the photographs, American artist Norman Rockwell created the front covers for a number of issues of *LIFE*, as he did for *Saturday Evening Post*.

The Rolling Stones released their album *Beggars Banquet*, which included the song "Sympathy for the Devil."

James Taylor's first studio album, the double-disk album simply titled *James Taylor*, was released under the Apple label. Peter Asher, Paul McCartney, and George Harrison played on the album.

Major League Baseball fired William Eckert as commissioner of baseball. Eckert, who had served previously as a lieutenant general in the U.S. Air Force, had been commissioner since 1965. Despite Eckert's efforts to promote the game on an international level (including a 1966 tour of Japan), he was criticized for poor management, including his decision not to cancel games after the assassinations of Dr. Martin Luther King and Sen. Robert Kennedy. In addition, team owners were expecting a players' strike in 1969, and they were concerned that Eckert would not deal forcefully with the matter. Eckert was replaced as commissioner by Bowie Kuhn, who would serve as commissioner from 1969 until 1984.

December 7 (Saturday)

In Ohio, Richard Dodd returned a library book that his great grandfather checked out in 1823 from the University of Cincinnati.

Born: Ricky Ervins, American football player, was born in Fort Wayne, Indiana. Ervins' touchdown run in the 1990 Rose Bowl won the game, and he was named its Most Valuable Player. He was a running back with the Washington Redskins and San Francisco 49ers, and helped the Redskins win Super Bowl XXVI.

December 8 (Sunday)

Motown Records released the Stevie Wonder album *For Once in My Life*.

Born: Mike Mussina, American baseball pitcher, was born in Williamsport, Pennsylvania. Mussina pitched for the Baltimore Orioles and New York Yankees from 1991 to 2008. Mussina was a five-time All-Star and a seven-time Gold Glove winner. Mussina pitched four one-hitters in his career.

December 9 (Monday)

In San Francisco, California, Douglas Engelbart performed a public demonstration for the ages involving computer technology. In that single demonstration, Engelbart demonstrated the computer mouse, the video conference, word processing, teleconferencing, and his pioneering hypertext system.

In Northern Ireland, the Derry Citizens' Action Committee called for a moratorium on all marches and protests for one month.

December 10 (Tuesday)

In Tokyo, the biggest heist in Japanese history took place, the "300 million-yen robbery." The robbery occurred when four bank employees were transporting nearly 300 million yen (the equivalent of about $818,000 in 1968 dollars, or $5.8 million in late 2017 dollars) in the trunk of a company vehicle. They were stopped by a young man dressed as a police officer, who warned them that there was a bomb in the vehicle. After they got out, he got in and drove away.

Died: Thomas Merton, French-American writer and Trappist monk, was accidentally killed at the age of 53 by electrocution in Bangkok, Thailand. Merton wrote 70 books on religion, spirituality, pacifism, and social justice, and he has been increasingly recognized as an important religious thinker of his time.

December 11 (Wednesday)

In Northern Ireland, Prime Minister Terence O'Neill fired William Craig as home affairs minister.

In the U.S., the unemployment rate dropped to 3.3%, the lowest it had been in 15 years.

The film *Oliver!*, based on the hit London and Broadway musical, opened in the U.S. after being released on September 26 in England. It went on to win the Academy Award for Best Picture.

Columbia Records released the album *Blood, Sweat & Tears*, the second album by the group with that name. The album included three consecutive Top 5 singles, and received the Grammy Award for Album of the Year.

The Rolling Stones Rock and Roll Circus film is celebrated with a promotional release party, but the film is not released until 1996. The film was the last appearance of the Stones' Brian Jones, who died seven months later.

December 12 (Thursday)

Born: Rory Kennedy, documentary film producer, was born in Washington, DC. Kennedy, the daughter of Ethel and Sen. Robert Kennedy, was born six months after her father was assassinated in Los Angeles while running for president. Kennedy won an Emmy Award for the 2007 documentary *The Ghosts of Abu Ghraib.*

Died: American actress Tallulah Bankhead died in New York City from double pneumonia at age 66. Bankhead starred in numerous productions on the stage and screen, including Alfred Hitchcock's 1944 film *Lifeboat.*

December 13 (Friday)

In Brazil, triggered by the growing unrest and spread of pro-communist terrorist actions, President Artur da Costa e Silva imposed the so-called Institutional Act number 5 (AI-5 or Ato Institucional Número Cinco), the fifth of 17 emergency decrees implemented to stabilize the country during its unrest. The provisions of the act went outside of the Brazilian constitution and overrode a number of personal guarantees of rights granted under the constitution.

The Hong Kong flu was reported as being widespread in the U.S. The flu had been spreading globally during 1968 and entered the U.S. in September via service personnel returning from Asia to

California. The 1968 Hong Kong flu was an H3N2 strain, the spread of which was classified as Category 2. The 1968 variation of the Hong Kong Flu killed an estimated 1 million people worldwide and 33,800 in the U.S. An estimated 500,000 people in Hong Kong contracted the flu.

December 14 (Saturday)

"I Heard It Through the Grapevine" by Marvin Gaye hit number one on the U.S. charts and remained there for three weeks. The single was featured on Gaye's album of the same name. The song, written by Norman Whitfield and Barrett Strong for Motown Records in 1966, had previously been performed by Gladys Night & The Pips, with their version hitting number two on the charts. In addition, in 1971, Creedence Clearwater Revival would release the song as an 11-minute single on the group's album *Cosmo's Factory*, with that version going to number 43 on the charts. Gaye's version was later selected as the number 80 on *Rolling Stone* Magazine's The 500 Greatest Songs of All Time.

Bobby Orr, regarded as one of the greatest hockey players ever, scored his first hat trick in the National Hockey League. Orr, then age 20, was playing for the Boston Bruins, and scored the three goals during the Bruins' 10-5 win over the Chicago Blackhawks at the Boston Garden. Orr scored two goals in the first period and one in the second.

December 15 (Sunday)

In Washington, DC, U.S. Secretary of Defense Clark Clifford expressed his disappointment in both North and South Vietnam, saying that the U.S. had "no obligation to maintain 540,000 men" in Vietnam while both sides delayed peace negotiations in Paris. Clifford said that representatives from both countries should "stop squabbling" over table shape and seating arrangements, and to get serious about putting an end to hostilities.

Guests on *The Smothers Brothers Comedy Hour* were The Doors and George Carlin. The Doors performed "Wild Child" and "Touch Me" live in front of the studio audience, with the Smothers Brothers Orchestra backing up the band on "Touch Me."

Born: Garrett Wang, American actor, was born in Riverside, California. Wang would portray Ensign Harry Kim in the television series *Star Trek: Voyager*.

Died: Antonio Barrette, the 18th premier of Quebec, died in Montreal at age 69. Barrette served as minister of labor from 1944 to 1960, and as premier January-July 1960.

Died: Former world heavyweight boxing champion Jess Willard died in Los Angeles at age 86. Willard had knocked out Jack Johnson in 1915 to win the heavyweight championship. He held the title for four years, losing the title to Jack Dempsey in 1919. Willard was a cowboy by trade, and did not begin boxing until the age of 27. Standing 6 ft. 6 ½ inches (1.99 m), Willard was one of the sport's tallest participants.

December 16 (Monday)

The Alhambra Decree, sometimes known as the Spanish Edict of Expulsion, was officially revoked by the Roman Catholic Church following the Second Vatican Council. The Alhambra Decree was an edict issued by the Catholic monarchs of Spain (Isabella I of Castile and Ferdinand II of Aragon) requiring all practicing Jews in Castile and Aragon to leave its territories and possessions. The decree had been issued on March 31, 1492, five months before Columbus left on his first journey to America. The revocation was somewhat of a formality in that Jews had been allowed into the restricted territories for more than a century before.

The film *Chitty Chitty Bang Bang* was released to theaters by United Artists. It was a story about a magical car, and was based on the 1964 novel by James Bond author Ian Fleming. The film starred Dick Van Dyke, Sally Ann Howes, Gert Fröbe, and Benny Hill.

December 17 (Tuesday)

In Newcastle on Tyne, England, 11-year-old Mary Bell was found guilty of murdering two small boys by strangulation earlier in the year. One victim was aged 4 and the other 3. Bell was 10 years old at the time of the first murder. She was sentenced to life in prison but released in 1980, at the age of 23, and put into witness protection. She and her daughter are still both believed to be living in the UK under new names. At the time of the investigation and trial, it was learned that Bell had been the daughter of a prostitute and was subject to cruelty growing up, including having her mother give her overdoses of sleeping pills.

December 18 (Wednesday)

Born: Rachel Griffiths, Australian actress who would play in the films *Muriel's Wedding* (1994), *The Rookie* (2002) and *Hacksaw Ridge* (2016), and in the television series *Six Feet Under* and *Brothers & Sisters*, was born in Melbourne, Victoria, Australia.

Died: Jill Tabor, American actress, died in Beverly Hills, California at age 36 after an accidental overdose of influenza medication. Her television credits included *The Red Skelton Show*, *Perry Mason*, *Have Gun – Will Travel*, and *Bat Masterson*. She had been married twice; her second husband was actor Broderick Crawford.

December 19 (Thursday)

Died: Norman Thomas, perennial Socialist Party of America candidate for president, died in Cold Spring Harbor, New York, at age 84. Thomas, who ran on the party's ticket six times, was a Presbyterian minister and pacifist.

December 20 (Friday)

In Benicia, California, near San Francisco Bay, the serial killer known as the Zodiac Killer shot Betty Lou Jensen and David Faraday on Lake Herman Road. The identity of the Zodiac Killer remains unknown.

In Northern Ireland, The People's Democracy (PD) announced that on January 1, 1969, it would conduct a protest march from Belfast to Derry.

December 21 (Saturday)

At Kennedy Space Center in Florida, Launch Complex 39A, Apollo-Saturn 8 was launched at 7:51 am Eastern time. Apollo 8 would be the first spacecraft in history to take humans outside of earth orbit, the first to take astronauts around the moon, and the farthest that a manned object had ever been from earth. It was also the first manned flight of the Saturn V rocket, the third stage of which had failed to restart on the last unmanned mission. Today, the launch of Commander Frank Borman, Jim Lovell, and Bill Anders was good, and after orbiting the earth to check out systems, the Saturn V third stage restarted perfectly, redirecting Apollo 8 on its path to the moon, and putting the three astronauts much closer to the moon than any human before.

In California, Crosby, Stills, and Nash performed together in public for the first time.

December 22 (Sunday)

Thirty-one hours after their launch from the Kennedy Space Center, the Apollo 8 crew of Frank Borman, Jim Lovell, and Bill Anders began transmitting black-and-white video back to earth. The camera used a Vidicon tube, a wide-angle lens, and a telephoto lens, which provided little flexibility for shooting. The crew was not able to see the moon due to spacecraft angle and window fogging, and earth looked like a glowing ball without details. But even though the picture quality was not good, viewers knew they were fortunate to see television from space for the first time.

In China, leader Mao Zedong, concerned with a prevalence of "pro-bourgeois" thinking among families, announced a policy of sending educated youth in urban China to the country. It marked the start of his "Up to the mountains and down to the villages" policy.

Married: In New York City, David Eisenhower, grandson of former President Dwight Eisenhower, married Julie Nixon, the daughter of President-elect Richard Nixon.

December 23 (Monday)

The crew of the USS *Pueblo*, which had been captured 11 months earlier by North Korea, was released. Upon their release, Captain Lloyd Bucher and the crew described their torture and poor treatment while in captivity. To gain the release of his crew, Bucher reluctantly agreed to sign an affidavit saying that the *Pueblo* was spying on North Korea. One crew member, Fireman Duane Hodges, was shot while trying to destroy classified documents during the capture of the *Pueblo*, and he died in captivity. His body was released with the rest of the crew. The entire *Pueblo* incident, happening at the time of the Vietnam War and other global unrest, was another blow to the lame duck Johnson administration and its policies.

While Apollo 8 was on its way to the moon, NASA's Chief of Astronauts, Donald K. "Deke" Slayton, told astronaut Neil Armstrong in a private meeting that he had been selected to be the commander of Apollo 11, which by that time was expected to be the first mission to land humans on the moon.

On *The Merv Griffin Show*, the guests were Judy Garland and Margaret Hamilton, who played Dorothy and The Wicked Witch of the West, respectively, in the 1939 MGM classic film *The Wizard of Oz*. Judy Garland would die the following June, at age 47, from a barbiturate overdose.

December 24 (Tuesday)

Sixty-nine hours, 8 minutes, and 16 seconds after leaving Florida, the Service Module engine of Apollo 8 fired for 4 minutes and 7 seconds, placing the spacecraft into lunar orbit. With the first orbit being intentionally elliptical (in case the crew needed to return early), the engine was fired again at the end of the first orbit, putting Apollo 8 into nearly-circular orbit 70 miles above the moon. The crew began to report back what the details looked like. They described a number of known craters, mountains, and other features, paying special attention to the Sea of Tranquility, where the Apollo 11 mission now planned to make the first landing. The crew, especially Bill Anders, spent much of their time in orbit taking photographs; they would take about 700 photos of the moon and 150 of earth during the mission. The crew became the first humans to see the far side of the moon, and the first to see an "earthrise" (earth rising over the horizon of the moon).

On the crew's penultimate orbit on Christmas Eve, they sent back the first live, black-and-white television signals from the moon. After each crew member described their perception and feelings about the moon, Anders said that "for all the people back on earth, the crew of Apollo has a message that we would like to send to you," the crew took turns reading the first 10 verses from the Bible's Book of Genesis. Borman concluded the transmission by saying "...and from the crew of Apollo 8, we close with good night, good luck, a Merry Christmas, and God bless all of you, all of you on the good earth." The message was seen or heard by an estimated 1 billion people, at a time when communications were still developing around the globe. The message of awe and optimism was in contrast to most of the news of 1968, which on the whole was decidedly bad.

The Disney comedy film *The Love Bug*, which featured a Volkswagen Beetle race car "with a mind of its own," opened to limited release in the U.S. The movie starred Dean Jones, Michele Lee, and Buddy Hackett.

Ten-year University of Michigan head football coach Chalmers "Bump" Elliott was appointed to the new position of associate athletic director at the university, and he resigned as head football coach.

December 25 (Wednesday)

Early in the morning of Christmas Day (Eastern U.S. time), after 20 hours completing 10 orbits around the moon, Apollo 8 fired its Service Propulsion Engine to return the spacecraft and its crew of three to earth. After Apollo 8 came around the far side of the moon for the last time and re-acquired communication with capsule communicators on earth, Jim Lovell radioed back home "Please be advised, there is a Santa Claus."

December 26 (Thursday)

In Athens, as Israeli-owned El Al Flight 253 was leaving a layover during a flight from Tel Aviv to New York City, two Palestinian terrorists attacked the aircraft, killing one passenger and injuring two. The two terrorists were captured and identified as being from the Popular Front for the Liberation of Palestine. One of the terrorists served more than 17 years in prison, and the other was released in exchange for Greek citizens who had been hijacked.

Led Zeppelin make their American concert debut in Denver, Colorado.

In Ann Arbor, Michigan, the University of Michigan announced that Glenn "Bo" Schembechler had been named as head coach of the university's football team to replace Bump Elliott. Schembechler had previously been an assistant coach for Ohio State head coach Woody Hayes. In his first 10 years as head coach at Michigan, Ohio State and Michigan would participate in a fierce "Ten-Year War" during which one of the two teams either won or shared the Big Ten championship, and were frequently at or near the top of the national rankings. Although Schembechler would be the Wolverines' head coach through 1987, the rivalry with Hayes would end in 1978 after Hayes punched an opposing Clemson football player during the Gator Bowl. Before retiring as head coach, Bo Schembechler's teams compiled a 234-65-8 record. He died in 2006 at the age of 77, the evening before the #1 Buckeyes and the #2 Wolverines brought identical undefeated 11-0 records into the final regular-season game at Columbus. Ohio State won the game 42-39.

December 27 (Friday)

Six days after its launch from Florida and two days after leaving lunar orbit, Apollo 8 successfully completed its 234,000-mile (377,000 km) journey home. It successfully re-entered earth's atmosphere, splashed down in the Pacific Ocean, and was recovered by the crew of the USS *Yorktown*. Eighteen days after their splashdown, in Miami, Florida, the Apollo 8 crew would lead the crowd at Super Bowl III in reciting the Pledge of Allegiance before Anita Bryant sang the National Anthem. The crew and NASA won an Emmy award for the live televised coverage of the flight. For the historic nature of the crew's journey and for bringing people together following such a turbulent and violent year, the entire three-man crew of Apollo 8, Borman, Lovell, and Anders, was named Time Magazine's Person of the Year. But perhaps most meaningful was a single letter from a stranger that Frank Borman received afterward, which said simply: "Thank you Apollo 8. You saved 1968."

December 28 (Saturday)

In Lebanon, Israeli forces launched an attack on Beirut airport, destroying 14 aircraft. The attack was in retaliation for the armed attack on El Al Flight 253 in Athens two days earlier.

December 29 (Sunday)

At Shea Stadium in New York City, the New York Jets defeated the Oakland Raiders, 27-23, to win the American Football League Championship. Jets receiver Don Maynard caught two touchdown passes from Joe Namath, with Pete Lammons catching a third touchdown pass from "Broadway Joe." Jim Turner added two field goals for the AFL Champion Jets. For the Raiders, quarterback Daryle Lamonica threw a touchdown pass to sure-handed Fred Biletnikoff, with 41-year-old kicker (and former quarterback) George Blanda adding three field goals.

Two weeks later, Namath and the Jets would go on to defeat the Baltimore Colts in the third AFL-NFL Championship Game, 16-7. The game was the first to officially be called the "Super Bowl," and with the Jets defeating the highly favored Colts, is still regarded as one of the greatest upsets in sports.

At Cleveland Municipal Stadium in Ohio, the Baltimore Colts shut out the Cleveland Browns in the National Football League Championship game, 34-0. With a 10-4 regular season record, the Browns had been the only team to defeat the Colts, who went into the NFL championship game with a 13-1 record.

December 30 (Monday)

The towns of Winthrop and Mazama in Washington state reached a temperature of -48 F (-44 C), a record low for the state, which still stands.

In Los Angeles, Frank Sinatra recorded "My Way." The song was written specifically for Sinatra by singer/composer Paul Anka. Although the song only hit #27 on the Billboard charts in the U.S., in the UK it spent 75 weeks on the chart, a record that still stands. Although "My Way" became Sinatra's signature song, his daughter Tina later said that he came to dislike it. According to Tina Sinatra, "He didn't like it. He always thought that song was self-serving and self-indulgent."

Died: Trygve Lie, the Norwegian politician and statesman who was the first secretary general of the United Nations, died of a heart attack in Geilo, Norway at age 72. Lie had served at various times as a politician, a labor leader, a government official, and an author. He was generally thought to be an honest, pragmatic politician and a good negotiator. In 1940, when Norway was attacked by Nazi Germany, he ordered Norwegian ships to sail to safety in Allied ports. In 1941, Lie became foreign minister of the Norwegian government-in-exile, a position he continued to fill until the end of the war.

December 31 (Tuesday)

The world's first supersonic transport aircraft, the Soviet Tupolev Tu-144, made its maiden flight. The aircraft, which looked much like the British-French Concorde, was capable of flying more than twice the speed of sound. The Tu-144 was designed by famed Soviet aircraft designer Andrey Tupolev and his son, Alexey. The aircraft would be flown above the speed of sound for the first time in June 1969, and was first publicly displayed in Moscow in May 1970. The first Tu-144 would crash at the Paris Air Show in 1973, and Tu-144s would be used for carrying passengers and mail until 1978, when another crash led the program to be canceled.

Epilogue

Thank you for your interest in this book. I hope that you found the events in it to be important, interesting, or both.

Like ripples in a pond, the events of 1968 caused changes that still make a difference. The differences of opinion over Vietnam War strategy caused changes in our national policy that still affect how we plan military involvement. Some of our more recent military leaders have written and spoken about lessons learned there. Colin Powell, who served as a captain and then a major in Vietnam, developed the "Powell Doctrine" in speaking of military involvement: only use military action as a last resort, but when the decision is made to go, to "use decisive force against the enemy." Norman Schwarzkopf, a Vietnam adviser and battalion commander who would later command forces during the first Gulf War, wrote about the importance of supporting the families of military personnel as well as service personnel.

The assassination of Rev. Martin Luther King Jr. continues to serve as a focus of improving civil rights for all. The assassination of Sen. Robert Kennedy led to Secret Service protection for presidential candidates in the U.S. There are still Americans who remember 1968 and regret that Sen. Kennedy was taken from us before he could have an impact on policy.

The election of Richard Nixon continues to have an impact, as the once solid Democratic South has been mostly Republican since. The election of Nixon, and his subsequent resignation in August 1974, established Watergate as the standard that most scandals would be measured against, and the suffix "-gate" would become common for creating names for scandals.

The successful missions of Apollo 7 and Apollo 8 led to 12 humans walking on the moon during the subsequent Apollo missions, one of the most unifying international experiences ever. The lessons of Apollo were key to establishing the Skylab, Space Shuttle, and International Space Station programs. As I write this, the new Orion and Space Launch System are scheduled to return humans to lunar orbit in 2022, and may take humans to Mars in the lifetime of some readers.

It's my hope that this book has triggered your interest in some of these events, and that you'll do further research on your own, if you haven't already.

Acknowledgements

I'm grateful for my supportive family and friends, especially those who like history and trivia as I do. You were my reason for writing this book. Thanks also to priticreative (at www.fiverr.com/priticreative) for designing my book cover. This was my first book, and I was very happy to have a cover designed by a professional who knew exactly what I wanted.

Following are the major sources of information that I used for information for this book:

airandspace.si.edu

aviation-safety.net

baseball-reference.com

bbc.com

boeing.com

historynet.com

mlb.com

nasa.gov

onthisday.com

pro-football-reference.com

vietnamwarcasualties.org

wikipedia.com

I'm appreciative of the information that people have posted on these sites and others, in many cases simply because they enjoy sharing knowledge. One of my personal goals in 2018 is to add additional events and details to online databases, in order to further share important information. I look forward to it, and I encourage you to consider doing the same. Everywhere, there are people who want to know what you've learned.

Take care.

Made in the USA
Lexington, KY
14 January 2018